CALLING OUT . . .

Calling out . . .

J. John

Authentic

CALLING OUT

First published 2000 by Authentic Media,
9 Holdom Avenue, Bletchley, Milton Keynes,
Bucks, MK1 1QR, UK.

Reprinted 2002, 2004

1-86024-359-2

Cover design by David Lund.
Typeset by Cyclops Media, 10 Bakers Lane, Norton, NN11 5EL, England.

Book production for Authentic Media by
Bookprint Creative Services, P.O. Box 827, BN21 3YJ, England.
Printed in Great Britain.

CONTENTS

PART FOUR
The 'Where' of Mission

PART FIVE
The Seven Pillars Of Mission

DEDICATION

I dedicate this book to
Andy Economides
who called out to me,
and continues to call out to others.

ACKNOWLEDGEMENTS

This book has a long history and many people have played a role in the growth of its various chapters. Thank you to Malcolm Down (Publishing Manager) who asked me to write the book – thank you for being a publisher and a friend.

I am grateful to Chris Walley for his skilful editing and meticulous support in preparing the final manuscript for publication. From the moment Chris Walley and I connected there was an instant rapport – his enthusiasm for this project has been unstinting and often contagious. Thank you for guiding me in crafting the manuscript, making it richer and deeper.

I am indebted to my dear friend Chris Russell, my invaluable researcher, who always illuminates my understanding and discovers appropriate seasoning.

I would particularly like to thank all the people who have talked so openly with me about their faith and the lack of it.

I owe a deep debt of gratitude to certain people who have shaped my thinking, challenged my ideas and encouraged me in research and writing. Thanks to many Christians and to pastors, teachers, evangelists, and worship leaders who have inspired, encouraged my own faith and motivated me to 'Call Out' – especially to Sharon Anson, Joseph Boot, Steve Chalke, Eric Delve, Chris Demetriou, Gary Grant, Michael Green, Mark Greenwood, Kenneth Habershon, Mike Pilavachi, Matthew Persson, Matt Redman, Rob Richards, David Shearman, Mark Stibbe, Yioula Taliadorou and Ashley Trask.

The Point Group, to which I am privileged to belong, led by Leighton Ford, including Stephen Abbott, Lon Allison, Doug Birdsall, Irv Chambers, Peter Chao, Caio Fabio, Steve Johnson, Graham Johnston, Susan Perlman, Perry Bowers, Carson Pue and Roland Werner.

To Michael and Yoma Rees (my in-laws) and to Clifford and Jeannie Hampton (uncle and aunt). Thank you for all your support and encouragement.

To my Trustees, Terry & Juanita Baker, Jamie Colman, Bob Fuller, Mike Shouler and Peter Wright, whose council and wisdom has guided and enriched my life and work.

To my colleagues Katharine Draper, Paul Wilson and Charlie Farmery, whose friendship and companionship in the service of the Good News of Jesus Christ is a Joy.

Special thanks to my wife Killy, for her sage advice. She is my devoted encourager and my most trusted critic. She brings balance and refreshment to a deeply satisfying, yet sometimes emotionally draining ministry. Our partnership makes every book hers too. And to my sons Michael, Simeon and Benjamin who are a delight and an inspiration, and who challenge me daily to 'practice what I preach!'

J. John, Summer 2000, Chorleywood, Herts, England

INTRODUCTION

I have been an evangelist for twenty-five years. As I see it, to be an evangelist is not ultimately about giving countless talks, much less is it earning your living through preaching. No, it is about passionately grappling day and night with communicating the Good News of Jesus Christ to people around you. Throughout the years that I have been an evangelist, I have struggled with what it is to be a bearer of that great message and how best to express it in our changing culture. And as I have wrestled with how to effectively share the gospel, I have wanted to be able to pass on what I have learned to others so that they might more effectively share Jesus.

This is what this book is about; it is me, passing on my thoughts and ideas to you. In doing this, I am not setting myself up as an authority on evangelism; it's just that when you do something day and night for a quarter of a century you have to be pretty thick not to have learned something!

Let me also say that I have written this book for everybody who is a believer in Jesus Christ. If you preach regularly in a church then I hope you will find something that will help or refresh you. If you do no more than talk to your friends about Jesus then I want to pass on to you what I feel may be helpful to you. There are two types of people that I have felt a special burden for as I have written this. The first is the new Christian; you may well feel bewildered about the whole thing of sharing

11

your faith. In writing this, I have tried to do all I can to take nothing for granted and to encourage you. As I will point out, we desperately need you and your freshness. The second is the Christian for whom *evangelism* is a word that induces attacks of guilt; it is something that you know that you don't do well, or it is something that you don't do at all. If you are in this category, first of all let me thank you for reading this far. Secondly don't worry; I am not in the business of making your burden of guilt any deeper. In fact, I think that guilt-driven evangelism is probably pretty useless. So relax and read on.

In writing this book for as wide an audience as possible, I have tried not to get bogged down in denominational issues or in matters of theology that do not seem to me to be relevant to the issue of witness. I have my own views and you probably know them or can guess them, but this book is not the place to air them. I should also say that because of my view that mission is to be at the heart of all that we do as Christians, this book inevitably interacts with a lot of issues, some of which are controversial. Where I have touched an area of controversy, I have tried to tread lightly. I hope that this lightness of touch is not mistaken for either frivolity or shallowness.

Who's calling out to who?

Let me explain the title *Calling Out*. It has at least three meanings.

First of all, it is *God calling out* to the darkened and lost world we live in. I don't suppose the shepherd in Jesus' parable went about his task of finding the lost sheep silently. He must have called out, hoping to hear at least a feeble bleat for an answer. God does the same. In the first part of this book, I want to talk about how God has taken the initiative in seeking those who have rebelled against him. Here I want to make an apology. Calling out is not very British (or at least English); it's frankly pretty bad form. After all the British are the race whose contributions to global culture have included men with stiff upper lips who make massive understatements in the face of crisis. Even when the Englishman is severely wounded in warfare, it is proper form for him merely to raise a bloodstained finger and quietly, smoothly and without urgency or panic say something along the following lines: 'I say old chap, I don't really want to make a fuss but I seem to have had a mishap. Lost a leg. Dashed nuisance. Couldn't you please look out a medical orderly for me?'

Now this aversion to calling out might seem amusing when it is a personal problem; it is a more serious matter when it is to do with another person. When you see someone about to drive over a cliff, politely muttering 'I wouldn't do that if I were you' under your breath is not the right response. You need to call out. Fortunately – and I hope this is not too unsettling a concept – God is not an English gentleman. He calls out.

Secondly, it is *you and I* together calling out to lost people. In Part Two I want to discuss what it is we call out and in Part Three why we call out. If the idea of you calling out to people about Jesus is something that simultaneously freezes your blood and dries your mouth then I want to try and help you here. If you are a Christian then you, not just your pastor, minister or vicar, need to be involved with mission. Even if you aren't a Christian yet, or if you aren't sure whether or not you are one, stick around.

Thirdly it is *me*, calling out to *you* to get involved in mission. You see I believe passionately that the church needs to speak and be heard today. This book is my personal appeal to you.

Words, words, words

Let me explain a little bit about how this book is written. I have a suspicion that there are not that many truly new books. I have wanted to be different here and have tried to be fresh. I have thrown away anecdotes or illustrations that I feel are stale or have passed their sell-by date. Can I suggest that this is a good policy for our use of language in communicating the Good

News? There is something bizarre about talking about the eternal ever-living God to people today, using words and illustrations that their grandparents might have used. If you find a well-worn clich in what you are saying then take it out and give it an honourable burial.

As a way of keeping this book fresh, I have tried to use plain, modern language; something that, if you are a new believer in Jesus I hope you find helpful. For instance, I see no reason to use terms like *epistles*. When was the last time *you* wrote an epistle? Here they are the New Testament letters. Antiquated terms like this make the Bible seem ancient and respected; that is good, but the price you pay is very high. By doing this the stories in the Bible acquire a sort of reverent 'once upon a time' feel to them. They are about men and women in robes with haloes around their heads and they are unreal and distanced from twenty-first century Britain. Yet the fact is, the Bible is about real people in real situations: the sort of things that you and I have to put up with. We may not face being thrown to the lions but we still have challenges that are nearly as threatening.

Where I have quoted the Bible I have used the New Living Translation. I find that in terms of communicating the meaning of the original text to our world today it is one of the best versions around. It is useful to remember that the New Testament was written, not in flowery classical Greek, but in the everyday language of the market and business world. The words the writers chose were those that communicated effectively to the people around them. It is a useful lesson. Another useful lesson is that it was written in contemporary Greek. Can I make a plea for you to use a Bible whose language you understand? By all means use sixteenth century English, if that is how you and your hearers normally speak. Otherwise, be contemporary. This is not me being trendy but me simply being anxious that God communicates effectively with us. If we are going to call out, we might as well do so that we are understood.

Can I make a comment about a number of specific words? I think there is no option but to use the word 'Christian', but as there are different definitions of what the word means, let me make the point that what we are calling people to is not church attendance, membership of a denomination, or even an intellectual acceptance that Christianity is true. We are calling them to a faith in which Jesus Christ has entered into their lives and is now the lord of all that they are.

I have struggled about what to call people who have not yet come to such a faith in Jesus Christ. It is hardly fair to call them 'unbelievers' as they may, in fact, believe strongly in another faith or believe in God (but just not follow him). A technical term is 'unchurched' but then what does that say to someone who has been in a church for decades but who has not yet come to a living faith in Christ, or someone who regularly goes at Christmas, Easter, weddings and funerals? You can hardly use the word 'pagan' either; that has negative overtones. Most of the time I have, in desperation, resorted to 'non-Christian'. In using that, I hope that no one feels that it is a dismissive or uncomplimentary term; it is here simply a convenient all-embracing phrase for the wide range of people of different faiths who are not (yet) followers of Jesus Christ. It also has the virtue of not trying to spell out what people do believe; it just says what they *don't* believe.

I have also tried to avoid using a number of words that older books might have done. The honourable word 'gospel' is now a problematic word; to most people it now means a sort of music. The alternative 'Good News' is perhaps better, but even that is bit tired.

In the Bible the Greek word for the Good News is the 'evangel'. From that we get three words that are often confused. An 'evangelical' is anyone who believes the Good News of Jesus; exactly what one is, is spelt out more clearly in Part Two. 'Evangelism' is the sharing of the Good News of Jesus in any way and an 'evangelist' is just someone who shares it. In fact I have tried to avoid using all these terms as far as possible, but as all of the alternatives are much longer, I have, in places, opted to save trees and have used the relevant E-word.

I also think that, although the word 'missionary' is now a bit elderly, there is little option but to continue to use the word 'mission'. No other word describes so well what God has done and what we are to do.

The road ahead

The seven chapters of Part One do something that I think is very important; they provide the foundations for mission by spelling out what God has done in history. In Part Two, I turn to the message of the Good News and in one chapter talk about what exactly it is and in a second, how much freedom we have to modify it. In the two chapters of Part Three I look at the reasons for sharing our faith and the obstacles that face us as we try to do this. The last part covers what I have called the 'seven pillars of mission'. There, in seven chapters, I cover the role of prayer, presence, proclamation, persuasion, power, praise and patterning to our sharing of Jesus. Finally, in the Appendix, I set out some of the answers that I have given to some of the difficult questions that I have been asked when I have discussed my faith in Jesus.

At the end of most chapters I have put in exercises and questions. These are not so much to make this a study book, but to force you to stop and think.

PART ONE

FOUNDATIONS FOR MISSION
or
A BRIEF HISTORY OF THE WORLD
AND YOUR PART IN IT

A little introduction to the Big Picture

A friend of mine became a Christian a couple of years ago and, as part of involving him in the church, he was asked to do a talk. The title was 'How and Why Should We Share the Good News?' Many of us in the church were more nervous than he was about this first speaking venture and so you can imagine our horror when he started off by saying, 'I think this title has got it all wrong'. He went on to say that how you told people about Jesus didn't really matter, the main thing to get straight was why we should tell others. And the reason why we should tell others, he said, is because of God: who he is, what he has done, what he can do, and what he will do.

I think he was right. That's why, in this book on sharing our faith, I want to begin with the reason why we should tell others about our faith: *God*. Mission is not about techniques or courses, nor is it about programmes and strategies. It is not really about something we do, achieve, plan for or even pray for. It's something that God has done, is doing and will do.

Now there are two dangers here. First, if we omit God from our idea of mission, soon we will have something so worthless that it will make no impact on the world around us. All we will have is a ragbag philosophy based on a few scrappy moral sayings: 'be kind', 'look after the world', 'you can change yourself' or 'have a nice day'. Not only is that worthless, but it won't work; we will end up being powerless pushers of an empty philosophy. That is hardly going to change lives and, however much we work at it, all we will do is run ourselves into the ground as guilt-ridden failures.

The second danger is to have God, but to have him in the wrong place. You see we have to remember who he is. God is eternal, present everywhere, all-powerful, all wise and totally holy, to name just a few of his characteristics. In fact, if we understood even a fraction of who God is, our brains would probably behave the same way as a domestic light bulb suddenly struck by a lightning bolt; it would not be a pretty sight. Because God is so big, it is important that we put him in the proper place when we think about mission. It would be foolish indeed to construct an entire system of how – and why – we do mission and then to try to tack God on the top like icing on the cake. It would collapse. God, being who he is, has to be the foundation and nothing else. So I want to dig foundations.

There are two ways of thinking about God. The first way is to deal with him in terms of trying to classify and describe who he is. You would start by talking about the nature of God (eternal, all knowing, etc.) and then move on to his character. Because God is not the sort of person who you can observe in a laboratory, you could only really base it on what he says about himself in the Bible. Now this sort of approach is taken in some theology textbooks and it is fine; it has its place, but that place is not here. The second way is to look at what God has done – to trace the story of his involvement with the human race. Now this is what I want to do in the first part of this book.

I have several reasons for doing this. Firstly, this method has a good pedigree. It is after all, the method that God uses; in the Bible he tells us a story. He could, I suppose, have listed who he was and who we are, but it would have been a bit cold and scientific.

Secondly, retelling briefly what really is 'the greatest story ever told' reminds us that the relationship between God and humanity is not cold and fixed. God does not stand there in heaven coolly staring at us as if we were goldfish in a bowl. He gets involved; he is a God that has acted – and acted spectacularly – in our history. In fact all through the Bible, we find an emphasis on what God has done. When we read in the book of Acts the summaries of what the disciples told people about the Good News of Jesus we find that much of what they said was the story of what God had done.

Thirdly, another reason for taking this approach is that when we see what God has done for us it ought to move us into a response. Imagine you were doing a television commercial for an appeal towards a new lifeboat. You could show pictures of the new boat and the stormy sea and tell people facts about how powerful the boat was and how it could save lives. And I suppose we might dig into our pockets for something, but it would hardly be an effective appeal. A better way surely, would be to have video clips of people (the young mother, the pretty little girl) who had been saved from the sea by the previous boat and for them to recount their experiences. That would bring home to viewers the reality of what this boat did and I have no doubt it would make a more effective commercial. It is the same with the Good News of Jesus. We should want to share it because of what he has done for us and for others.

Finally, when we look at the past we see how God is an example for us. You see the most extraordinary missionary of all is God. God is the prototype missionary, the one who started it all and the one who all the best missionaries model themselves on.

So in the following chapters we are going to think about God – what he has done and the story of the Good News he has given us to share. Now some of you, especially those who have been Christians a long time and have been in churches with good teaching, may say that you know all this. Wonderful! (I mean it). Well, think of what follows as a revision lesson. You may also want to ask yourself how would you tell the story; after all, in mission you may have to. But there will be others, especially new followers of Jesus, who need to see the big picture. I also think that there is a temptation to get distracted; to get absorbed in the fascinating byways that centre on such things as Noah's flood, the lost tribes, and the exact time and precise manner of the Second Coming. In short, we need to be sure we don't lose the plot. We need to get the 'big picture'.

But before I start, let me make a brief diversion to talk to you about the way the Bible tells the great story. I want to point out that there are two sorts of history. There is what we can call Ordinary History and there is Deep History. In explaining the difference, let me give you an illustration that may help. Imagine you are far out at sea in a boat and all around you are waves moving past. They are all you can see on the water and by looking at them you tell yourself that you know which way the water is moving. In fact, they are probably misleading; it is highly likely that, just a few metres below the surface, the water masses are, quite invisible to you, really moving in another direction all together.

Now to the Christian, history is like that. What most people call history, the drama of kings and queens, empires, and wars that we read about in books and are taught at school is what occurs on the surface; it is Ordinary History. Many people have written about it because that is what catches the eye and it is what seems to be the most important. But there is more to history than this and below the noise and spray of surface events there is something far more important going on. This is the vast, powerful and often silent movement of God's plans and purposes; this is Deep History. Now we pay heavily if we ignore it. For one thing, Deep History is actually far more significant than Ordinary History; it is actually real history. Ordinary History is quite frequently no more important than the froth on a pint of beer. I mention these two sorts of history because we need to understand Deep History when we think about sharing our faith in Jesus with someone. Because sharing our faith is linked, not with the shallow noisy tumult of what we see in the newspaper and on television, but with the eternal, massive and unstoppable motion of God's plans and purposes.

In the next chapters I have divided Deep History into seven great episodes that are marked out in the Bible. In summarising these episodes, do remember that I am concentrating on what these events signify for mission. There is, of course, much that I have missed out or skimmed over.

At the end of these chapters, I have put in some exercises and questions. I have written these exercises and questions as if they were addressed to you. That is purely a convention. In fact they are addressed to us all and I need to think about them too.

Chapter 1

EPISODE 1: GOD'S GOOD EARTH

'In the beginning God created the heavens and the earth . . .
And God saw that it was good'

Genesis 1:1, 4

The Bible's account of Deep History opens with a vision that is mind-blowing in the vastness of its scale. It is the making of the entire universe. In the first two chapters of Genesis this awesome picture starts with the first moment of the creation of the cosmos and then rapidly focuses down onto our world and our species. These two chapters are short – barely a page and a half long in my Bible – yet what is said here echoes through every page that follows and has a fundamental bearing on everything that we are as individuals and as a species. When I recently wrote a book on the Ten Commandments I found myself constantly referring back to these two chapters. In them we see, spelt out in the very briefest of words, who God is, who we are, and what we were designed to be.

Now before I look at these topics, all of which are critical when it comes to sharing our faith, can I make a plea? It is very tempting to look at these chapters and say 'Ah yes but how does that fit with the "Big Bang"?' 'How long is a day?' or 'Did Adam have a navel?' I'm sure you know the sort of thing. There are two problems with these questions. First, by some mysterious process of mental physics, they take a lot of time and energy and convert it into a great deal of heat with very little light; they really don't get us very far. I like to think of these chapters as if they were a painting done in broad, impressionistic brush strokes or a film shot in soft focus. I have no hesitation in saying that some of the Bible's language here is symbolic or pictorial, but how much is hard to say. Of course, we must remember that language using images can be truer than non-pictorial language. I could say to my wife, 'Killy, when I think of you, various glandular and hormonal processes go into operation which result in elevated mood feelings'. Now I could also say 'Killy, I love you with all my heart'. I know which statement is more correct scientifically, but I know which conveys the truth more accurately. I know too which she would prefer.

Secondly – and more seriously – they are the wrong questions. They almost totally obscure what these passages are really about. These chapters are about God and who he is, creation and what that is, and humanity and who we are. I refuse to be sidetracked by these secondary issues and so should you. You can ask Adam about his navel when you see him in heaven.

Let me summarise, as briefly as I can, what we learn in these chapters.

We see who God is?

- In the beginning, we read, God made everything out of nothing. Everything out of nothing. At this point, you really ought to stop to think a few awed thoughts, or at least, say 'Wow!' God is that sort of God. Let me tell you a story that makes a serious point.

  Finally, after centuries of work, a scientist with a test tube stands before the Angel Gabriel in the vast echoing hallway of heaven.
  'We've done it! We too can make human beings,' he announces proudly.
  'Really? From the dust of the earth?' asks Gabriel.
  'Absolutely, from pure dust,' comes back the confident answer,

'that puts us equal to God.'

'I see,' says Gabriel, rather coolly, 'well let me check a moment.' He vanishes behind the great golden doors at the end of the hall.

A few moments later he returns, shakes his head sadly and gestures the scientist back out to the door.

'But what did he say?' protests the scientist indignantly.

'He said', Gabriel answers quietly as he closes the door on the departing scientist, 'that you have to make your own dust'.

- God is the eternal and infinite one. There is much that the Bible tells us about God, but eventually we reach limits. Quite simply, we cannot begin to comprehend God because there are limits to our brains. Think about something that is smaller than God: the universe. That is at least 30,000 light years across (and each light year is a mere nine million, million kilometres). The number of stars is around 30,000,000,000,000,000. If it helps you, that is about the number of grains of sand on all the beaches of the entire world. But it is not just scale or size that make God impossible for us to comprehend, it's the fact that however many dimensions there are, God can see all of them at once. Time itself poses no limits to him. Speaking as someone who finds London hard to visualise, that is pretty humbling. And if we cannot handle the universe we cannot hope to understand the One who made it and keeps it all going.

- God has always existed. In the beginning, we read, there was God. He is the one who is immortal and who has no beginning and no end. However old the universe is – and it may well be many billions of years old – God was there before it started. Time doesn't bother him. No one made him or brought him into being, he just was, and is and will be. To ask who made God is like Mickey Mouse asking Goofy, 'So who drew Walt Disney?' We need humility as we come before God.

- God is all-powerful. In a simple string of commands, 'let there be . . . let there be . . . ' God makes everything. At a mere word the heavens are formed, the land and sea separate, living things arise.

- God is personal. He thinks, creates, acts and feels. He is not some force or power. He is a person and that means we can know him as we can know any other person. It makes sense to talk about relating to God or talking to him in a way that would be crazy if he ('it'?) was a force, like gravity or electricity.

- God simply chose to create. Freely, deliberately, graciously and wonderfully, he chose to make the universe, galaxies, the nebulae, the stars, the moon, the planets, and this world that we call Earth.

- God has ultimate freedom. He made things without the help of others. He was not forced to create and he is not to be limited by anything or anyone else. In Genesis, there is a cast of one.

- The combination of these characteristics is, I think, unique in religion. Many tribes and peoples have believed in personal gods (think of the Greeks and Romans) but they have always been limited. Many others have conceived of a single, infinite, all-powerful God (as in some forms of Hinduism) but that sort of God is always impersonal. Only within the Bible do you get the combination of the two: a God who is personal *and* infinite.

We see what creation is

- All that we see is God's handiwork. On the one hand, it is not some mysterious and half divine New Age 'Nature'. On the other, it is not merely the atheist's wishful fantasy of something produced by random chance over time. It is a *creation*, like a picture, a poem or a symphony. And, just as an artist's work reflects them, so God's creation reflects who he is. The diversity and complexity of the creation speaks to us of God's power, wisdom and care for detail. The enormity of what he created and the awe-inspiring nature of so much of it; from the mountains to the stars to the intricacies of the cells of our body, speaks to us of an awesome God; all mighty, all powerful and all wise; who is concerned with both the largest and very smallest of things. Creation is a mirror in which we see God's image.

- Creation was good. We are told, time and time again in Genesis 1 that God took pleasure in what he was making, '. . . and God saw that it was good.' God made his universe good. Much of it still is.

We see who we are

- People are created in God's own image. This, as I have said, is not literal language (after all, God has no head, arms or feet) but it means that we can relate to him. Although there is much that we cannot understand about God, the fact is that we have been made so that we can have knowledge of him adequate enough for us to relate to him. There is something complementary about him and us. Now part of being made in God's image seems to be that we have the ability to choose. God didn't make humans to do what he wants them to do automatically, like some kind of programmable biological robots. God gave us freedom. He wants us to love him, to live in relationship with him, but he does not force us to do that. Even though that is what is best for us, he has made us able to choose for him, or against him. Now I know there are complex issues here to do with the fact that God somehow remains in control of us while allowing humans freedom to say yes or no to him. This is what God does; he never compels or forces, but freely gives people the option to accept or reject him.

- We see that we were meant to have an unbroken relationship with God. At first, there were no barriers between God and people. God, we read, talked to Adam and Eve and in Genesis 3:8 we learn that God walked in the garden of Eden.

Behind the symbolic language is the idea of free, open communication.

- Men and women were intended to have a deep and lasting relationship with each other. We read that woman was made out of man and then, in marriage, they are allowed to rejoin to become one flesh.

Lessons for mission

This first episode of the Bible's Deep History is vital. For a start, it tells us who the God that we seek to share with people actually is. It tells us that he is the one that made everything out of nothing. He has not lost that skill. He is still the one who, in the darkest of minds and situations, can bring in light. He is still the one who we cannot fathom and who is frustratingly, maddeningly and lovably independent of us. We may try to tame God, we may pretend that we understand him and that we can predict his activity but we cannot. I was reading only last week about how many Japanese are currently being brought to faith in Jesus by listening to performances (sung in German!) of Bach's church music. Yes, that J. S. Bach, the one who died in 1750. In an age when the aims, goals and methods of mission are made by men and women in boardrooms as if they were defining some corporate business strategy, I find the idea that God is independent and imaginative refreshing. He cannot be tamed.

Yet if God has not changed, creation and humanity have. Here the witness of the Bible is especially vital. Imagine a great piece of sculpture that has been broken into a hundred fragments. In order to restore it, it would be of enormous help to see a picture of what it was originally like. These two chapters give us 'the world as it was'.

Creation still reflects God in some way, although it is now a tarnished mirror and the image is not as clear as it was. Even so, we still see in it something of the goodness and greatness of God. Many people, who would never say a prayer, come closest to worship in the presence of mountains, sea and sky.

As we will see in the next chapter the image of God in humanity has also been damaged. Yet here too there are, even in the most ravaged of lives, the remains of what we once were. All human beings are still in God's image, however defaced that may be. Deep in every heart is the desire to be in a right relationship to God our maker and to be back with him. The very heart of mission is spelt out in these chapters. On the one hand we have an awesome God, all powerful, all magnificent and all wise, but one who also stoops down to create a humanity that can relate to him. On the other hand, we have a human race wonderfully designed to have fellowship with God and to know him. That original pattern has, unfortunately, gone very badly wrong. The goal of mission is this: to bring back to God this species that has so badly strayed away from Him. God has a project, a rescue mission to bring men and women back to him. He wants you and me to be involved in it.

Exercises

1. Read Genesis chapters 1 and 2 (remember to use an up-to-date translation!). Imagine you knew nothing about God other than these verses. What would you learn?

2. Make a trip into the countryside if you can, or a garden or park if you cannot, and force yourself to look at how wonderful things are. Think about what God must be like if what you see around is a just a tiny, flawed reflection of God.

Questions

1. About God

- How does it help our mission to realise that the God who we talk about is the one whose power made the universe?
- Does it encourage you that Christianity is not about us seeking God, but about God trying to restore the lost relationship with us?
- If God is 'independent and imaginative', what does that mean about our efforts to share our faith
- Is mission us telling people about God, or God revealing himself to people through us? Does that make a difference?
- If God decided to hide, could we ever find him?
- How might the idea that the God who made entire planets at a word, help you to reach out to someone whose life seems in a total mess?

2. About Creation

- Do you think that the natural world is a mirror of God? Does God speak in nature to people?
- If God does speak in nature, isn't that enough? (This is an idea that we will pick up again later.)
- How might you encourage someone who was

interested in landscape painting, walking or bird watching to think about God?

3. About Humanity

- If, as we see in the next chapter, our species has rebelled against God, why does he not just force us back into line?
- When you look at people, do you see God reflected in them? How about your friend? Your colleague? Your neighbour?
- If we are made in God's image how can we reflect that fact more clearly?
- How does the fact that all people are made in the image of God affect how we witness? What limitations does it put on our methods?

Chapter 2

EPISODE 2: THE GREAT REBELLION AND ITS CONSEQUENCES

'Their judgement is based on this fact: the light from heaven came into the world but they loved the darkness more than the light, for their actions were evil.'

John 3:19

If the creation of the world and humanity is recorded in a mere two chapters, the disaster that descended on the human race is even more briefly told. In the third chapter of the Bible we read how, through disobedience, paradise is lost and how a cursed humanity becomes separated from God.

Before we look at the events surrounding what Christians have always called 'The Fall' let me say again that I think it is quite unprofitable to wonder where and when all this took place. The relation of this important event in Deep History to the timescale of Ordinary History is not clear. The key point is that it happened and that it has messed up the human race ever since. There may be some symbolism (we will meet the trees and the serpent again in the last two chapters of the book of Revelation), but if there is symbolism, there is far more reality. The psychology of what happens (for instance the way that Adam blames Eve and Eve blames the serpent) is so realistic that it could have been drawn from twenty-first century life.

In Genesis 2:16-17 we read how Adam was given total freedom in the wonderful paradise of Eden. There was only one minor restriction; he was not to eat of the fruit of the tree of knowledge of good and evil. To eat that was death. He and Eve had freedom to choose to obey or disobey. Tragically, we read that they chose to disobey. Eve is enticed by a mysterious serpent into questioning the good words of God about the tree and its fruit: it is a plot. The serpent says, 'God knows that if you eat of it you will become just like him'. Eve, it says, has nothing to fear – and everything to gain from going against God's ruling. Eve eats the fruit and Adam with her. As they eat, their eyes are opened and they feel shame – at their nakedness. They have indeed come to know good and evil but in the worst possible way.

At the heart of this temptation is the whole issue of whether or not Adam and Eve trust God and his goodness and kindness to them. In the end, they chose to rebel against him, to disobey and to take his crown and put it on their own heads. They have chosen to try to be gods themselves. This also is all too modern.

For me the big question is why? Why did they do this when they had everything they could possibly need with God? Why did they believe the Devil (or Satan, as he is termed later) when he raised doubts about God's good ways for them? Why did they choose to turn away from a God who was so loving, liberating and generous? How, we say, could they be so stupid! Frankly, the answer to the cause of this first act of evil is a mystery. And evil continues to mystify us; every time there is some horrific crime we ask, 'Why?' Everybody, from psychologists to politicians, gives their opinion on the origins of these terrible evils that have been committed.

In part it is because, as a result of committing that first act of rebellion, the virus of disobedience entered so deeply into humanity that it has been with us ever since. We are slaves to what the Bible calls *sin*; the state of rebellion against God. But at the heart of all turning away from God, all sin, there is a mystery: why do we choose to act wrongly, badly, selfishly?

Much as we might like it to, the Bible does not spell out the theoretical, psychological, or spiritual basis for sin. Instead, in its pages it gives us the answer. It is a manual of practical medicine, not a treatise on how diseases occur.

The reason why the human race rebelled from God might be mysterious, but the consequences for our ancestors are plain and terrible. From happy innocence, they go to guilt-ridden shame and flee from God. The open and fearless relationship with God that they had has been irreparably breached and shattered. Now their lives are characterised by fear and hiding, by guilt, by blame and counter blame. The breach of their relationship with God also has side effects. The relationship between the man and the woman starts to fracture; they realise that are naked and they start the first of all those rows ('It was your fault!' 'Oh *really*? You started it!'), that sadly, we all know.

In Genesis 3, God solemnly announces the results of the rebellion. Eve is told that pain will be added to her life and that her relations with her husband will be distorted (Genesis 3:16). Adam is told that from now on his life will involve painful hard work in tilling the ground (Genesis 3:17- 20). Somehow, humanity's relationship with creation itself is now twisted. Above all, death in all its horror is to descend on them. The sad final words of God's sentence upon Adam and Eve echo down solemnly through the ages to us, 'For you were made from dust and to dust you will return.'

The chapter ends with both the man and the woman being banished from Eden and God sealing its entrance by mighty angelic beings and a flaming sword. There is no direct way back to Eden. As we will find out, there is a road back to Eden but it is a long one; and to make it cost God an almost inconceivable price.

Lessons for Mission

This chapter of the Bible spells out the reason why we need mission. Ever since Adam and Eve, with one exception, the human race has joined in the rebellion against God. The virus of sin has taken such a deep hold that no amount of prosperity, education or social work can remove it from our system. Every aspect of our lives – social, psychological, physical and even religious – is now affected by this rebellion and its consequences.

Let me summarise the state of humanity that it reveals.

- The open and friendly relationship that humanity once had with God is now shattered. There is an enormous gap between him and us.
- The basis of this separation is that we are guilty before God. When we seriously consider the matter, we become conscious of our shame and moral nakedness. Instead of embracing God, our natural reaction is now to hide from him. He now has to come looking for us.
- So deep is our ruin, that even our attempts at being religious and doing good things become flawed. Without God's help through the Holy Spirit (a subject to which I will return), religion leads simply to pride and intolerance.
- Our relationships with human beings are fractured. In particular, male-female relations are distorted.
- Our relations with our world are also warped. We have gone from being those who were to tend and care for the garden (Genesis 2:15), to being a species whose struggle for survival in the wilderness has vandalised the rest of God's creation.
- Finally, over all our lives now hangs the terrible certainty of death. Deep in our hearts we know that we have fallen short of God's standards and the idea of meeting and being judged by a Holy God is something that appals us.

Now I have spelt this out in detail for two reasons. First, it is a motive for mission. The entire human race is in serious trouble. We all suffer from a chronic ailment that unless treated will have permanent and appalling consequences. Telling people about Jesus Christ is not like offering someone a cosmetic remedy for baldness or wrinkles. It is instead offering them the radical surgery that is the only chance of saving their life. Jesus is not an optional extra to our lives; he is life itself.

Secondly, it affects how we do mission. So deeply ingrained within us is the virus of sin that it even affects how we view the world. The Bible talks about sin as blindness (John 9: 39-41) and this is a good description of what it does. Do you remember the distinctly sick sketch in *Monty Python and the Holy Grail* where King Arthur fights the Black Knight, played by John Cleese? As limb after limb is severed from him, the Black Knight refuses to admit there is a problem, protesting that 'tis but a scratch', 'I've had worse!' and it's 'just a flesh wound'. People are often similar about the state of their lives; you can tell them there is a problem, you can point out all the symptoms, but they will still not face up to it. Sometimes too, people do not even want to change. In fact, we can actually prefer staying in a familiar, if unpleasant, condition, rather than face dealing with a change. A well-known psychological phenomenon occurs if people are in jail for a long time; the prospect of freedom can come to almost terrify them. They prefer the cell to liberation. That is what sin can do to us. Sometimes, the idea of being set free by Jesus is scary. The old ways can seem safer.

It is for these reasons that I believe we need to work at mission. The quiet fireside chat may not be enough to break through the mental and spiritual chains that bind people. Our gentle, carefully reasoned, arguments may make as much impact as a feather blow on our listeners. That is why the Holy Spirit must be involved in our mission, because only he can make people see that they are in desperate need of God's love and forgiveness. Only he can shed light into the darkness of people's minds. Equally, it is not enough to quietly request to people that they come to Jesus – we have to *call out*.

However, I also think that this dark chapter hints at something in human nature where the Good News about Jesus may find fertile soil. It is that the idea of being expelled from Paradise comes up again and again in our lives. In the midst of our species' exile from the Garden of Eden, we get repeated dreams of what might have been. If you look at the great themes that regularly occur in art, whether it is poetry, cinema or music, perhaps one of the strongest is the longing to return to Eden. It is that strange, inescapable and tantalising feeling that somewhere, just around the corner, is the place where it will all be all right; where we will be home at last. You get it in the film *The Beach* with Leonardo DiCaprio, which had the slogan of longing, 'Somewhere on this planet it must exist', and you get it in a thousand other places. Much of literature tells us that this is not just a modern youth phenomenon.

If we are to engage in mission, we have to acknowledge that people are in darkness to such an extent that they do not even want to meet God. But we also have a toehold in that when we talk of God and heaven to men and women who do not know Christ, it may be that it reminds them of what they know that they have lost.

Exercises

1. Read Genesis chapter 3 again. Concentrate on seeing how the various relationships (humanity and God, man and woman, humanity and creation) start to become distorted.

2. There are two major treatments of sin in the Bible. In the Old Testament, Isaiah 59:1-15 is a devastating analysis of the sinful state of humanity while in the New Testament in Romans 1:18 - 2:16, Paul the Apostle (an appointed church leader) is equally frank about the state of humanity. Read both passages in a modern translation and notice how widespread and deep- seated the effects of sin are. If the passages make you depressed, remember that both Isaiah and Paul hold out the hope of a redeemer from sin (Isaiah 59:20-21; Romans 5:1-11).

Questions

1. The Bible teaches that well-educated and respectable citizens are sinners as well as inhabitants of prisons. Which do you find it harder to believe? Why?

2. Does how we do mission depend on whether we believe we are dealing with people who, spiritually, are merely slightly or terminally ill?

3. Why does conversion have to be supernatural?

4. Do you agree that people still long for a lost paradise? How does it show itself among your family and friends?

Chapter 3

EPISODE 3: THE RESCUE BEGINS

'Oh how can I give you up, Israel? How can I let you go?'

Hosea 11:8

If I had made the world and Adam and Eve had rebelled against me, I would have been pretty annoyed. Think of it – you go to all that trouble to make the world, you do everything you can possibly do to bring into being the most wonderful forms of life, you place people in a beautiful garden with everything they could want. And instead of living in gratitude, they turn their backs on you, disobey you and go their own foolish way? Frankly, I'd be tempted to wipe out the lot. Drop a big meteorite on Eden and start all over again. Alternatively, if I were feeling especially mean I'd have said something like this: 'Obeying the serpent eh? Very well, you can serve him. You'll make a perfect match. Don't bother to write.'

Then I'd have cleared off and started work on Humanity Version 2.0 no nearer than Alpha Centauri.

But God does not do that. Instead of giving up on the human beings that have so devastatingly turned away from him he starts a process to bring them back. There is a wonderful image in Genesis 3:8-9 'Towards evening they [the man and the woman] heard the LORD God walking about in the garden so they hid themselves among the trees. The LORD God called to Adam, "*Where are you*?"' (italics mine).

I love that picture of God, straight after the rebellion, going out to search for the disgraced man and woman. '*Where are you*?' That cry from God's own heart is found on every page of the Bible from there on.

God does not give up. In the almost total darkness that descends on Adam and Eve in Genesis 3, there is the tiniest flicker of hope. Amid the solemn sentences of judgement, God tells the serpent that from now on he will face hostility from the woman and her offspring. Mysteriously, God says that 'he will crush your head, and you will strike his heel' (Genesis 3:15). Who the '*he*' is that will do this is left unsaid and will not be revealed for a long time. Yet, it is a hint that God has not given up on the rebels. He has started a rescue mission.

Again we find that God's way of doing things is not the way I would do it. For a start, he takes time: lots of it. Unknown years pass. The account of Deep History passes quickly over those events Ordinary History gets excited about: technology, new farming methods, writing and empires. They are just background. At first, it simply recalls how humanity falls further into spectacular chaos of war, violence and judgement. Finally, the camera of Deep History focuses down onto one man. To this man, known to us as Abraham, God gives promises as part of a covenant, a solemn binding agreement. 'From you,' God says, 'will come a great people ... All the families of the earth will be blessed through you'(Genesis 12: 2-3).

The rest of the Old Testament, the first three-quarters of our Bible, is about that rescue project and how God takes Abraham's offspring, the Jews, and over the best part of two thousand years, makes them into a people that are exclusively his own. Behind all the tales of kings, prophets and priests, at the back of all those genealogies, beyond all the strange names like Elimelech, Ahithophel and Maher-shalal-hash-baz lies one thing; God's great rescue mission.

Nothing else matters. Most of the great empires and kings of the Near East that we know from Ordinary History make appearances in this story, but always in supporting roles.

Indeed, the Bible's attitude to them is almost absurdly arrogant. Take the great Babylonian Empire: its entire purpose, the Bible implies, seems simply to have been as God's tool for the refining of his people.

I could follow this tale in detail but I won't. This is not because I want to downplay the significance of the Old Testament; on the contrary, I feel that we would benefit a great deal by digging more deeply into it than we do. I just don't have the time or the space here to do that. Instead, what I will do is try to summarise what God had taught the Jews (often in the 'School of Hard Knocks') by the time that Jesus was born. At the end of this chapter, I will explain what the implication of this great tale is for our mission today.

I think we can say that by time of the birth of Jesus the Jews had, as a result of God's patient disciplining, gained four things.

1. They knew who God was

Throughout the Old Testament, God revealed himself repeatedly to the Jewish people. He did this through the prophets, people like Moses, Jeremiah and Isaiah. He revealed his nature (unique and almighty) and his character (holy and caring) to his people. A key thing was that he had given them his personal name *Yahweh* ('The LORD' in our English Bibles). By doing that, he personally confirmed any covenant agreements he made with his people. They were his people and he was their God.

After various unfortunate episodes involving dabbling in idolatry and other religions had resulted in God passing down unpleasant disciplinary action (like the seventy years in exile in Babylon), the Jews had finally decided that there was indeed only one God and that he was Yahweh. There was no one else. They knew they couldn't make images of him and they knew that he was the almighty God who had made everything. They also knew that Yahweh was holy and righteous and that care and reverence was needed in dealing with him. In fact, they were so careful in their transactions with God that they didn't even use his name. (The belief that they called him Yahweh – or didn't call him, if you take my meaning – is actually a bit of guesswork.)

Now this idea of one holy and all-powerful God may not sound like much, but it was streets ahead of the other religions around. For example, it was after this time that the Romans, generally a pretty sensible bunch, started to consider their emperors as gods.

2. They knew what God had done for them

To the Jews of Jesus' time, their history was precious. They may not have used the term Deep History but they would have understood the concept; indeed, they believed that as the nation of Israel, they were at the centre of history. As they looked back on their past, they saw how God had been gracious to them. He had led them out of slave labour in Egypt and in the desert, God had given them his laws, made covenant promises to them and given them his name, Yahweh. Then he had led them to the 'Promised Land' and fought alongside them so that they had, finally, a land of their own. And in the thirteen or so centuries since they had taken the land, God had been kind and loving to them. He had disciplined them again and again, but nevertheless had preserved them. They must have thought that their history was remarkable: it was. They had been threatened by a 'Who's Who' of the Ancient World. The extinction of their tiny nation must have seemed a safe bet on numerous occasions. The Egypt of the Pharaohs, Sennacherib's Assyrians, Nebuchadnezzar's proud Babylonian forces, the mighty Persian empire and Alexander's Greek armies along with various alliances of second-division nations seeking promotion had all seemed poised to erase them off the map. Yet the Jews had survived, and Egypt, Assyria, Babylon, Persia and Greece (not to mention the Philistines, Edomites, Moabites, Amalekites *et cetera*) were now gone. There were still the Romans, but there must have been a quiet confidence that one day, Yahweh would sort them out too.

God had also protected Israel against internal enemies. Somehow, despite moments when it looked as if the whole nation would slide into the worship of idols, God had intervened and raised up faithful prophets and wise kings and they staggered back on track. God could be trusted – their history demonstrated that. Yahweh not only made covenants – he kept them.

3. They knew what God expected

The Jewish faith at the time of Christ was more than a set of beliefs in God and how he had acted in the past. Jewish life focused on God; the whole of their lives was, at least in theory, devoted to him. They knew by now what he expected. They were a religious state; in theory again, God was their king. There were three areas where they saw God particularly involved:

a) They had a God-given Law

The Law or the *Torah* was the set of rules for life that God had given his people after Moses had led them out of Egypt. Although we may only be aware of the Ten Commandments, there were many more laws, as a brief glance at the Old Testament books of Leviticus and Deuteronomy will show. There were also a vast number of extra rules that had been created by scholars since. Memorisation of the Law, meditation on it and obedience to it, were seen as vital duties. As a result of human additions, some of the rules, particularly on keeping the Sabbath, were so extensive and numerous as to be almost impossible to keep. Nevertheless, there was a widespread belief that their holy God, who had saved them, expected them to be holy and devout in return. Linked with law were the various festivals. The most important of these was the spring festival of Passover that commemorated God's deliverance of Israel out of Egypt.

b) They had God-given intermediaries.

In the long history of the Jewish people, three positions or offices had become established for people who stood between them and God.

- There were the *kings* who ruled over the people in the name of God. Under the rule of the great King David and his son Solomon, the Israelite Kingdom had seen a short-lived period of glory and regional expansion. By the time Jesus was born, it had been many centuries since the last true king of Israel (the Herods – ethnically only half Jews, and politically Roman puppets – didn't count). But under the harsh, and what must have been seen as the disgustingly pagan rule of the Romans, the idea of a king of the type of David was an attractive one.
- There were the *prophets*. These were men (more rarely, women) who spoke God's words to the nation. Far from simply predicting the future ('war and plague imminent'), they often just announced God's verdict on society (mostly along the lines of 'must do better!'). Although the great prophets (of the Isaiah, Jeremiah and Hosea calibre) had not appeared for centuries in Israel, lesser prophets and prophetesses were still around at the time of Jesus' birth.
- If kings and prophets were not what they had been in the past, there were still *priests*. These men carried out the sacrificial offices in the temple in Jerusalem. Their offerings, mostly of animal sacrifices, filled the gap between humanity's sinfulness and God's holiness. To use a technical term that has passed into common use, they 'atoned' for sin.

One minor point: kings, prophets and priests were all offices that were anointed by oil. The Hebrew term for such an 'anointed one' was *Meshiach*, from which we get the word 'Messiah'. The Greek equivalent of this word is *Christos*: Christ.

c) They had a God-given land.

Yahweh had promised Abraham a land, his descendants had been given it and somehow they had managed to hold onto it since. Mind you the habit every up-and- coming regional superpower had of invading Palestine, as if conquering it proved you'd made it in the world, made holding onto it a touch and go business. Yet, even if it was only by reluctant Roman permission, the Jews were still there. At the centre of their land, they had the temple at Jerusalem. A huge structure, a third version of which was approaching completion in Jesus' day, was where the sacrificial system was based. It was the heart of the Jewish faith, the heart of the nation and, in popular thinking at least, was the house of God.

4. They knew what God promised them

As well as knowing who God was, what he had done and what he expected of them, there was something else that made the Jewish people special: the promises that God had given them. Throughout Old Testament times there had been prophecies of a future kingdom grander than David's under a yet greater king of David's line. Under this deliverer-king, the Messiah, Jerusalem would be the worship centre, not just of the Jews but of 'the nations', the non-Jews or Gentiles who, in the glorious age to come, would travel to worship God there.

Yet there was no firm agreement on how the prophecies would be worked out. Was the Messiah to be man or God? How did Daniel's vision (Daniel 7) of a God-like 'Son of Man' fit in? How could the Messiah's role as triumphant warrior-king relate to the prophecies (in Isaiah 53) of the Servant who was to suffer for the sins of others?

So, two thousand years after Abraham, and unknown years after the rebellion, everything was finally ready for God to act. The preparations were over; the great intervention could begin.

Lessons for mission

There are many lessons here for us in the Old Testament. I think it is unfortunate that we often neglect the first three-quarters of our Bibles. Jesus came to fulfil and complete the Law, not to replace it. This was his Bible and what he and the early Church grew up on. If we overlook this, then we are in danger of misunderstanding both him and his message.

There are some general points that I see in this long episode. One of the most important of these comes out of the fact that it is such a long time. You see it reminds us that God doesn't ever give up. God's love is so great that he persists even though the objects of his affection continue to rebel against him. When you read the Old Testament, you marvel at God's patience. It almost seems as if his people are looking around for idols, unwise political alliances or just plain corruption to get involved in. There are endless opportunities for God to say, 'That's it! I have finally had enough. I'm cancelling all my initiatives to save you'. Yet, God continues to love them. God has not changed in his character.

We also see how God's purposes work out. The promise to Abraham is not broken by all the powers of kings or empires. The line of David from which the Messiah is to come hangs on a thread more than once. Yet, almost miraculously, it survives. Under the constant turmoil of the Middle East, God's plans – what we have called Deep History – work steadily towards their goal of preparing the way for the Saviour of the world to come. I find that encouraging. God is *God*. God makes promises and he keeps them, even over centuries of turmoil. Circumstances do not defeat his purposes. He can be trusted.

There are other points in the Old Testament that I think are relevant to mission. I feel that there is significance in the many different ways in which God dealt with his people in Old Testament times. There is not just a single monochrome message rammed home in a single way. Of course preaching, whether in the delivery of a prophetic message or in the routine explanation of the Law, was vital. Yet in the Old Testament we also find a rich variety of rituals, festivals and institutions, and constant reminders in everyday life of God and his claims on his peoples' lives. God used prophets, priests, kings, ordinary men, women and children in many ways. Perhaps we need to be more open to new ways of relating to people today. Britain is not a holy nation in the sense that ancient Israel was, yet it seems rather sad that Christians have been largely relegated to the edges of society, often only talking openly about Jesus in churches or chapels on Sundays. I think too, I see here a better picture of what mission is about. Too often, we have the picture of mission as someone giving a message, seeing conversions and then leaving. Yet the Old Testament picture is different; it is much more down-to-earth. It's about conversions yes, about acknowledging that Yahweh is a redeeming God, but it is also about producing a holy people who live in holy ways in a holy community and who reflect God in every area of their lives. And without in any way undermining the need to preach the gospel, I want to say that we need to recover that vision of the God-centred life and community.

Exercises

1. Read the story of the appearance of the resurrected Jesus to the two disciples on the Emmaus Road (Luke 24:13-34). How does Jesus use what we call the Old Testament? (See especially verse 27).

2. Read Hebrews 1:1-3. How, according to the writer, is Jesus similar to the Old Testament writings? How is he superior?

Questions

1. If the Old Testament had somehow never been translated into English how much would we lose

2. It is traditional in Christian thinking to see Jesus as being the final and ultimate king, priest and prophet. What do you think? If he is, then how should it affect our attitude to him

3. How do you feel about the fact that it was so long from Adam to the birth of Jesus? Are you impressed by God's patience or puzzled at his delay

4. In Britain, previous generations were brought up knowing the Old Testament so that they could use its images and symbols to explain who Jesus was. Today the position is different. Can we use the Old Testament in any way to talk about Jesus to people today?

5. What was good about having the name of God so sacred that it could not be written down? What was bad about it? It could be said the name Jesus has now replaced the mysterious Yahweh for those people who are believers in Christ. How should that make us feel when we pray to him

6. Imagine that you and someone really important (the Prime Minister perhaps?) had made a solemn covenant. How would you view your responsibilities towards such an agreement?

Chapter 4

EPISODE 4: THE GREAT INTERVENTION

'In the beginning, the Word already existed. He was with God and he was God. He was in the beginning with God. He created everything there is . . . So the Word became human and lived here on earth among us.'

John 1:1-3, 14

Finally, it is time. God comes personally to this troubled earth. He does not come as an imitation man, as God merely disguised as a human; he comes as the authentic article in every way. It is almost as though God wants to avoid the accusation that he has cheated, that the Messiah is not really one of us. It is as if he wants to be sure that he cannot be in anyway disqualified from being fully human: and to be human means to be born as a baby.

In one respect it all seems extraordinarily insignificant, indeed by the standards of Ordinary History it is. An attempt by Roman bureaucracy to work out who they have in this out-of-the-way fragment of their sprawling empire, summons a young pregnant bride and her husband to a strange town. There, in the most basic lodgings, she gives birth. But in God's plan, this birth in this place – Bethlehem, the town of David – is the point that all Deep History has been working to.

Somehow, in this infant Jesus, God became one of us, in every way. He had a mother and father who cared for him, who taught him to walk, to write and to read. He grew up in a small

51

village in a remote northern part of Palestine learning his human father's trade of carpentry. He would have spoken with the heavy (and much mocked) accent of Galilee, would have worn normal worker's clothes, and probably had the leathery, scarred hands of any labourer in the developing world today. He would have been like everyone else and in a crowd: you and I would probably not even have noticed him. The only thing that would have marked him out was an unusual devotion to God and his word, but his humility was such that he would not have paraded that.

This is not the place to retell Jesus' ministry; that would require another book. The account given of his life in the Bible is something we need to master by regularly reading and re-reading the four Gospels. A good up-to-date guide to Jesus' life and culture may also be helpful to explain the background.

There are however, some aspects of Jesus' teaching that I want to highlight here.

• Jesus' ministry centred on himself. For all his transparent humility, there was an astonishing focus in his ministry on himself. Either directly or indirectly, Jesus claimed that all the great symbols, images and institutions of the Old Testament were fulfilled in him. He was, he claimed, the true and final Prophet, Priest and King; in him, everything that the Sabbath, the Land and the sacrifices meant was fulfilled. He was even, he indicated, the fulfilment and replacement of the temple. He called himself the Good Shepherd, the True Vine, the Living Water, and the Bread of Life. In his ministry Jesus deliberately referred, in word or deed, to the great figures of the past such as Abraham, Moses, David, Solomon, Elijah, Elisha and others and then stated or clearly implied that he was greater than they were. Most astonishing of all, Jesus took terms that were applied only to God in the Old Testament and applied them to himself. Bearing in mind the reverence the Jews applied to God this was extraordinary and, more than once, nearly led to his premature death. In his hands, all the Scriptures point to himself. Jesus also stated that he himself was going to be the judge of all people at the end of the world and that it was how we related to him that would either bring us into eternal joy or cast us into eternal loss. Finally, he called God his 'Father' in an intimate family way that caused offence. He was altogether too familiar with God for some people's liking. People sometimes express surprise that Jesus was crucified: given the statements that he made, I am more surprised that he lasted three years.

- Jesus preached about the Kingdom of God. However, to the dismay of the nationalist elements, he was at pains to point out that the Kingdom of God was not an earthly political kingdom. Now, he said, it was the rule of God in people's lives. In the future – at the end of the age – the kingdom would come in power and glory and under God's reign all evil would be eliminated. But not until then.

- Jesus emphasised both God's holy demands and his gracious love. On the one hand, Jesus took the Old Testament law and tightened it so that to be perfect was not simply to avoid murder and adultery; it was to avoid anger and lust. What Jesus did was to make the law apply to what we think, not just what we do. On the other hand, he taught that God was forgiving and gracious to the humble, repentant sinner (Luke 18:9-14). Jesus had the boldness to suggest that a certain type of religious observance could be a barrier to getting to heaven. In fact, he said that those that knew they were sinners were closer to heaven than those who were confident that they had earned their way to God's good favour. Can you imagine how this must have gone down amongst those whose lives had been dedicated to negotiating the endless rules of the law? Significantly, despite his strict teaching on what sin was, Jesus is never recorded asking for forgiveness for himself. In fact, no allegations of sin emerge at his trial; only his claim to be Messiah is challenged.

- Jesus especially emphasised God's love to those who were outcasts under the Jewish faith of his day. He taught that

God could forgive people such as prostitutes and corrupt tax collectors. It was a thought that was not popular in the religious hierarchy and was widely considered insulting by many. There was also a suspicious breadth to Jesus' teaching about the Kingdom. Some of his stories-with-meanings (the 'parables') suggested that not only would there be Gentiles in the Kingdom but that some of his Jewish hearers might not be there. Unlike the religious leaders of his day (and many since), Jesus plainly considered women worth teaching and even had women followers (Luke 8:2-3). One challenging fact summarises Jesus' concern for those who were outside the exclusive and respectable club of official religion in his day. It is this: the longest theological discussion of Jesus that is recorded in the gospels, is in John chapter 4 where he talked with a woman of dubious morality who belonged to the half-breed Samaritans who were, in Jewish eyes, contaminated both by foreign blood and false worship.

- Jesus taught that he would die, but that this death would be central to what he had to do. Increasingly, he gave detailed predictions of the manner of his death: in Jerusalem, at the hands of non-Jews and on a cross. He also suggested that his death would be sacrificial and that it would involve a substitution for others. In Mark 10:45 we read that he said 'For even I, the Son of Man, came here not to be served but to serve others, and to give my life as a ransom for many'. Jesus made the nature of his death plain at the Last Supper where he said that the torn bread and the poured out wine were pictures of his body and blood 'given for many'.

- Jesus looked beyond his death. He promised that he would rise from the dead. He also said that one day in the future he would come in his kingdom as Judge and King.

The manner of Jesus' ministry was as remarkable as his message. None of his close followers, the twelve disciples, appear to have had theological training. From the gospel accounts, we have to say that they do not appear to have been especially talented in the area of intellect. They were actually very ordinary people: a fact that has encouraged many very ordinary followers of Jesus' since. It encourages me!

There is something gloriously unpredictable about Jesus' earthly ministry. If you did not know the stories, you would be hard-pressed, on reading them, to guess what came next. Jesus and his followers travelled light and he seems to have kept moving. On the one hand, he had to keep one step ahead of those vast numbers who wanted to mob him because of his healing powers. On the other, he seems to have wanted to avoid the inevitable final fatal showdown with the authorities until it was at a time and a place of his choosing. Although much of Jesus' teaching, especially to the disciples, is uncomfortably blunt and radical, he appears to have often been hard to pin down over what he claimed. His use of parables, illustrations and references to the Old Testament seems to have put off the shallow-minded sensation seekers and troublemakers, while giving those who were genuinely searching something to think about. Sometimes he used parables to make hard criticism about the state of religion in his day. But by leaving the interpretation to his hearers, he was able to escape the force of directly criticising them. Only in the last week in Jerusalem did Jesus openly confront the religious leaders.

Jesus of course performed miracles in a way that no one has done before or since. None of them were to draw attention to himself; in some cases, he (rather optimistically?) asked the healed to stay silent. Some of the miracles seem to have been done out of simple compassion, while others were done because they made a point about who he was. John, in his gospel, describes the miracles as 'signs'. Let me give you an example. In Mark 4:35-41 we read how when the disciples cross the Sea of Galilee a sudden fierce storm arises. Panicking, the disciples wake Jesus, who with an order 'Quiet down!' stills the wind and waves. As the boat settled back on an even keel I'm sure the disciples would have remembered this passage

about a storm at sea from Psalm 107; after all what Galilean
fishermen would not have memorised it?

> Their ships were tossed to the heavens
> and sank again to the depths;
> the sailors cringed in terror.
> They reeled and staggered like drunkards
> and were at their wit's end.
> 'LORD, help!' they cried in their trouble,
> and he saved them from their distress.
> He calmed the storm to a whisper
> and stilled the waves.

Psalm 107, 26-29.

I can imagine them looking at each other with widening eyes as
– hairs on the back of their necks rising – they made the
following steps of logical deduction:

1. Yahweh, the LORD, is the one that stills storms.

2. Without so much as a quick prayer, we have just seen our
   teacher, Jesus, order the wind and waters to be still. Just like
   a man orders a dog. And we saw the elements dutifully obey
   him.

3. If steps one and two are true then Jesus must be ... *Gulp*

No wonder we read at the end of Mark's account, 'The disciples
were filled with awe and said among themselves "who is this
man, that even the wind and waves obey him?"'

And many, if not all, of the other miracles were like this.
They were the sort of thing where people must have gone away
afterwards and said, 'Yes that healing was marvellous but I'm
sure it meant something. Now didn't Isaiah say somewhere that
the Servant would bear our diseases?'

Finally, of course, it was all too much for the authorities.
Jesus went to a village near Jerusalem, before the Passover

festival that commemorated the deliverance out of Egypt, and raised Lazarus from the grave. As Lazarus was not only very firmly dead, but also decomposing, this was sensational and could not be overlooked. Jesus then entered Jerusalem on what we call 'Palm Sunday', and over the next few days the temperature rose as the religious authorities were challenged again and again. Finally, aided by the defection of Judas Iscariot, they arrested Jesus on the very eve of the Passover feast. After a series of speedy sham trials, the religious leaders persuaded the Roman Governor, the brutal but weak Pontius Pilate, to have this 'King of the Jews' executed. After being treated with brutal mockery by the soldiers, Jesus was taken out and crucified. Weakened by the torture, he lasted a few hours on the cross before dying. His body was taken down by a wealthy sympathiser and buried in a stone cave.

And with anyone else, that would have been that: birth, life, death and burial; the whole cradle-to-grave experience. Of course, with Jesus, it was not at all the end of the story, but I will look at the resurrection in the next episode. Here I want to focus on the cross for the simple reason that the Bible does.

The emphasis on the cross comes over strikingly in the way that the Bible tells the story. We are told the life of Jesus four times, almost as if the four gospels are God's way of underlining its importance. Within each of the gospels the trial and crucifixion gets a remarkable detailed coverage. The first thirty years of Jesus life are almost entirely omitted as we flash forward from the birth to the start of Jesus' ministry. His teaching and miracles are recorded in a series of sometimes disjointed scenes as we cut from one location to another. But as we come to the last week of Jesus life there are fewer and fewer jumps and we have some idea what happened on almost every day of the last seven days. Over the events of the Thursday night to the Friday afternoon, the detail is such that we can work out what is happening almost by the hour by terrible hour. For the writers of the gospel the cross is central to the story they have to tell.

The gospel writers outline what happened next: the whipping, the crown of thorns, the carrying of the cross, the mockery from Roman and Jew. They do not, thankfully, detail the appalling physical pain of the cross. They do however hint at something far worse. 'My God, my God, why have you forsaken me?' Jesus cries out. In every other prayer of his in the gospels, Jesus calls God 'Father'. Somehow here, he is separated from his heavenly Father, becoming cursed and broken for our sake. What was going on in this terrible event I will try and explore, as best as I can, in Part Two.

There are many pointers to the fact that, in this execution – just another piece of everyday bureaucratic nastiness in the Roman world – something awesome is happening. Let me sketch some of them.

- The crucifixion took place on the afternoon of the eve of Passover. This was when the lambs would have been slaughtered as a reminder of the first Passover. Then, the lambs had acted as a sacrifice for God's people, allowing him to deliver them unharmed out of Egypt. This time, another ultimate lamb, the Lamb of God, was being slain.

- By a careful reading of the four accounts of Jesus' death it is possible to work out what Jesus said on the cross. I have already mentioned that most appalling plea of 'My God, my God, why have you forsaken me?' Jesus final words however, seem to be a pained but confident cry of 'Father, I entrust my spirit into your hands!' (Luke 23:46). What swung the balance from the bleakest despair to faith? The clue is found in the previous statement he made where, John 19:30 tells us, Jesus said, 'It is finished!' The single Greek word used here means more than 'finished'; it also means 'completed' or 'accomplished'. In his last moments, Jesus was aware that something had been achieved. And with that awareness the darkness lifted.

- Things happen around the cross, which refer unmistakably to various key Old Testament passages. Psalm 22 for example, refers to the shameful execution of a man, surrounded by gloating enemies, thirsting and with pierced hands and feet; his executioners gambling for his clothing. Even if Jesus had not quoted its dreadful opening words ('My God, my God why have you forsaken me?') any who knew the psalms would have remembered it. There are other references, notably to Isaiah 53, where the mysterious figure of the Servant of God is led 'as a lamb to the slaughter' and killed, then buried 'like a criminal' and 'put in a rich man's grave'.

- Mysterious signs are recorded as occurring with the crucifixion. Darkness, possibly symbolising God's judgement, falls across the land (Matthew 27:45). At the moment when Jesus shouts 'it is finished', the curtain in the temple that sealed off the sacred Holy of Holies is mysteriously ripped open. It is an act that points to the fact that, with the death of Jesus, the way to God is no longer restricted.

- In the trial and crucifixion of Jesus, all sorts of themes from the Old Testament surface. One is the question of who is the king of the Jews. The Jewish leaders try to persuade Pilate to have Jesus executed because he has claimed to be the Messiah king. John tells us that, desperate to have Jesus crucified, the leading priests tell Pilate that they 'have no king but Caesar'. Out-manoeuvred, Pilate is forced to agree to crucifixion but – as if to spite the priests – has a placard placed on the cross with the inscription on it 'Jesus of Nazareth, King of the Jews'. On one side, Israel's leaders deny Jesus as their real king and in doing so break the covenant with God. On the other, the Gentiles unintentionally proclaim Jesus as king.

- The cross is central in the preaching of the first followers of Jesus. In fact one of the early church leaders, Paul, summarises the Good News of Christianity in a single phrase; it is he says, 'the message of the cross' (1 Corinthians 1:18). He even says in Galatians 6:14 'As for me, God forbid that I should boast about anything except the cross of our Lord Jesus Christ'.

- One of the few things that Jews and Romans agreed on was that the cross was an abomination. The Romans, not known for their sensitivity, felt it was a dreadful way to die and banned it for their own citizens. Crucifixion was not mentioned in polite society. To the Jews, it was not only a horrible fate but it drew upon the crucified person the divine wrath; after all the law said that 'anyone hanging on a tree is cursed by God'. Yet so central was the cross in Christianity, that it, not the manger or the open tomb, became its symbol.

In the account of Deep History we have been following, the image has zoomed in. We have moved in time from the creation of the cosmos, uncertain billions of years ago, to an eerily darkened spring afternoon in Palestine. We have moved in space from the almost infinite cosmos of stars and galaxies to a few square feet – a man on a cross takes up little room – on a bare hill just outside Jerusalem. Although they are not of great importance, we can be even more specific about the time and the place. Scholars consider the date is most probably the 3rd April AD 33, and the site is probably that now covered by the church of the Holy Sepulchre. What is important is that in a real man, at a real place and a real time, God in Christ suffered death and worse than death for us.

And at the end of that desolation Jesus was able, almost with his last gasp, to cry out in triumph '*It is finished*!' It is the strangest possible statement for a dying man to make. 'It is completed' is more appropriate for a climber as he clambers to a summit, or a marathon runner as he breaches the winning tape. There is only one situation I can think of in which it would make sense for a dying man to say such a thing. He would have to know that his death had accomplished something.

Lessons for mission

The lessons here are extraordinary.

In Christ we see who God is. I think there are two things

that are significant here; we see God's character and we see God's methods.

- Gods *character* is seen in the way that he loves to the extreme limits. Think of what you or I might say if we had been God and had looked at the mess that humanity had got itself into. We would probably have said, 'Well, I did warn them. It's their fault. And I have done all I can. I'm sorry but there are limits. Enough is enough.' And to say such a thing would actually have been quite fair. As a species we, as they say, 'had it coming to us' and 'deserved all we got'. But God does not say that. He is driven by his love to this unimaginable and inconceivable costly rescue mission.
- God's methods are seen in the way that he becomes one of us. In Jesus, he has a normal birth, a normal childhood and a normal life. There were no exemptions for him. He did not even come to this earth as a comfortable middle-class Briton of the twenty-first century, cushioned by the health service, central heating, antibiotics and dentists: he came to a life of poverty, pain and manual labour. And to save us he even went lower than that. He was rejected by his family, falsely accused, treated as a criminal, tortured and bloodily executed in a way that made him cursed by his religion. *That* is how much God loves us.

If we see in Christ who *God* is, we also see, in how we treated Christ, who we are. We see the darkness at the heart of humanity. You see those that killed Christ were not savage, ignorant sub- humans with a particularly mean streak. They were ordinary people like you and me. In fact they were possibly better than us; they were the educated representatives of the race that God had dealt with over many centuries. Religion and morality were their specialities; they would have memorised much of their Bibles. Yet when God came to these typical human beings they took a long hard look at him and delivered the briefest of verdicts: 'Crucify him!'

We are no different. God is all too uncomfortable for normal human beings. And *God among us*, telling us to our faces what we really need to know, offering us life (and life in all its fullness) is more than we want. We try to push him away from us. He is light; we prefer darkness. And when he will not stay away, we nail him down.

I'm not really bothered about whether aliens exist or not; all that Roswell/Area 51 stuff leaves me cold. But if aliens do exist, can you imagine what would happen if a human being were introduced into some great intergalactic assembly? The human representative would walk in to be greeted by a sudden hushed silence and a sea of intense curious gazes. Then, out of the sides of mouths muffled by tentacles or claws, would come the quiet, appalled whispers, 'Yes, two legs, two arms, single head. *That's* the species. *They* are the ones who crucified God.'

There is one final point. I have avoided using theological jargon throughout this book but there is one useful word that I cannot avoid. The act whereby God became human is called the 'Incarnation' from the Latin word to *become flesh*. Now the incarnation provides a wonderful model for mission. You see, I suppose that God might somehow have found a way of saving us without leaving heaven. There might have been some way that he could have skipped the whole messy and bloody business of becoming a man, and living and dying as one of us, but he avoided it. The fact is that he came to this earth and he got his hands dirty (and bloody) doing it. And Christians ever since have said 'well, if that's the way he did mission, it is the way that we must do it too.' So they have gone to poor, developing countries and lived in them and they have moved into violent inner-city slums and set up home there. They have got alongside people, learnt the language and culture, and shared their hopes, fears and often, their diseases. And many of them have paid the price, but it is part of the incarnation model of mission that Jesus set the pattern for. Now we need to realise this again in our age; it is easy to say that we can reach people with religious pamphlets, satellite TV, radio and the Internet.

We can do all those things, but they cannot replace being there alongside people; 'mission by incarnation' is the rule. And, as what happened to Jesus shows, incarnation costs.

Exercises

1. If you have not done so recently, read through a gospel in one go in a modern translation like the New Living Translation that I have used here. (Mark's gospel is the shortest.

2. In the Old Testament read Isaiah 52:13 – 53:12. Written around seven hundred years before the crucifixion, it is widely quoted in the New Testament. Isaiah not only foresees the crucifixion, but he also goes some way to providing an explanation of it.

3. Try to read a good and reliable account of the last week of Jesus' life, which will fill in some of the details of the trial and the horrors of the crucifixion.

Questions

1. How does Jesus' teaching differ in style and substance from ours? Are there any lessons we can learn?

2. Do you love people as Jesus did?

3. We are often tempted to say to God 'You have no idea what I am going through!' or 'It's all right for you. You don't know what it's like!' If we believe that, in Jesus, God was here among us, how are these sorts of accusations true?

4. What strikes you as unique about the life of Jesus?

5. What must it have been like for someone who had perfect loving fellowship with his Father to experience separation from him? And to have known his wrath?

6. Think of some of the groups of people around you who do not know Jesus. You may think of the teenage gang that terrorises the nearby estate, the Muslims who use the mosque and speak a strange language, the alcoholics on the park benches or those people at the Yacht Club. If someone was to do 'mission by incarnation' with that group, how would they do it? Why don't you?

Chapter 5

EPISODE 5: THE RESURRECTION – HISTORY'S TURNING POINT

'But the fact is that Christ has been raised from the dead. He has become the first of a great harvest of those who will be raised to life again.'

1 Corinthians 15:20

With the sound of the stone being rolled in front of the rock tomb at that dark day, we come to the lowest point in all of Deep History. It is as if we have descended into the very depths of some dark valley. The hope of humanity has come and we have crucified him. Hell has won.

'And *that* is the end of that!' many people must have said that Friday evening. Some, such as Jesus' followers, must have said it between their tears. Others, such as his enemies, must have said it with sighs of relief. But they all knew, as we know, that death is the end. And one of the unsubtle attractions of crucifixion for those that practised it, was that it provided a very visible, very certain and utterly final death for the victim.

Yet, Jesus did not stay dead. When I write those words, I realise that they do not seem to make sense. I almost expect the computer to put a green squiggle under them and suggest that, in writing *'did not stay dead'*, I must have made a mistake. After all, we know that being dead is a state you stay in. By any definition, *death* is the ultimate in final and irreversible things.

That Sunday morning however, an exception occurred and

67

Jesus ceased to be dead. He became alive again. Indeed, if we take the hints of scripture, what he had become seems best described as being in a state of being 'more than alive'. We can only speculate about what happened. I simply offer the suggestion that if there is Deep History then there is also Deep Science. Somehow, the dead body changed its physical form, became alive and left the grave clothes that had been wrapped around it. Over the next few days, the risen Jesus appeared to a considerable number of people of differing backgrounds under different circumstances. Finally, after forty days, Jesus announced his return to his Father and, with a promise of the coming of the Spirit in the near future, ascended to heaven.

From the reports of the eyewitnesses, two statements can be made about the resurrected Christ:

- The appearances were of Jesus himself, as the body bore the evidence of crucifixion and the spear wound to the chest. He also had the same personal relationship with his followers as he had done before his death. Yet, there were changes that meant that an immediate identification of him was not always made.
- The appearances were not hallucinations; they were real and physical. The writers are at pains to make it clear that this was no delusion or psychic illusion. The risen Jesus allowed himself to be touched, embraced and he ate food, specifically to make the point that he was not just a ghost. Yet, he passed through walls and locked doors.

The data suggests a new, and so far unique, form of existence, with similarities *and* differences to ordinary human life. But then, given who Jesus was, something unique would not be surprising.

It is easier to say *why* the resurrection took place rather than *how* it took place. The logic of the resurrection, although never spelt out, seems to be like this: death is due to sin, therefore, sinless people cannot stay dead. However, what had been a theoretical possibility – there are no sinless people – became a reality with Christ. As Peter said in Acts 2:24 'for death could not keep him in its grip'. Although Jesus went down into grey chill waters of death, he soon bobbed back up to the surface. An illustration might be of a famous man arrested and taken into police custody where he is charged with a serious offence. The outside world sees him descend into police cells and waits. A few days later he is declared innocent; all charges against him are dropped. He is released and his public exit from the police station demonstrates the fact of his innocence.

The resurrection appearances occurred over a short period and ended with Christ returning to heaven in an event that we call 'the ascension'. The ascension of Christ into heaven is, in a way, the completion of the resurrection episode. The ascension visibly demonstrated to the disciples the end of Jesus' earthly ministry and prepared the way for the coming of the Spirit at Pentecost. Some people have been puzzled by the idea of Jesus ascending into some sort of physical heaven 'up there' that not even the Hubble space telescope has found. To our minds, used to the language of modern physics and science fiction, it is easier to conceive of heaven as being in some sort of parallel dimension to ours. The idea that heaven is all about us rather than a billion light years away is a comforting one to many people. The idea the hell may be just as close is less so.

It is hard to overestimate the significance of the resurrection. You may remember that Bill Shankley commented about football, 'Some people think football is a matter of life and death; I can assure them it is much more serious than that.' There are few things that are genuinely more important than life or death, but Jesus' resurrection is one of them. Simply put, the resurrection changes *everything*. Let me again make several brief points.

• The resurrection declares that Christ is vindicated by God. The shameful circumstances of Jesus death were such that even those who knew Jesus might have thought that he was a deceiver and not the Messiah. By raising him from the dead, God states very simply, that Jesus was all that he claimed to be. The resurrection is God's signature of approval over Jesus, his life and his teaching. Most of all – and we will look at this later – it is God's signature of approval over the cross. 'Paid in full' it says.

- The resurrection declares 'Christ is King'. He has conquered death, sin and Satan. Now, passed beyond death, he is indeed Lord of all. He can now be worshipped and prayed to, not just by his followers in Palestine, but by all people everywhere. He has taken up the throne that he vacated when he became a human being.

- The resurrection points the way to the final triumph of God. As the first snowdrop announces that spring is on its way, so the resurrection of Jesus declares to all that the days of Satan's rule over this planet are limited. The Apostle Paul wrote this to the church in Corinth, barely twenty years after the resurrection: ' but the fact is that Christ has been raised from the dead. He has become the first of a great harvest of those who will be raised to life again. So you see, just as death came into the world through a man, Adam, now the resurrection from the dead has begun through another man, Christ,' (1 Corinthians 1:20,21). As Archbishop Desmond Tutu says, Jesus' resurrection shows us that:

> Goodness is stronger than evil,
> Love is stronger than hate;
> Light is stronger than darkness;
> Life is stronger than death;
> Victory is ours through him who loved us.

- The resurrection starts the spread of God's kingdom. During the ministry of Jesus the Good News of the kingdom was effectively concealed and confined to the Jewish people on earth. Now, with the resurrection, the time of concealment and restriction is over. In the thick, fearful and total darkness of this world, the resurrection is like a match being struck. From the blazing flame of the resurrection other lights will be lit. And gradually, the darkness of the world will retreat before them.

That first Easter morning was where Deep History changed direction. Those hours from Friday afternoon to Sunday morning were, in their way, the darkest in the entire history of the world. When we went over the account of the crucifixion of Jesus in the last chapter, its shock and horror was neutralised by the fact that we knew the outcome. Having grown up with the Easter story, it is hard to put ourselves in the position of the disciples. Numbed by events, they missed all the meaning of the cross. To them, it must just have been the ultimate tragedy; all hope had gone and the worst possible disaster had happened. This was the end; darkest night was upon them.

Yet it was not the end. In the darkness, at a moment of time planned before the creation of the universe, death was reversed and light broke into the tomb. And with that, everything changed. Hell's retreat had begun. From then on, the path of Deep History, however winding, has been upwards, towards the light.

Lessons for mission

Looking back over the last two thousand years, we have to say that without the *fact* of the resurrection, the church would never have been born and without the *reality* of the resurrection, the church would never have survived. Nothing has changed. In the third millennium, we need to know both the fact and the reality of the resurrection of Jesus Christ.

The *fact of the resurrection* is critical for Christianity and for mission. On it stands all that we preach and talk about. No one has put the significance of this better than the apostle Paul, writing around AD 55 when many of the eyewitnesses of the events of that first Easter must have still been alive.

For if there is no resurrection of the dead, then Christ has not been raised either. And if Christ was not raised, then all our preaching is useless, and your trust in God is useless. And we apostles would all be lying about God, for we have said that God raised Christ from the grave, but that can't be true if there is no resurrection of the dead. If there is no resurrection of the dead, then Christ has not been raised. And if Christ has not been raised, then your faith is useless, and you are still under condemnation for your sins. In that case, all who have died believing in Christ have perished! And if we have hope in Christ only for this life, we are the most miserable people in the world. But the fact is that Christ has been raised from the dead. He has become the first of a great harvest of those who will be raised to life again.

1 Corinthians 15:14-20

Christianity rests on an extraordinary claim: it is that in the death of Jesus of Nazareth God was *himself* paying the price for *our* sin and *our* wrongdoing. It was, if you like, as if we were lined up ready for execution and Jesus came over and said 'if you are willing, I will take your place'. The proof that this almost too-good-to-be-true transfer was acceptable to God is to be found in the unique event of the resurrection of Jesus. The fact that he was raised from death tells us that Jesus' mission was a success.

Let me give you an illustration to help. In 1999, the body of George Mallory was discovered high on the slopes of Everest, raising again one of the greatest mysteries of climbing: did Mallory and his companion, Andrew Irvine manage to conquer the summit of Everest in 1924, nearly thirty years before what the history books describe as the first ascent? Mallory and Irvine were seen, still climbing upwards, just below the cloud-capped summit but whether they succeeded is unknown, as neither man returned. If they had made it back, we would have known whether they had made the summit or not. But they didn't return, and as Mallory's frozen body did not resolve the matter the doubts remain. We would be in the same situation if the crucifixion had occurred without any resurrection. There would still be the nagging doubt as to whether it had been satisfactory. The resurrection confirms, beyond all argument, that the great exchange was acceptable to God.

However, it is not just the *fact* of the resurrection that is important, it is also the *reality* of the resurrection which is critical for Christianity and for mission. You see we can only pray to Jesus and know his presence if he is alive and in heaven. That may sound obvious, but it is worth thinking about. There is not much point in praying to a corpse, or even some soul asleep in the grave. Luke, who wrote the gospel named after him, also wrote the sequel, the book of Acts. It begins like this. 'Dear Theophilus: in my first book I told you about everything Jesus began to do and teach until the day he ascended to heaven after giving his chosen apostles further instructions from the Holy Spirit.' I like that 'began to do'. What Luke is saying is that the gospel story was simply what Jesus started to do; the book of Acts is the continuation. Jesus continues his work. The rest of the New Testament repeats that extraordinary news: he is alive. 'He is risen' is the great cry of Christians throughout the ages. Because Jesus is risen, we can know his presence personally; we can talk to him, listen to him and know his comforting (and sometimes challenging) presence.

If Jesus Christ did not rise, then the disciples (now termed apostles) were either fools or frauds. Were they gullible and naive? In fact, they themselves were so far from being eager to believe the resurrection that, when the three women came back from the tomb with the news that it was empty and that Christ had risen, 'to their minds the story was madness' (Luke 24:11).

Such men would not be content with any second-hand evidence and they did not have to be. Later, Christ came to them and they saw him with their own eyes. They saw him, not just then but many times afterwards. They saw him, not at a distance, but close-up. They saw him not just then, but many times afterwards. They saw him not just in a flash, as if he was some magician's trick, but over the period of six weeks before he returned to heaven. They saw him not just when there were only one or two witnesses, when hallucinations might occur, but with a dozen other people. He was also seen with a hundred, two hundred and once five hundred people.

Most of the apostles eventually died the violent death of martyrdom. Frauds do not die for what they have lied about. It is far easier to believe that someone is telling the truth when they're willing to have their throat cut for their testimony. The apostles did just that.

I like to think of resurrection as being a *proof*, a *pledge* and a *plea*:

- The resurrection is a *proof* that Jesus Christ is the Son of God. By defeating death God is shown as the master of nature and the death of Jesus on the cross is demonstrated to be the key that can open the lock of death; only the Son of God could sleep in death and then through God's power, rise to life.
- The resurrection is a *pledge* that authenticates Jesus' teaching; because he rose, we know that all his words are trustworthy.
- Finally, the resurrection is a *plea* for us to meet the risen Christ with all our wounds, mistakes and hurts of the past and to be forgiven and healed by him.

If Jesus had not risen, Christianity would have been a mere footnote in some multi-volume encyclopaedia. Instead, Christianity proceeded to topple great empires, to form the ethical and moral framework of our civilisation, to give rise to the best of art and music and to become the teacher of people's consciences. All this only happened because the founder of Christianity rose from the grave.

Can you grasp how important this is for mission? You and I are not going out into the world on our own, telling people about someone who was a pile of dry white bones a thousand years before William the Conqueror got his moment of fame.

We go out telling people about someone who is alive today and will be alive tomorrow. Not only that, but that person goes out with us. Becoming a Christian is not about following a code of practice or even trying to imitate the lifestyle of a first century Palestinian preacher, it is about knowing Jesus as a person.

There is also an encouragement to us when we face difficult situations. You see we worship a God for whom resurrection is a speciality. He likes to take dead things and make them alive. The history of the church is full of disasters that appeared to be final; times when it seemed that a particular congregation or church was dead or that some enterprise had died out. The obituary of the church itself has been written on many occasions. Yet, suddenly from out of the ashes, new life has sprung.

There is a lovely story about the evangelist David Watson that goes something like this. When as a young minister, his bishop offered him the parish of St Michael-le-Belfry in York he warned David that it was 'dead', but said that if the church closed it wouldn't be held against him. 'Your Grace,' David Watson replied, 'I believe in the resurrection of the dead.' And as things happened, God honoured David's faith and the church saw remarkable growth.

A final point about the significance of the resurrection is this: it offers hope for humanity in the face of death. Death, the great unmentionable, hangs menacingly over our culture as it has done over every other culture. It strikes without warning – remember Princess Diana? – and makes all our efforts meaningless. Imagine a man: one day – perhaps today – he is a captain of industry, gliding in his spotless suit from his office to the boardroom and back, giving decisions, sending emails, making phone calls, planning meetings and new ventures, arranging meals with friends, or holidays with his family. Then a heart attack strikes. The next day he is nothing, except a still and silent cold lump on a slab, and everything about him is now said in the past tense: he *was* this, he *did* that, he *went* there, he *said* this, he *had* hoped for that. Without the hope of the resurrection, death renders everything futile. And everyone on this planet knows that some day death will visit them.

For the Christian though, Jesus resurrection changes things; death is reduced from a fearsome and eternal reality to a temporary shadow that falls over our lives. For us it is not the end of living; it is the beginning of eternal life.

Did you notice what Paul said at the end of the passage I just quoted, from 1 Corinthians? 'But the fact is that Christ has been raised from the dead. He has become the first of a great harvest of those who will be raised to life again.' Jesus is the prototype of the new humanity; the first of the new humanity, who will no longer be subjected to death. He is now beyond death and alive for evermore. One day we will be like that. Death for us, who know Jesus, is merely to fall asleep with the certainty of waking in glory. And that hope, unique to those who know Jesus, is something that should drive us forward into mission.

At the end of his discussion of the resurrection, in 1 Corinthians 15, that I have already quoted from, Paul says this: 'How we thank God, who gives us victory over sin and death through Jesus Christ our Lord! So, my dear brothers and sisters, be strong and steady, always enthusiastic about the Lord's work, for you know that nothing you do for the Lord is ever useless.'

Did you get that? Because of the resurrection, 'nothing you do for the Lord is ever useless.' When you see people's successes in this world and are tempted to be discouraged about what may seem to be meagre results in your own life, repeat that to yourself.

Exercises

1. Read the resurrection accounts in all four gospels carefully. Notice:

   - The apparent inconsistencies (i.e. was there one angel [Matthew] or two [Luke] at the tomb?)
   - The awkward facts (i.e. the first appearances being to women who were ruled out from being witnesses under Jewish law; the lack of belief of the disciples; the inability to recognise him at first).
   - The frankly irrelevant details (i.e. Peter being outpaced to the tomb in John 20:3).
   - The evidence of the psychological state of the disciples (fear, bewilderment, doubt, etc).
   - The low-key nature of the resurrection itself (no trumpets or massed choirs of angels. Hollywood would have done a better job!)

   Do you think these are fictional accounts or eyewitness reminiscences? They have to be one or the other.

2. The book of Acts has a number of speeches in it. Look at those in Acts 2:17-42; 11: 34-43; 13: 17-41; 17:22-31. These are by different people in a variety of cultural settings. Notice, in each case, what the speaker claims about the resurrection. How significant do you think the resurrection was to the early church

3. Read 1 Corinthians 15:1-58. How important is the *fact* of the resurrection to Paul? Why?

Questions

1. How do people today handle the 100 per cent certainty that they will die?

2. If the living Jesus is present with Christians, why do we not always feel that he is?

3. Is the Good News of Christianity about a) an event, b) a teaching, or c) a person?

4. How does Christ's resurrection affect our attitude to a) our sin, b) our deaths, c) the future of the world?

5. If there is no resurrection from the dead, aren't all human lives ultimately tragedies? In contrast, if Christ does raise his followers from the dead, aren't all Christian lives, however undistinguished they may seem, ultimately triumphs?

NOTES:

Desmond Tutu, *Bread of Tomorrow*, ed. Janet Morley (Christian Aid/SPCK)

Chapter 6

EPISODE 6: THE UNFINISHED STORY

'But it is actually best for you that I go away, because if I don't, the Counsellor won't come. If I do go away, he will come because I will send him to you.'

John 16:7-8

'And I will ask the Father, and he will give you another Counsellor, who will never leave you. He is the Holy Spirit, who leads into all truth.'

John 14:15-17

'But when the Holy Spirit has come upon you, you will receive power and will tell people about me everywhere – in Jerusalem, throughout Judea, in Samaria, and to the ends of the earth.'

Acts 1:8

For ten days after Jesus went back to heaven, the disciples waited. In that quiet period, where it almost seems as if God was allowing the disciples to catch their breath, they must have thought a lot about what Jesus had taught them. He had often said things that were quite incomprehensible when you first heard them, but which made sense later. Some of those sayings centred on the Holy Spirit. In particular, during the traumatic night before he died, Jesus had said many things about the Spirit who he would send. The risen Jesus reinforced that teaching in the forty-day period between the resurrection and the ascension. As Luke records, 'In one of these meetings as he was eating a meal with them, he told them, "Do not leave Jerusalem until the Father sends you what he promised. Remember, I have told you about this before. John baptised with water, but in just a few days you will be baptised with the Holy Spirit"' (Acts 1:4-5).

When Jesus was promising the Holy Spirit, he was promising someone who would stand alongside his followers. The Spirit is, in many ways, Jesus' replacement and indeed in Acts he is sometimes referred to as the Spirit of Jesus. What Jesus was on earth to his disciples, the Spirit was to them (and is to us) after the ascension. This is borne out by what Jesus says the night before the crucifixion. In John 15 and 16, the Greek word *paraclete* is used for what the Holy Spirit will do. This word has defied translator's attempts to render it simply into English but it basically means 'someone who stands alongside another' and it could be translated as 'Counsellor', 'Helper', 'Comforter', 'Encourager' or 'Advocate'. In fact, the rest of the New Testament (and nearly two thousand years of Christian experience) suggests that he is all these things.

Finally, ten days after the Ascension, at the Feast of Pentecost (when devout Jews offered to God the first products of the year's harvest) the Spirit descended on the gathered disciples. And from then on, everything changed. Counselled, helped, comforted and encouraged by the Spirit the disciples started to spread the Good News of the risen Jesus. Such was the power of their message and their zeal that, despite travel being slow and dangerous, the message of Jesus spread out from Jerusalem so rapidly that, within twenty years, churches were being founded throughout the Roman Empire and even beyond it. If the resurrection of Jesus was the lighting of a match, the effect of the coming of the Spirit was like the application of that match to dry grass.

The priceless testimony of the Acts of the Apostles is how, fanned by the Spirit, those flames spread. So important is the work of the Spirit in this early explosion of the Good News, that a number of people have actually said that instead of being called 'The Acts of the Apostles' Luke's second book could have been better called 'The Acts of the Holy Spirit'. The same pattern is picked up in the letters of the New Testament.

As the Good News spread, the hopes of the Old Testament were fulfilled, but in a far greater way than could have been imagined. The Old Testament vision for the future was of a very physical and purely Jewish kingdom of Israel, centred in Jerusalem, to which all the nations would come. From Pentecost onwards it is superseded by a new vision: that of a spiritual kingdom of God with no geographic boundaries, centred in heaven, and which extends out across the world. In this new kingdom are included all who know Christ, regardless of racial and cultural background. God, while fulfilling the Old Testament vision, has wonderfully turned it inside out. The nations are not coming to the holy people and their earthly kingdom; instead, the new holy people (the church) and their heavenly kingdom are going out to the nations.

As we trace the story of the spread of the church in Acts, it is as if the camera angle is broadening. Jerusalem, and even Palestine, ceases to be the focus and the picture now includes the Mediterranean and the edge of Europe. In the power of the Holy Spirit the Good News is spreading. The end of the book of Acts represents the last piece of history in the Bible. There are hints in the later letters about churches expanding but the long span of history in the Bible ends around AD 62 with Paul in Rome – at the very heart of the empire – under arrest.

Let's take a look here at how the Holy Spirit works. With the same foolhardiness that has characterised the previous chapters, let me here try to summarise what we learn from the New Testament about the Holy Spirit. Any good study book or guide on the Bible will give you chapter and verse for these statements.

In terms of *who* the Holy Spirit is, we learn the following:

• The Holy Spirit is a *person*. That means that the Spirit is a 'he' not an 'it'. This is not simply a matter of grammar. I can have a relationship with a person; I can't with a thing.

- The Holy Spirit is *Spirit*. Although this may sound obvious, it is a reminder that the Spirit is not a force or an influence. Neither is he someone we can manipulate or understand entirely: we have little understanding of what happens in the spiritual world. There is a mystery to the Spirit and his workings and we need humility in dealing with him.
- The Holy Spirit is *God*. In order for the Spirit to be another helper like Jesus, he has to have the characteristics of Jesus. After all, the Spirit could hardly be helping you in one place and me in another unless he was also God.

In terms of *what* the Holy Spirit does, we learn the following:

- As we have seen, the Holy Spirit is someone who will stand alongside Jesus' followers to help and support them. Through him, we know Jesus' presence and power in our lives.
- The Holy Spirit reveals the Father and the Son to Christ's people. He speaks truth into our minds about God. A characteristic of the Holy Spirit is that he does not draw attention to himself; instead, he focuses on the Father and the Son. He is, if you like, transparent, and seems content for it to be that way.
- Because the Holy Spirit is holy, he confronts sin. He brings light into the sin-obscured minds and hearts of those who do not know God, and rebukes sin and evil in the lives of those that do know him.
- The Holy Spirit unites us with God and with other followers of Jesus. We can now have fellowship with God through the Spirit: after all, through the Spirit, God lives in Christians.
- The Spirit acts as a guarantor of our future. His presence in us is evidence that we are indeed born again and that we belong to Jesus. And in that case, as Jesus rose from the dead, so at the end of time will we rise from the dead and be with him.

- Finally, and it is very definitely a case of last but not least, the Spirit equips and energises us for mission. Because this is so important, it is something that I will return to later, but I want to say here that it is the Spirit who gives us power and insight when we speak about Jesus. Only the Spirit can gives us the ability to love those who are unlovable.

You may have noticed that I have not mentioned when this episode ended. There is a good reason for this – it hasn't. We are still living in this episode. The church is still expanding the horizons. Of course, it has not been straightforward growth over the last 1900 years. There have been long periods when, with the church apathetic or cold, the kingdom has stagnated and even retreated. Yet the church is still growing; the story is unfinished.

Let me leave you with a final thought: the story the book of Acts tells is, in a real way, an unfinished one. As the church has spread on through the world there have been millions of sequels to Acts. Only patchy and fragmented summaries of these accounts are ever published on this earth, but I am certain that full details are recorded in heaven. As I write this – and as you read it – I can imagine volumes are being written up about the growth or decline of the church wherever you and I are. As I think about these sequels to this great, and still unfinished, story, I hear a hard question:

Am I playing the part that I should be playing? . . . Are you?

Lessons for mission

As we are in this episode of Deep History, some of the lessons for mission are things that I will be covering later. Nevertheless, there are some things about the way that mission was done that are highlighted in the book of Acts, which I want to talk about.

The first important thing in the records of the early church is this: we see *what they saw mission as*. For them, it was not just making appeals; producing intellectual agreement to the facts of Christianity; or even filling churches: it was generating new believers in Jesus, who then became part of living communities. All the people who followed Jesus were given the gift of God's Spirit and, through him, had fellowship with God and with each other. The result was the body of Christ on earth: the church. This pattern continues in the church today. Through the power of the Spirit, God's people celebrate God's life and enjoy his presence among them. Such a view balances out seeing evangelism as just making appeals and counting the numbers of those going forward for counselling.

The second thing we see is *how they did mission*. There are many aspects to this. For a start, it seems that, while there were clearly specialised evangelists in the early church, almost certainly, most of the telling of the Good News was done by ordinary believers in Jesus. Now we make a distinction between 'professional' ministers, pastors and preachers and the rest of the church. Rather nonsensically, we call the 'non-professionals' *ordinary* believers. Really! Can you call a man or woman with God's Spirit living in them *ordinary*? Anyway, it is an artificial division that is not found in the Bible. In the early church, mission seems to have been something that everybody did. Young and old, slave and free, men and women. Equally, it seems that much of the mission was done on a day-to-day basis in ordinary conversation. Yes, there were debates (like Paul in Athens, Acts 17), lecture series' (like Paul in Ephesus, Acts 19) and (at least, at first) they used the synagogues: but there were no mass rallies and no campaigns. Ordinary Christians just shared the Good News. I am impressed by the almost total silence of the book of Acts and the New Testament letters on either 'evangelistic technique' or on trying to motivate them for mission. The writers seem to have felt that teaching Christians how to witness was about as necessary as training rabbits to breed.

The third thing is this: we see the *vital role of the* Holy Spirit. As I have mentioned, the Acts of the Apostles is full of the mention of the Holy Spirit. His name occurs over sixty times in that book and a similar emphasis is found in the New Testament letters. The Holy Spirit is critical to mission. In Acts we find that it is the Holy Spirit who gives the power to do mission and to change lives. Now we need to think here about the fact that the Spirit's work is supernatural. This is not just in the area of producing the sort of things that we would think of as supernatural miracles (healings, exorcisms etc) but in producing conversions and in guiding the whole strategy of mission. This is so important that I want to talk about it at length later. But it is useful to remember that the extraordinary progress of the church in the first century can only be explained by God's power. They did not have much else going for them!

I want to end my thoughts on this episode by making one particular point. The main missionary in the early church was not Paul or Peter; it was God. Through his Holy Spirit, we see God driving forward his mission. The same God who called out after Adam and Eve is now at work in the whole world calling out to men and women. Behind every conversion to Jesus in Acts, or in the long history of the church since, lies God.

This episode is not over; the story is still unfinished. When you or I share Jesus with our friends or neighbours, whether from a pulpit, a stage or over a cup of coffee, what we are doing is simply what Peter, Paul and Priscilla were doing in the early church. We are letting God call out through us.

Exercises

1. Read John 14:15-26; 15:26; 16:5-15. If you only knew these passages, what would they tell you about the Holy Spirit?

2. Find the following references to the Holy Spirit in Acts: Acts 1:2; 1:8; 2:4; 4:8; 4:31; 8:29; 9:31. As you look at them, ask yourself what they tell you about the work of the Holy Spirit in mission.

Questions

1. What practical difference does it make that the Holy Spirit is a person and not an impersonal force or power?

2. It has frequently been said 'In many churches the presence of the Holy Spirit could be withdrawn and no one would notice.' On the basis of what you have read in John and Acts what things ought to characterise a church where the Holy Spirit is present?

3. Why do you think that the Holy Spirit does not work in our lives as effectively as he might? What can we do about it?

4. What difference should it make in our lives that, in the Spirit, we have God with us?

Chapter 7

EPISODE 7: THE FINAL VICTORY

'Then the seventh angel blew his trumpet, and there were loud
voices shouting in heaven: "The whole world has now become the
kingdom of our Lord and of his Christ,
and he will reign forever and ever"'.

Revelation 11:15

I said that the last episode, the one I entitled 'The Unfinished Story', was the one that we are still in. What more then, you may ask, is there to say? The answer is that actually, there is quite a lot, because history isn't complete. There is still a further episode to come: the last episode of Deep History has not yet dawned.

The Bible does not leave the future open-ended; we are not left in a state of ignorance about it. Equally, the Bible does not talk about the future in tentative, wishful terms. God does not have his fingers crossed that, somehow, it will all work out. The Bible proclaims, as strongly as words can, that the kingdom will come. Again and again, we have statements that the future is God's and that – in his time – the eternal kingdom will come in all its power and glory. At the cross, the decisive battle against evil was won completely; Satan's power has been crippled. God's ultimate victory, in this greatest of all wars, is now assured, even if there are still some bloody battles left to be fought.

What is to happen in our world's future is hinted at by the

prophets in the Old Testament, often in images of a universal judgement, or of a new heavens and new earth. In a number of sayings, Jesus sketches in details of the future more fully. Some of the letters tell us more. The final book of the Bible, the strange but wonderful Revelation to John, is entirely devoted to the end of this world and the start of eternity.

What the Bible gives us is not like any human prediction of the future. You know the sort of thing; they come in optimistic and pessimistic flavours. From the optimist we get full employment for all, the thirty-hour week, a cure for cancer, free electricity from nuclear fusion and computers that actually do what we want them to do. From the pessimists we get nuclear holocausts, total loss of the ozone layer, genetically modified mutants and 'the end of civilisation as we know it' (see Hollywood for further details).

The Bible's vision is extraordinarily different. In the pictures of the future that the Bible gives, three great and awesome events are marked out as occurring one after another. These are the return of Jesus in glory; the judgement of all creation; and the making of a new heaven and a new earth. I am aware that generations of false alarms, doomsday cults and wild-eyed, unshaven men (why are they never women?) with sandwich boards proclaiming that 'The End is Nigh!' have meant that many people are uneasy about the idea that Jesus will return. Let me therefore, briefly, and with a great deal of caution, outline these three events.

The first of these three events is the Second Coming of Jesus Christ. There has been so much said about Jesus' return that is either wrong or misleading that it is worth while spelling some truths out.

- The idea that Jesus will return in glory is not a minor or obscure belief of the lunatic fringe of Christianity. In fact, it is to be found in more than 330 places in the New Testament and Jesus himself frequently talked about it. One whole book of the Bible, the book of Revelation, is based around the coming again of Jesus. The Second Coming is not something that was added to the teaching of the Jesus. It was always there and it cannot be removed from our Bibles without making a total nonsense of the text.

- Jesus' return will be personal, visible and unmistakable and in great power and glory. Unlike his last coming, it will not be done quietly; this time it will be no manger and stable job. When Jesus returns, it will not be an inconspicuous, unreported event. It will not merely be the end of our civilisation, but the end of our universe. No one living is going to overlook *that*. In fact, as the dead will be raised at the same time, even they won't miss it. Attendance at the Second Coming is going to be one hundred per cent compulsory.

- Jesus said very plainly that the date and time of his return were unknown and would remain so until the event happened. That has not stopped some people trying to guess the year and month: so far with a spectacularly consistent total failure rate. We would like to know dates and times but, of course, that would be fatal; we need to be kept on our toes. While some Christians feel that some prophecies are yet to be fulfilled, most believe it perfectly possible that the Second Coming could occur at any time. Christ's coming again *might* occur before you have you read the end of this book, but equally, it might not come for another ten thousand years. No one knows: we were not meant to.

- At Jesus' return all evil will abruptly and finally be ended; the great rebellion will at last be over. Do I need to point out that when Jesus comes it will be too late to join his side? You can hardly bet on who is going to win a horse race when the winner has crossed the line. It is far too late. If someone has rejected Jesus, a change of heart will be impossible when he turns up. Their decision will have already been permanently made. And, in this context, *permanent* means for all eternity.

I cannot disguise the fact that this is all very hard to envisage, and there seems no doubt that, as with the Bible's account of the creation of the world, some symbolic language is used. Yet the reality behind the repeated and varied images is clear: one day, without warning this world will abruptly dissolve and Jesus Christ will return in awesome glory. And it isn't going to be presents all round.

Let me give you a picture that may help. In the film *The Truman Show*, Jim Carrey plays Truman Burbank, a man who lives in a world that, unknown to him, is a total illusion. It is merely a monstrously large stage set in which Truman is being constantly filmed for television. The plot revolves around Truman's dawning realisation that there is another world beyond his own, and his resulting escape from the studio set that has been his entire life. Now the Bible indicates that in some ways we are like Truman: our world too is a theatre set. One day though, instead of escaping out of it like Truman, God will suddenly take down the scenery and come in. As we see, beyond the wreckage of all that we thought was reality, the truly real world, Jesus will stride out gloriously onto the set.

Now some people may smile at the notion that this solid world of ours might, one day, be totally transformed. Yet what we call solid objects are made up of scattered atoms held together by atomic forces with an awful lot of nothing in between. And the atoms themselves are made up of scattered particles held together by subatomic forces with – you guessed it – an awful lot of nothing in between. Indeed, according to modern theories, at the time of the Big Bang the entire universe was compressed into something the size of a basketball. These days even *solid* doesn't seem to mean what it used to mean.

The Second Coming will lead into the second of the three events. This is the great and final judgement when Jesus will judge the world. For those who have, before death, repented of their sins, and said 'yes' to Jesus' gift of forgiveness, there will be a welcome, and they will go to be in joyful fellowship with him for forever. Jesus repeatedly spoke about this event when people would be divided into two groups: healthy crops and weeds (Matthew 13:24-29), fish that are edible and inedible (Matthew

13:47-52) and into sheep and goats (Matthew 25:31-46). The divisions correspond to either eternal life or eternal death. This verdict, the Bible reiterates, is not going to be given based on being a religious person, a regular churchgoer or even having 'done our best to live a good life'. That is not enough. The only way of being sure that we will have God's approval and not his condemnation, is to confess our sins now and to believe and trust in Jesus as our representative and substitute.

I will talk about hell more in Part Two when I discuss the nature of the Good News that we have to share. Here I will simply say that, even when we make all the allowances for the images of the Bible, there is still the very strongest teaching that a most terrible fate awaits those who reject God's offer of forgiveness through Jesus Christ. Jesus' language of hell (and no one spoke in more detail about it) may well be symbolic but, even if there are no literal flames or undying worms, I suspect no one there will accuse him of having exaggerated how truly dreadful it is.

With relief, I turn now to the third of the three last events: the making of the new heavens and the new earth. Now there is a problem today whenever we talk of heaven and hell because most people's images of both are totally inadequate and based on cartoons. For instance, heaven is believed to be a place where angels with robes and halos play harps on clouds forever. And hell! Well, let me talk about *that* later. These views are distortions of such a magnitude, that if they were about almost any other area of life, the government would launch initiatives to remedy the situation. Imagine if people went through life seriously thinking that atoms were little ball bearings or that all French men were called Pierre, had moustaches and walked around with baguettes under their arms? As they say, 'get real'!

The Bible's picture of heaven is very different, and harps and clouds get barely a mention. It uses very large brush strokes to paint the picture of what it will be like; it will be a place of abundance, feasting, dancing and enjoyment. The commonest image that Jesus used for heaven was of a banquet. I see no reason (other than that of causing heart attacks in some churches) why we should not call it a party. There will be no more sin, sorrow or pain, only joy. If hell is the place where nothing good can exist, heaven is the place where nothing bad survives. The apostle Paul uses some words from Isaiah to encourage his fellow Christians: 'That is what the Scriptures mean when they say, "No eye has seen, no ear has heard, and no mind has imagined what God has prepared for those who love him"' (1 Corinthians 2: 9). Not only will heaven have a wonderful quality about it; there will also be a wonderful *quantity* about it. Quite simply, unlike every other wonderful time we have ever experienced, heaven will go on forever.

Lessons for mission

This final episode should *encourage* us in our mission. The final victory is guaranteed. Imagine you are a football player at a match who has been sitting on the bench as a substitute. Your team has amassed an unassailable lead, say six–nil, and you are well into the second half. Suddenly, you are called on to the pitch to play for the last few minutes. Now is your moment. That is how we are; the match is won and at any moment, the referee's whistle will blow. In the meantime, confident of victory, we play as best we can.

This final episode should also give us an *urgency* in our mission. Underneath all the events of our world, Deep History is moving steadily and unstoppably towards its goal. One day, the nature of the entire universe will undergo an awesome transformation. God has directly intervened once before in human affairs, with the arrival of a helpless baby who came in obscurity. He will intervene again, with the arrival of a mighty king who will come in public glory. Unless men and women have been brought to know Jesus before then, his arrival will bring a terror and shame that we cannot imagine. We must do all we can to lead people to Christ: that day may be sooner than we think.

Exercises

1. Read Matthew 24 and 25. Try not to get bogged down in details of how and when the end will come. What do you learn about the role of the Son of Man (Jesus) in these events? What practical lessons are there for you?

2. Read Romans 8:18-25. What is Paul's emphasis here in his teaching on the day when Christ will return? Do we share it?

3. Read Revelation 21 and 22. Try not to be put off by the symbolism. What do you learn from this about the future? Does everybody live happily ever after?

Questions

1. Why are people so reluctant to believe that God's intervention could end this world suddenly

2. Jesus' resurrection appearances were not to everybody. The last view most people had of Jesus was when he died on the cross in shame and disgrace. How does the Second Coming address this? (Revelation 1:7)

3. How does the fact that evil will one day be judged console you when you see injustice going unpunished? Could you live with the thought that the evil men and women would suffer no punishment?

4. How does the idea that good wins in the end encourage you? Does this have any practical implications for you?

5. What would you say to someone who was terrified of dying and of God's judgement? a) If they were a Christian and b) if they were not?

6. In the light of this perspective on the future, are Christians optimists or pessimists?

7. The penultimate verse of the Bible includes a prayer calling out for Jesus to return. Can you pray it?

Your part in the Big Picture

This then, as near as I can tell it, is the grand story of the Bible. This is the big picture, the great plot line of history.

It is a remarkable story. The fact that the Bible begins in Genesis 1:1 with the creation of this world and ends in the last chapter of Revelation with the creation of the new world in the undated future, is something that strikes us as obvious, yet it is not. No other ancient book does anything like this, running in a straight line from the farthest past to the ultimate future. This remarkable road is even stranger when we realise that at least a thousand years passed between the writing of Genesis and the penning of the last book of the Bible.

I want to also draw your attention to the fact that, not only is there a straight line to the Bible's view of history, but there is also extraordinary symmetry to it. We start in Genesis with a cosmic vision painted in such broad brush-strokes that a precise time frame is hard to determine. In the first chapters of Genesis, we read of a beautiful garden set amidst rivers; of the tree of life; and of God dwelling with his people. Paradise ends as, with the entry of an evil serpent-like tempter, disobedience occurs and a curse is placed on humanity. In the last chapters of Revelation, we find ourselves within a similar impressionistic vision of uncertain time and place. Here though all is reversed. We see the destruction of the Serpent, 'the deceiver of the nations'; a new heaven and earth is brought in and we see again, the tree of life in a beautiful garden set by a river. Now though, the curse is lifted and God again dwells with his people. Of course, it is not a complete mirror image, but the parallels are stunning. But then if God is the Bible's author, this should not be surprising.

What I have given above is just an outline of the Good News. More could be added but we need to get this big picture straight in our minds. If the cross of Christ is a great jewel, then this vast history is the splendid mounting in which it is set. This great history, Genesis to Revelation, is one that is vital for us. It is important for us to get clear what we believe and why we believe it, so that we can share our faith with confidence. It is important that everything we do is rooted in everything that *God* has done for us.

I also find that I am stirred to action by this epic picture of how God has worked over so long to save the Human Race. God's mission was begun thousands of years ago with the announcement to Adam and Eve of the one who would crush the serpent, and it continues today. We are a part of this, or at least we ought to be. What you and I do in sharing our faith today and tomorrow is all part of the task for which God called Abraham, Moses, Mary and Paul. From their vantage-point in heaven, these and all the other great men and women of the Bible are looking down at what we are doing. We – and it is an unnerving thought – are their successors. Imagine the delight and pride that a designer of a spacecraft must feel as, years later, he or she sees an astronaut actually using it. '*This*', you can hear them say in excitement, 'is what it's for! *This* is what I worked for'. So it is with us. We are linked into that great mission that began so long ago. And now it is now our turn.

Above all, we see in this great saga the awesome fact that God loves us with a love that cannot be measured. Our undertaking to tell others about Jesus is not our own idea. Behind it is God's great driving purpose. When you or I call out to people to come to Christ, it is not us alone who speak: it is God who calls out through us.

PART TWO

THE MESSAGE OF THE GOOD NEWS

THE 'WHAT' OF MISSION

With the foundations laid, it is now time to look at the Good News and how we share it. In talking with people about Jesus, two dangers face us. One of these is to change the Good News and to twist and distort it so that it is no longer what it was. The other danger is to be so inflexible in what we say that the world around us cannot relate to the message.

In Chapter 8, I want to look at what the message of Jesus really is and what its basic elements are. Then, in Chapter 9, I want to put down some guidelines regarding how far we can adjust the message of Jesus to suit the people we meet.

Chapter 8

THE SIX BUILDING BLOCKS OF THE GOOD NEWS

Introduction

What I want to do in this chapter is to look at what makes up the Good News of Jesus. There is a message to share but we need to know exactly what it is. I once saw a poster outside a church that merely said 'Have a nice day!' That was not the message of the early church. You don't throw people like that to the lions; you merely yawn at them. Even if we don't go as far in watering things down as that church had done, there is always a temptation to remove the unpopular elements in the Christian message.

Without wishing to be dogmatic over every detail, I think that there is a broad pattern to the message of the Good News that we can follow. I think we can think of it as being based around six building blocks and I want, briefly, to go over these in turn. For some readers these blocks will be obvious. 'That?' I hear you protest,' I learnt *that* in Sunday School!' *Exactly*! Do you know how few people attend Sunday school these days? Do you know how little religious education there is at school?

As we go through these building blocks, you will probably find the pattern familiar if you have read the first part. The reason is that we have already seen these blocks because they are in the Big Picture that we looked at in Part One. The message of the Good News follows that picture. That is why I spent so long on that history; it is in itself a framework for our message. Incidentally, can I give you a warning? One way of testing whether you, or your fellowship, are starting to go away from traditional Christianity and heading off into the wild, wacky, but deadly lands of the cults, is to check your message against the big picture that the Bible gives. If you are starting to hear more about the Flood, the dimensions of the temple, the Lost Tribes of Israel, or of how Daniel's prophecies are being fulfilled in modern Iraq, and you can't remember when the focus was on Jesus and the cross, then a small, private alarm bell should sound.

The first building block of the message is no less than God himself.

1. God

Behind all that we say, lies God. Becoming a follower of Jesus is not about joining a club; it is about knowing God. In this generation, which is very literally 'God-less', who God is, has to be spelt out in some shape or form. Now I am not saying *proved* – that is beyond any of us – but the basic truths of who God is need sketching out. We are helped in this difficult task by the fact that there is a consciousness of God, however buried, in the hearts of all men and women. But today most people below forty know very little about who God is. This is a major difference between evangelism today and a hundred years ago. Then, when you talked about God, people had a vague idea who you were talking about. Now they either know nothing of God, or their ideas are influenced by Eastern religions. We have to start much further back than any preacher or evangelist in this country for over 1,600 years.

Let me list three broad areas of things about God that it might be important to sound out. Of course, by ransacking some huge theology book I could add very much more to this list. These though, are pretty much the basics:

a) God's Nature

Four concepts come to mind here:

i. God is *eternal*. He always is, was and will be. He is not affected by time.

ii. God is *totally powerful*. As an all-powerful being, he can do anything that it is consistent with his character.

iii. God is *present everywhere*. This is not the same as the New Ager's 'everything is God'; rather it means that he is everywhere. On the one hand, he cannot lose us, on the other we can never escape from him.

iv. God *knows everything*. He knows the present, the past and the future. He knows what we have said (even when we would rather forget it) and he knows what we think.

Yes, I know that I could use the words *omnipotent*, omnipresent and *omniscient* for these last three aspects of God. One day, when I am invited to talk about Jesus to the 'Society of Crossword Fanatics' or the 'Association of Scrabble Players', I will use them. Until then, like lots of other long words, they will stay in my mental file marked 'For Private Use Only'.

These combine to give us a God who is *GOD* not 'a god'. The God we talk about is not some spirit who lives in an oak tree and who is seriously menaced by a man with a chainsaw. The God we talk about sets off supernovas as if he was a boy on 5 November. On the positive side, presenting a big God is helpful to people who have big problems. On the negative side, we must remember that this is a serious business: you do not mess around with this God.

Another important concept, which overlaps with the character of God, is that God is a personal God. He is not a force or a power, but a being to whom we can relate. He has emotions: of care, of love and even of anger. Now some people might say here, 'there you are, you have made up an imaginary God!' This is just a 'big dad in the sky' figure. Surely, they might further protest, the real God, especially an all-holy, all-wise God, would be so distant and different to us that we could not know him. After all, how can a spider relate to us? The answer is that we are designed to relate to God. We are so constructed that our brains have the necessary wiring to be able to understand him sufficiently for a relationship to exist. God is not made in our image – we are made in his.

b) God's Character

When we think, of God's character and personality there are, I think, two main things that are important. In fact, they are so important that they lie at the very core of the Good News.

- God is *holy*. God is someone who is morally perfect; he makes promises and keeps them. He is never inconsistent. Frankly, God's holiness is a hard concept to put over in modern British society. There is so little respect for anything or anybody; everyone is fair game to be mocked or sneered at. This is a major difference from the world of the Bible where, at least amongst Jews, there was a widespread awareness that God was holy. After all, every time they made a sacrifice they were rather bloodily reminded of it. Fortunately, one of the tasks of the Holy Spirit is to bear witness to God and he can convict people of God's holiness where we cannot.
- God is *loving*. God cares for us deeply; he wants to relate to us, wants us to be friends with him. God longs for us to know him in this life, and throughout eternity. I should remind you that he did not create us because he was lonely. He does not, in any way, actually need us. He loves us just because that's just the sort of God that he is.

Now we need to be aware that holiness and love are not simply God's attitudes, but are also how God acts. We, as human beings, sometimes keep our attitudes and our actions separate. 'I know I really *ought* to visit Mary, but I can't be bothered', we say. God however, cannot hold back either his holiness or his love. He must act on them.

c) God's Actions

Philosophers love the concept of God. The thought of a supreme being sets their nostrils twitching. He (she, or it) is a fun idea to play with in university seminars or over coffee in the Senior Common Room. Yet the God we talk about is not a philosophical concept: he is a person and he acts. For some people, who have used the term 'God' in the cold, theoretical sense all their lives, the realisation that he may be alive is profoundly shocking. It is like seeing a statue every day of your life and then one day, suddenly observing it move.

God does act. That is what Part One was all about; at its deepest level, all history is about his interventions. In English we can say '*History*' is '*His Story*'. God acts: he has acted, he is acting today and he will act in the future. He is capable of acting in my life, your life or any other life on this planet. God delights to intervene in lives; he prefers to do it with our permission but he is capable of doing it even if we say no. In fact, a key part of the message of the Good News is this: God has acted; God has intervened!

Presenting God: some reflections

There is much that is good news here. For a start, we can present God to people. He is not some unknown mystery; the 'great unknowable' or some 'make him up yourself' deity. God is someone who has revealed who he is to us in word, deed and – most clearly of all – in the person of Jesus Christ. God is the God who paints us a picture of himself so we can know that we can trust him. That picture is a vast and rich one that is both challenging (he knows our thoughts; he is holy) and comforting (he is all-powerful and he acts). Another piece of good news is the fact that God *wants* to be known; in fact, it is his desire that people come to him.

All this, though, raises an interesting question. Do we need to cover all this material in sharing our faith? Does any discussion about the Good News of Jesus have to bring in all this? This is a hard question and part of a larger problem that I will look at in the next chapter – do you have to give people grounding in the things of God before you invite them to know Jesus?

I think it may help us here to think of normal human relationships. Imagine you are introduced to someone and soon make a firm friendship in which you meet and talk regularly. Now, there may still be enormous areas of the other person's life that you do not know about; yet, as the friendship continues, the gaps in your knowledge slowly decrease. It is even possible that months into the friendship you stumble across things that really surprise you: he turns out to be a keen golfer; it emerges that she is fluent in Greek. You adjust your opinions, but your friendship adapts to these new facts. So it is with God: we always go on learning about him. Frequently what we find out causes us to turn to him in renewed repentance or worship.

Now I think the things that we have looked at above (God's nature, character, etc) are all critical elements to having a relationship with God. Some are, doubtless, more important than others. For instance, by definition, you can hardly enter into a relationship with God if you haven't realised that he is personal. Equally I would be a bit uneasy about how genuinely converted someone was who, after a few weeks, had not realised that God was holy.

2. Sin and judgement

The second great building block is the unpopular subject of sin and judgement. I discussed the background to this in the previous part, where, in Chapter 4, I told the story of the Great Rebellion and its consequences. While this may be unpopular, it is vital. After all, if the human race had not rebelled, there would be no need of this book: you and I would have had unbroken fellowship with God since our birth. The only reason Jesus is 'good news', is because there is 'bad news'.

The bad news in this case is very bad, and the Apostle Paul spells it out plainly in the letter to the Romans. After a long discussion of how sin controls all human lives, whether they have been exposed to the written law of God or not, he sums up matters like this: 'For no one can ever be made right in God's sight by doing what his law commands. For the more we know God's law, the clearer it becomes that we aren't obeying it' (Romans 3:20). His final summary is devastating in its scope: 'For all have sinned; all fall short of God's glorious standard' (Romans 3:23).

Our human nature has been affected by sin is so completely, that there is no area of our lives and personalities that has not been affected. It is common to refer to it as a disease (I have already done so myself), yet there are other illustrations. For example, it is possible to think of human beings as a vast series of interlinked biological computer systems. These complex systems control not just our bodies, but also our thoughts and our desires. Sin is like some computer virus that has infiltrated every level of the programming in every system. Everything that we do is warped. Oddly enough, the Christian view of how humanity works has, in this area, been boosted by psychology. The recognition by Freud and others that, beneath the conscious mind lies a barely sensed subconscious with its own pulls and pushes on our behaviour and thinking, is close to the Bible's picture of our whole lives being controlled by sin's power.

We are all under the power of sin and are, the Bible says, slaves of sin. Jesus said 'I assure you that everyone who sins is a slave of sin.' (John 8:33-37). Paul goes even further. 'Don't you realize that whatever you choose to obey becomes your master?' (Romans 6:16-18).

Now it seems to me unwise to downplay the seriousness of

sin. For one thing, if we are only guilty of a minor misdemeanour, the whole business of hell and Jesus having to save us from it by the cross, seems to be a bit of an over-reaction. If, on the other hand, we have committed a terrible act of rebellion against an infinitely good and great king, and incurred an eternal death sentence as a result: then hell and the cross make perfect, if appalling, sense.

In Chapter 7, when I talked about the Final Victory, I briefly mentioned hell. The topic of hell cannot be avoided, although it is something of a disputed issue these days. Some people have removed the entire topic from what they talk about when they share the Good News. Some, have done this out of reaction to what they see as the abuse of the concept of hell by preachers in the past: the sort of 'repent, or fry for ever' sermon. Now if that is indeed their motive then, to some extent, I am sympathetic to them. Others though, have ceased talking about hell simply because it is not socially acceptable these days to mention the topic. That is a very different matter; and I have no sympathy there.

Plainly, the Bible teaches that there will be some sort of awesome and dreadful final destiny for those who reject God's offer of forgiveness in Jesus Christ. In many parables, Jesus himself talks about the fact that, in the end, there are only two roads that each of us walks down. One is that which leads to a glorious eternity with him and the other is that which leads away from him into an awful and eternal darkness. Now part of the problem is that, when people think of heaven and hell today, they tend to think in cartoon images. For most people hell is something like an enormous oven, in which a crimson-robed devil with horns is prodding people with a pitchfork. God, if he plays any part in the picture at all, is merely keeping a watchful eye on the thermostat in case it cools down.

Now of course this is such a major distortion of the symbolic imagery in the Bible that it would be laughable if it were not about such a serious topic. But what, we must ask, do we put in its place? How can we be sensitive to those we talk to and at the same time faithful to the fearsome scriptural warnings? Cautiously, let me make some suggestions. In doing so, I am happy to acknowledge that I am merely following up some of the ideas that C. S. Lewis outlined.

- It may be helpful to think of hell as being a self-chosen destiny. If we consistently choose to have our way rather than God's, after death we must exist on our own. If men and women have rejected Jesus, and have chosen not to receive him but to live for themselves, separated from God, then they will have to face the consequences of that decision. Quite simply, they will be given what they have sought and they will be separated from God forever. God's final judgement, in this case, largely confirms the choice that we make ourselves. God says, in effect, to the lost, 'you want to live without me? Well now you shall. I shall never bother you again.'

- If hell is a self-chosen destiny, it may also be helpful to think of hell's punishments as being largely self-inflicted. Following on from what I have just written, someone might be inclined to say that spending eternity apart from God was not that bad a thing. Yet, a moment's thought reveals a problem. To be separated from God must also mean to be separated forever from anything good. In hell, there will be no trace of anything like friendship, cheerfulness, peace, love or hope. These things are gifts of God and those who have chosen to live without God in this life will live without God's gifts in the next. Hell will be eternal aching agony, loneliness and self-hatred, without the faintest ray of hope. I doubt whether this is any better than flames and undying worms.

The extent to which we share all of this in the course of telling the Good News is, I think something that depends on where – and to whom – we are talking. But the reality of an awful fate for those who have rejected Christ, needs to underlie all that we

say. The Good News is only really *good news* if there is bad
news in the first place.

Before we move on, let me mention that a whole group of
hard questions exist about whether God will send to hell those
who have never heard of Jesus. Many people have felt that this
is hardly fair, as they had no chance of being saved. A firm
answer to this is hard to give. One factor is that, although never
really spelled out, there are hints in the gospels of varying
degrees of eternal punishment (Luke 12:48). On this basis,
some people in the medieval church solved the problem by
having a tiered hell where the good pagans were confined to a
rather bleak, but not actually awful, first circle. Maybe? But as
a wise man said, 'insufficient data: mind open and mouth
closed'. All we can say is that a) God's love is such that we can
be certain he will do all he can to save all he can, b) the
overwhelming thrust of the Bible is that we must preach the
Good News to everyone or they will suffer an appalling loss.

3. Christ and his substitution for us

Unless you read all of Part One in your sleep, you will know
that I believe that the Christian message centres on Christ.
Without Jesus, there is simply no good news at all. The issues I
want to raise here are what we believe about Jesus. After all
many people will say that they believe in Jesus. He was, they
will say, 'a good man', 'a great teacher', 'a holy man', 'a
prophet', or even perhaps, 'a son of God'.

Now all these views – and many others – are inadequate. I
would suggest that knowing Jesus properly is based on two
things. It is based on knowing the *right things* about Jesus and
knowing him in the *right way*.

In terms of the *right things*, we need to know that Jesus is
both perfectly man and perfectly God. We also need to know
that Jesus is the only go-between that God has appointed
between himself and the human race. There is no one else we
can deal with. He is the only mediator.

In terms of the *right way* to know Jesus, we need more than to know about him – the Devil does that – we need to know him personally. He is not simply to be *the* Lord but he is to be *my* Lord.

We also need to know what he has done for us. Now I spelt out a great deal of this in the first part and I do not want to go over that again. I will, however, remind you that the focus of Christian teaching is the cross. In dying on the cross, the Bible says, Jesus was doing something for us that could be done no other way. In our sharing the Good News, we need to be sure that, in some way or another, the cross is in it.

But what did the cross achieve? Let me briefly summarise what we think it was all about. Many books have been written on the 'logic of the cross', 'why the cross?' and so on. Some of the more or less technical books on theology that I have listed in the Appendix will help you pursue these ideas further and give you the full Bible references. The way that the New Testament explains what occurred on the cross is to use a number of different overlapping images. Some of these images are unfamiliar to us, while others are easily identifiable. They do, however, help us to understand what happened.

One image is that of a *temple sacrifice*. The idea that the anger of a god (or gods) can be turned away by a sacrifice is widespread across the human race. In this view of things, when we commit sin, we incur guilt. That guilt can only be removed by a sacrifice of something living, so that the blood of the sacrifice (rather than our own blood) pays the price and offsets the guilt. The technical term here is to 'atone for' or to 'make atonement for' sin. Of course, in the Jewish faith of the Old Testament the sacrificial system was well organised with the temple, a whole class of priests and a full range of animal offerings. Other societies have gone even further and have brought in human sacrifice, something strongly disapproved of in the Old Testament. To us in modern Britain, the sacrificial system seems a rather strange and even brutal business. Yet, among people who regularly butcher animals for meat (instead of getting other people to do it for them behind closed doors) the idea of animal sacrifice is less repulsive. But despite us not being familiar with the act of sacrifice, the concept of sacrifice is well known in our culture. We may hear that someone 'sacrificed her career' for her children or that some soldiers 'sacrificed themselves' to save their comrades. This image is widely used for Jesus' death in the New Testament. Jesus himself was responsible for this: at the heart of the Last Supper (and every communion service since) is the gory language of sacrifice.

A second image used is that of a *law court*. Here the picture is of a person, having been tried and found guilty, standing before a judge and awaiting sentence. Yet, as the punishment is announced, someone else stands in for them and offers to bear the penalty instead. The substitution is accepted and the accused person is set free and is declared innocent; the penalty has been paid. In the legal language of the day, the accused person would be declared *justified*. In our modern legal system we are, I think, more familiar with this sort of concept in the case of fines where no one objects if one person pays the fine for another. The idea that, in the case of a serious crime, one person can be substituted for another seems strange to us. However, in cultures where the family, not the individual, is the building block of society, it is not unusual for one member of a family to stand in for another.

Still another image is that of a *slave market* where slaves were bought and sold. Here Jesus takes our place and ransoms us. We are set free or, to use the technical term that has passed into common usage, we are *redeemed*. This theme of being redeemed, of being delivered, of being set free, has been very popular in societies where slavery or oppression is widespread. I suspect it meant a lot to slaves in the first century Roman world. They knew only too well what slavery was and they knew how important it was to be set free. To us, this is (thankfully) a distant image, but we can imagine what it must be like to be a slave.

A fourth image, perhaps the strangest of them all to us today, is that of a *curse*. A curse hangs over someone and a substitute must be found who the curse can be passed on to. In the Bible's picture, Jesus is the one on whom the curse, due upon on humanity, falls instead. Under an ominously blackened sky, Jesus hung on a cross (and 'anyone hanging on a tree is cursed by God' said the Law) accursed of God and under his wrath. He bore the curse upon himself. Now if we are modern, technological people, the idea of curses may seem a most primitive superstition. Yet the idea never quite goes out of fashion, and in some religions and in New Age circles, the idea of being cursed is nothing strange.

There may be other images that we can explore. Consider the idea of being adopted into God's family that lies at the heart of being a follower of Jesus. At the cross Jesus, the eternal and perfect Son of God experienced separation and rejection by his heavenly Father. It is almost as though he yielded his place temporarily as the Son of God, in order that we might be adopted as sons and daughters of God.

Which of these images is the best? I suspect it depends who you are talking to and what their background is. All the images I have outlined above have their strengths and weaknesses, and none tells the complete story; I suspect that none of them could. Taken together they make a consistent picture because the one thing that all these images have in common is the idea of substitution. And that, I think is the most important concept that we have to try to put over when we talk about the Good News: the idea that somehow, in some way, Jesus stood in our place.

The idea that Jesus was our substitute is not popular with some people. I think it may be worthwhile here just looking at some of these objections.

- One criticism is this: *how can God take the place of guilty people*? The answer is that, in Jesus, God became fully and completely human. As I write this, there is much animated argument in the rugby world about exactly who is eligible to play for England, Wales or Scotland. Ancient birth certificates are being subjected to hostile scrutiny to be sure that X's grandmother really was Welsh or that Y's grandfather was Scottish. I have no doubt that the Devil must have mounted an even more intense examination of Jesus' credentials to stand as a human being. That is why Jesus had a normal birth and a normal existence; he lived in every way like one of us. He did not simply pretend to be human; he was human. He was as representative of humanity in saving us, as Adam was in condemning humanity in the first place. There are no grounds for his disqualification as our substitute. God made sure of that.

• Another criticism is this: *how can one man's death possibly do anything for so many others*? Now there is a sort of logic in this. For instance, if I chose to sacrifice myself by standing in for someone else I could only do it for one other person. It presumably works on a one-for- one basis. One J. John is worth one other human being. And I can only do it once; to make an obvious point, dying is not (thankfully) something that you do repeatedly. Now there are two answers to this. In the first place, Jesus was not simply a private individual when he died; he was the representative head for the entire people of God (remember Pilate's placard on the cross, 'Jesus of Nazareth, The King of the Jews'?). In a hostage situation, kidnappers may let many ordinary people go in exchange for a one single important person. This is similar. In his death, King Jesus was able to substitute himself for his entire people. In the second place, Jesus was God, and to my mind, we must think of the cross in mathematical terms. Jesus being God puts an infinite element into his side of the equation. If one human's death might pay for another's, then surely the death of an infinite, eternal being, can pay for an infinite number of people?

Incidentally, do you notice that this is exactly the opposite argument to the first criticism? There the argument swung around whether Jesus was completely human; this hangs on whether he is also God.

Still another criticism is this: *isn't it unfair of God to punish the innocent for the guilty?*

The picture here that is presented is that of a father torturing his innocent son. Here though, the answer is that, because Jesus was God, this is not at all the case. Although this is a complex area, it seems that when Christ was crucified God, Father, Son and Spirit must have suffered. The whole Trinity was involved in planning and carrying out the great mission of salvation. God doesn't punish someone else for us – he punishes himself.

So much, you see, hangs on who Jesus was and how he related to humanity and God. It was for precisely these reasons that the theological experts in the early church spent several centuries trying (sometimes, it has to be said, rather clumsily) to make sure that Christianity had its definitions right in this area. They knew that when they thought about Jesus, unless he was perfectly man, perfectly God and perfectly linked to the Father and Spirit, the whole business of the cross was undermined.

Now of course we do not need to tell people all this when we talk to them about the Good News of Jesus. You do not tell someone how the internal combustion engine works when you teach them to drive a car. The key thing is surely this: Jesus willingly made a vital and costly substitution for them. But if we are interested in telling people about Jesus, knowing the various ways that the cross can be explained are important. I think it is also vital to know that despite attacks, the cross is something that can, if needed be adequately defended.

4. The Gift of the Holy Spirit

If we are faithful to our Bibles, we ought to mention that becoming a follower of Jesus is not just us holding onto him. In fact, the term 'follower of Jesus' can have rather negative implications. Did anyone else gasp their way round cross-country races following – at an ever increasing distance – the leader? The truth is that while we do follow Jesus, God also goes alongside us. The way he does that is by giving us his Holy Spirit to live within us. The Holy Spirit is God linked with us. A better image might be of a mountain climb, where we are roped to our leader Jesus.

Now it is important to distinguish between the fact of the giving of the Spirit and the manifestations of the Spirit being given. The Bible teaches that everybody who is a believer in Jesus receives the Spirit at conversion. The effects of that awesome gift vary: for some people there may be spectacular emotional effects, while for others almost nothing may happen. What you say, do or feel like is relatively unimportant. In fact, most things are relatively unimportant compared to the mind-blowing idea of God coming and living in you.

In some church circles, the gift of the Holy Spirit is played down to the point of almost non- existence. In other churches it becomes a major – or even *the* major – feature of the Good News. Both are extremes to be avoided.

Now although I do not have time to develop this here, the idea of the Holy Spirit living in us is a very helpful one. You often meet people who have failed at so many things that the idea of becoming a Christian seems an impossible demand for them. Oh yes, they say, I might make a decision to follow Christ, but I could not keep it; my old way of life would catch up with me very soon. Here though is where the Holy Spirit makes a difference; he works alongside us and, if we let him, provides the power to overcome and follow Jesus.

5. The implications of making a response

A criticism of some types of Christian mission is that it hides the cost to potential converts. People are sometimes so keen to persuade others to become followers of Jesus, that they overlook telling them the implications of making a response. Now this is something that Jesus never did; he told would-be converts that if they followed him they ought to pick up their cross. He warned them that, if they wanted to follow him, they had better take note that he had no home and had only stones for a pillow. He told one man to give up all his possessions, and promised hostility, family rejection and persecution to others. In his own words, he said that people ought to count the cost before joining him.

There are two reasons why I think that it is important that we follow Jesus' pattern. This first is simple; if Jesus did it, then so should we. Our mission should imitate the one who we serve. Secondly, it is only honest. Becoming a follower of Jesus is entering into an arrangement with him. He agrees to save us from the consequences of our sin and to protect us, while we agree to follow him and obey him, whatever he demands. When we take him as our Saviour, we must also take him as our Lord. We need to warn people that while, to follow Jesus is to be sure of life in heaven for eternity, there are no guarantees about this life. We may be in for a rough ride in the short term. But then on the scale of eternity, even seventy years is a short term. I also have to say that I think that this is good advice. There is a fall-out rate amongst people who make decisions for Jesus. It is actually surprisingly low: many leading Christians today date the start of their following Jesus to decisions they took at evangelistic rallies twenty or thirty years ago. Nevertheless, even a few cases is a few too many. The problem, in some situations, is that sometimes people have a false expectation that following Jesus will solve *all* their problems, *forever and instantly*. In fact, one day he will solve our problems, but in the meantime, there is hard work to be done.

I think that in the future this will need to be increasingly emphasised. My reasons for saying this are simple. In the past, Britain was, to some extent, a Christian culture. You could be spectacularly converted on a Sunday, and you might be able to get through a whole week without your new faith making any real demands on you. After all, in your work and social life you were already expected to be living as a Christian (whatever that meant). Now though, Britain is a 'post-Christian', 'non-Christian' or just simply a pagan country. Someone's conversion on Sunday is likely to cause conflicts from the moment they wake up the next morning (if not before). The current is very firmly against us, and new believers need to be warned that they may face opposition. Thirty years ago, you had to apologise for adultery; now you have to apologise for chastity. For those who are coming to faith in Jesus from, say, Hinduism or Islam, the cost may be even higher than having to make apologies.

6. The need for a response

The final building block is this: we need to make it plain that there has to be a personal decision to follow Jesus. It is very easy for people to say, at the end of a discussion or a presentation of the Good News, 'yes well, that's very interesting, I need to think about it.' They may even be intellectually convinced, or emotionally moved. Yet, they have not become followers of Jesus: that requires an act of the will; the making of a decision to follow Jesus.

I feel that many visual images are helpful here. We can think of the offer of Christ as being like a rescuing hand extended to someone drowning in the water – the hand must be grasped; like a cheque offered to someone – it must be cashed; like a contract – it must be signed; like an offer of marriage – it must be accepted. 'Look! Here I stand at the door and knock. If you hear me calling and open the door, I will come in and we will share a meal as friends' (Revelation 3:20), is a very helpful verse here.

Let me suggest, by way of a variation, another image: it is that of parachuting. Imagine that you have persuaded me that parachuting is safe and desirable. I have talked to many of your friends who have impressed me with their enthusiasm and tales of how great an experience it is. I have done the training. Now though, is the big day. I have put the parachute on and we are in a plane at five thousand feet up. The door is open and far below I can see the countryside. You gesture for me to jump out, I gulp and, with my stomach churning, make a final decision. Now, notice some helpful points about this situation:

- I have to act in order to jump. Sitting on my seat will not cause me to jump. I have to get up, walk to the door and throw myself out. So it is with becoming a Christian. No amount of waiting will make me into a follower of Jesus: I must act.
- I can only either jump or not jump. There is no halfway 'sort of jumping'. Equally, you either are a follower of Jesus or you are not. He has no 'halfway followers'.
- My intellectual agreement that parachuting is safe is tested. I must act upon it now; my beliefs must be turned into action. So it is with becoming a Christian, head knowledge alone will not do.
- There is no turning back once I have made the decision: I jump out and that is that. Following Jesus is like that: you can never go back.
- Finally, the time is limited. The plane will not stay in this position for more than a few minutes. I must make a decision to jump now or I will not jump. Well, here too there are parallels: none of us knows how long we have to choose, but time is limited.

The people who we talk to must be made aware that a whole-hearted response is needed. You see there is one major difference between the real world and my parachuting illustration. In that, all that happens if I do not jump is that the plane will return safely to ground and there, shame faced and embarrassed, I will get out and walk away with no more than my pride injured. The choice of becoming a Christian is far more serious: this world is a plane that is not returning safely to base. We either jump, or perish with it.

The Good News is more than Facts

Let me end this section with something of a warning. I have listed in this part, some of the main building blocks or components of the Good News about Jesus. But by using such language and by talking about 'components' and 'elements' there is a danger of treating the gospel as a mechanical process, almost as if becoming a Christian was like building a house. It could suggest that simply understanding Steps 1-6 will make you a Christian, but that overlooks something very important. The Good News is more than learning a factual piece of knowledge; it is about having a relationship with God.

There are different kinds of knowledge in the world. There is, for example, logical factual knowledge. As children we learn many such facts: perhaps that the earth is round, or, more usefully, that falling off a wall hurts. There is also, a scientific knowledge where, on the basis of research and experiment, we are able to predict things. But in this context I want to point out that there is also another type of knowledge and that is what I can best call *personal knowledge*.

For example, when my wife, Killy, kisses me, I don't say to myself, 'Ah, I know what this is! It is the contact of two lips to two more lips, with a bit of suction thrown in, along with the exchange of microbes and carbon dioxide.' Nor do I hypothesise about the specific measure of pressure needed on the component parts, in order to produce a measurable response! I could know all those things and perhaps (poor wives!) there are men who think this way. But I feel very sorry for their wives, because when Killy kisses me what I *really* know is none of the above; it is simply that she loves me. Now this type of personal or relational knowledge in no way contradicts the other sorts of knowledge; it is just different. In fact, I'm not even sure it is the same sort of knowledge at all – but I'm sure it is the most important source of knowledge.

It is this type of warmly personal knowledge that mission is all about. Christianity is not ultimately about facts or theory. It doesn't exclude scientific knowledge and logic – but it can never simply be just that. It is about us knowing God in the deepest way that we can know a person. It centres on establishing personal relationship between God and another person. Of course, solid facts ('factual knowledge') enter into it, but it is not ultimately what it is all about. It will, I'm sure, soon be possible to teach a computer the basics of the Good News, but getting all the answers right would hardly make the computer a follower of Christ. In fact, we have it on very good authority that demons know all the facts there are to know about God; yet, obviously they do not know him in the sense of a personal relationship.

Telling someone the Good News about Christ is not simply persuading them of facts; it is introducing them to a person in the hope that they will respond positively.

Exercises

1. Read Exodus 33:7 – 34:8. Here we have an account of how Moses met with God. From this passage, what do you learn about a) God's nature? b) God's character? c) the gap between God and human beings?

2. Some of the greatest descriptions of God in the Old Testament come from the prophet Isaiah. In Isaiah 6, the prophet recounts a vision he had of God. Read the passage. What aspects of God struck Isaiah most forcibly?

3. Read Isaiah 40:1-24. What more do we learn about God here?

4. Read Romans 11:33-36. Midway through discussing a technical aspect of theology, Paul bursts out into praise. What aspects of God does Paul rejoice in here?

5. Read Revelation 1:4-8. What do we learn here about God the Father and Jesus (God the Son)?

Questions

1. Why is an adequate knowledge of God vital for a) worship, b) witness?

2. How can we find out who God is and what he is like, if he is too great and too wonderful for us to understand? How does Jesus answer this problem?

3. Why do we need to spell out who God is? Can't we just let people define who he is themselves?

4. What, if anything, can we find out about God from nature?

5. How would you express who God is to a) a small child who knew nothing of him and b) a learned non-Christian philosopher?

Chapter 9

MAKING THE GOOD NEWS CLEAR WITHOUT CHANGING IT

Can we miss anything out?

As you read the previous chapter, I'm sure this question arose: 'In sharing the Good News do I need to cover every one of these building blocks?'

Now, how much, or how little, we tell a person, has been the source of a great deal of debate within Christian circles, some of it, sadly, not very loving. Some people have accused others of preaching a 'populist' or lightweight gospel that is weak on sin, judgement, or other things. For them, a person's conversion must be rooted on nothing less than a firm conviction of personal sin, a recognition that they lie under judgement and an awareness of the fact that Jesus paid the penalty for their sins on the cross.

In response to this, let me say two things. Firstly, it is very easy to pick holes in preaching. If we look at any of the sermons recorded in the book of Acts it is quite possible to point out that they omit some of our key building blocks. The great speech in Acts 2 by Peter is, for example, very weak on the fact that Jesus died for humanity and Peter's outline of the gospel to Cornelius, the God-fearing Roman in Acts 10 is, similarly, sketchy on why Jesus died. Paul's sermon in Pisidian Antioch, in Acts 13, makes no reference at all to the Holy Spirit. Later, in

Athens, Paul's address is basically an appeal to turn from idols to God before there is judgement: there is no mention of God's dealings with Jews, and Jesus gets a mention (and there not by name) only in the last sentence. I know that these reports are abbreviated and the speeches (especially Paul's in Athens) may have been interrupted. Nevertheless, the point is significant: it is easy to criticise preachers on the grounds of what they omit.

Secondly, the full content of the Good News is actually quite substantial. In fact, what I have been doing in this and the preceding part, is spelling out what the Good News is. Although I skimmed through what God has done in history and raced through what the components of the Good News are, it has still taken me a long time.

I think my answer to the question of whether, in sharing the Good News, we need to cover all the components would be this: ideally, *yes*, but practically, *no*. I think we are duty-bound to present as fair and full a presentation of what Christianity involves as we can. Nevertheless, God, in his grace, seems to allow people to start to follow Jesus with less than a full understanding of what is involved. Of course, when you put it that way it is obvious that he does. Can any of us put our hands on our hearts and say that we had sorted out all the vital aspects of Christianity before becoming Christians? Of course not! In fact, can any of us say that, before we became Christians, we realised exactly how sinful we really were?

God, and specifically God the Holy Spirit, seems to specialise in what teachers call 'remedial education'. Actually, there are some spectacular examples in the Bible of people who appear to have entered into a relationship with Jesus on what we might feel to be an inadequate basis. In Acts 18, for instance, we read of Apollos, 'an eloquent speaker who knew the Scriptures well [and who] had just arrived in Ephesus from Alexandria in Egypt. He had been taught the way of the Lord and talked to others with great enthusiasm and accuracy about Jesus. However, he knew only about John's baptism. When Priscilla and Aquila heard him preaching boldly in the synagogue, they took him aside and explained the way of God more accurately.' Somehow, Apollos had missed out on being baptised in the name of Jesus! In Acts 19, we find an even more startling case. 'While Apollos was in Corinth, Paul traveled through the interior provinces. Finally, he came to Ephesus, where he found several believers. "Did you receive the Holy Spirit when you believed?" he asked them. "No," they replied, "we don't know what you mean. We haven't even heard that there is a Holy Spirit."'   Now the Holy Spirit is hardly an inessential point of Christian belief!

Of course, I am not defending sloppy teaching, nor am I saying we can throw out what we don't like when we talk about Jesus. What I am saying is that God is gracious and if some one has genuinely decided to make a response to Jesus on the basis of a limited understanding, then God, I believe, will allow them to fill in the missing bits later. A key thing is, surely, to have the childlike trust and willingness that Jesus praised in Matthew 18:3.

Clearly, there must be a minimum level of knowledge needed for someone to come into a relationship with Jesus. It's just that God has not told us what that minimum is and I suspect it may vary from person to person. If people do come to faith with big holes in their beliefs, then we need to try to fill the gaps as quickly as we can.

With that said, it is now time to discuss how we can sensitively shape the message of the Good News.

Shaping the message

Taking into consideration the fact that there is a core message of the Good News that cannot be changed I think there are at least four things that we need to take into account when we share it.

a) We need to take into account the setting

There is no single 'right' setting in which to share the gospel. In fact, I am hard pushed to think of a wrong one (a too-noisy disco? somewhere where you shouldn't be?). A conversation about Jesus could open up to you on the train to work tomorrow or with friends tonight. In fact it is a cunning strategy of the Devil to make us think that we need the right time and the right place before we can talk about Christ. If you do take such a view, you will find yourself saying again and again, 'but this is not the right time or place for this'.

The settings in which we share the Good News vary. It may be a quiet one-to-one conversation over a coffee with a friend. It may be meeting a stranger on a train or a plane. It may be talking over a dinner table where others can hear us. It may be to many people in a pub lounge. It may be where we alone do the talking, or it may be a dialogue where we are asked questions. Sometimes all we can say is a few hasty words. On other occasions, we may have the liberty to talk at length. What we say should reflect our setting. How we react to our setting is, I think, a mixture of the guidance of the Holy Spirit and the work of our own brains: a sort of partnership of prayer and perspiration.

b) We need to take into account our hearers

To say that 'people vary' is hardly novel. Everyone brings their mental baggage with them, whether it is their background, their temperament, their problems or their education. We are all unique. On a one-to-one basis, what we say will take account of this. The variation in how Jesus spoke to people strongly suggests that he did not apply any rigid formula and was led in what he said by who he was talking to.

Now it may be that we find out that there is a good deal of common ground between our hearers and us. For instance, if some one is a practising Jew then there is much that we can build on. Or if it turns out that the person we are talking to used to attend church, then we may be able to take some things for granted. It is rather pointless spending a long time trying to prove something, only to find out that they already believed it anyway! Some people may have had a long struggle over their guilt and how they can find forgiveness. Clearly, we can lead them straight to the one who can forgive them, without talking to them in detail about sin.

It may be, though, that what we find out, may warn us. So, if we find out that our friend is from a troubled family background, we may want to steer clear of talking about God as a heavenly father. We may need to refer to this aspect of God in some other way. People may also have had some previous experience of some form of religion that has left them scarred. We need also, to adjust our language. It is easy to go over people's heads; it is hard to go under them. But in simplifying things, we need to avoid being condescending.

Of course, this poses dangers. The temptation exists that we so adjust our message to our hearers that what we say ends up being less than 'the truth, the whole truth and nothing but the truth'.

c) We need to take into account who we are

I'm sure all Christians have a mental picture of what an evangelist really is. An evangelist is someone:

- so gifted that they say the right thing all the time and, if needed, can quote John 3:16 in Serbo-Croat, or flawlessly perform Japanese ritual greetings
- so learned that they have a complete knowledge of art and culture ('You know, Sartre said something very relevant here')
- so sensitive that they are masters of psychology and counselling ('I can really sense you have a problem of self-worth here')

- so steeped in Bible knowledge that they have a verse for every occasion ('Let me read you something from the book of Obadiah that may help')
- so sharp that they never lose an argument, but are always able to turn things round with a quietly devastating punch line
- so holy that they have that presence and charisma that has sinners praying for repentance within minutes
- so cool that they always look and dress perfectly: sweat stains never darken the armpits of *their* shirts

And so on . . .

Of course, the cunning thing about this fantasy, which I'm sure comes from the Devil, is that it makes us feel inadequate. I'm not up to it, we say grumpily, and decide our ministry is that of prayer. Or, even worse, we try to pretend that we are this sort of person and make a total hash of it.

Such 'super-evangelists' do not exist and would probably be a total turn-off even if they did. For one thing, God almost certainly would not use them. The fact is that God delights in using ordinary people. After all, the twelve disciples fitted into the 'ordinary' category with room to spare. We all (and that means you) have different personalities and gifts. Let God use what you are, rather than what you are not.

Now this also applies to how we tell people about the Good News. You must find a way that is natural for you. Some people have knocked into them the idea that to talk about Jesus it is always necessary to talk in the sort of gloomy tones more suited for men in dark suits standing about in graveyards. Of course, there is a serious side to the gospel (didn't I just write about hell?) but it is not called the 'Good News' for nothing. The note of joy is sounded throughout the New Testament.

May I suggest that, in this area, you turn yourself over to God? Ask him, through the power of his Spirit to develop what is good in your personality and to overrule what is bad. Then ask him to use you as you are.

d) We need to take into account the Spirit

I cannot emphasise too much, how we need the Holy Spirit's help in telling people about Jesus. He is vital for any effective witness of the Good News. After all, why do you think Jesus told the twelve disciples to stay behind in Jerusalem and wait until the Spirit came? They knew everything about him already. Did the church loose ten days waiting for the Spirit? I don't think so.

There are many things here that I could talk about. Let me list a few important areas:

- *We need the Spirit's power to love.* I shall talk more about this vital matter later, but I want to make the point very strongly that at the heart of mission lies love. We tell people about Jesus not because we want more Christians (we are not recruiting for a political party), or even because we want the church filled. We tell them about him because we have the deep, caring, committed compassion for them that the Bible calls *love*. Now some people (a very few) are easy to love: most people are not. Of course, you may be someone who is naturally able to love everybody all the time. If you are, can you tell me how you do it? Personally, I find it hard to love a whole range of people: these include terrorists, wife-beaters, child abusers, and arrogant and greedy businesspersons. I am not either, I confess, overly fond of drunks with vomit on them. Yet, all of these people need the Good News of Jesus. Only the power of the Holy Spirit can help us show love to these people, so that we can befriend them.
- *We need a sensitivity to the Spirit's leading.* The Holy Spirit knows the hearts of everybody so we need to listen to his prompting. Can I suggest that when we talk to people we try to listen with 'both ears'? Obviously, we need to listen to what our friend is saying, but we also need, with an 'inner ear', to listen to what the Spirit is saying. Anybody who has done even a small amount of talking to people about Jesus

will know how you sometimes feel constrained to say
something that, at the time, may feel odd to you. Yet often it
turns out that this is the very thing that needs to be said. We
need to remember that, especially in the sort of deep areas
that are likely to come up in when we talk about Jesus,
people play games and hide behind endless levels of masks.
It is not uncommon for someone to say 'I have worked with
Bill for years but I haven't a clue who the real Bill is'. The
Spirit does know who the real Bill is, and we need to listen to
his quiet prompting.

- *We need a faith in the Spirit's power.* It is all too easy for us
to try to talk to people in our own strength, trusting in our
own ability and learning. After all, you may say (often sadly,
after reading a book like this), 'I know the Good News about
Jesus and how to tell it'. Very soon – I can guarantee it – you
will meet someone who will shatter that self-confidence. It
may be someone who seems to be in such a hopeless
predicament (perhaps bereaved, abused or drug-addicted)
that your words will seem inadequate. Or it may be someone
who will take some argument of yours and then smash it into
a thousand pieces and leave you crushed. I know, it's
happened to me. We must remember that any hope we have
of results lies only in God's mighty power, through his
Spirit. And that power, which made worlds, can turn around
even the most disastrous of lives.

- *We need to pray for the Spirit's working.* We cannot
command the Spirit to change people's lives and make them
turn to Christ. But, in prayer, we can plead with God to work
in people's lives through his Spirit. Individual prayer, prayer
in small groups, prayer as a church: it is all vital. Bringing
the light of Jesus into minds that have been darkened is not
something that we can do by argument: it is God's work.
There is also a real sense in which mission is a battle against
forces of spiritual evil, and that the Spirit's power is
essential to overcome the works of Satan in binding and
blinding people (2 Corinthians 4:4). Of course, like almost

anything else, it is possible to lose one's balance in this area and start to see demons everywhere. But it is foolish to overlook the fact that we face more than simply changing people's habits or opinions.

- Finally, *we need to be open to extraordinary workings of the Spirit*. Much of what I have described is what we could call the 'normal working' of the Holy Spirit; the conversion of people when they are presented with the Good News of Jesus. Now, of course to call this 'normal' is unfair; it is still supernatural, but you know what I mean. There are, however, unusual and more direct ways that Jesus works with people through his Spirit. It is fairly common, for example, for Muslims to have dreams or visions of Jesus and to suddenly want to know more. Other people can have their lives turned around abruptly by God's power. Sometimes whole communities (as in the Revivals in Wales and elsewhere) can fall under God's power. I do not claim to understand phenomena; in fact, I have a suspicion that God sends them partly to keep people like me humble. But we need to be open to the possibility that wonderful and out-of-the-ordinary things may happen. Please, never ever limit the power of the Spirit!

Exercises

1. Read the speeches in Acts 2:17-42; 11:34-43; 13:7-41 and 17:22-31.

2. Notice who the hearers were, and imagine how different their backgrounds would have been.

3. Try to find common elements in the speeches.

4. Try to find ways that the message is altered for the different hearers.

5. How much change is there? Is the core message altered, or is it only the wrappings?

Questions

(NOTE: let me apologise, these are both very difficult.)

1. You are asked to give a short talk on Jesus to the following groups. Without any further information, what approaches might you think of trying, to effectively communicate the Good News to them?

   ■ Some young adults who have been meddling in spiritualism and who have been badly scared.
   ■ People who have come to Britain as homeless refugees after their land has been stolen. (Would what you say be different if they were from a Muslim or a Christian background?)
   ■ A bunch of people coping – with only varying degrees of success – with alcohol problems.
   ■ A support group for mothers who are grieving over the deaths of their children.
   ■ A gathering of wealthy business people the day the stock market has slumped dramatically.

- A gathering of wealthy business people the day the stock market has surged dramatically.

2. Traditionally, in Britain, evangelists addressed the issue of sin and forgiveness first in their witness. Today's hearers are quite likely to have little appreciation of their own guilt before God; it's not 'where they itch'. Do you:

- try to make them realise how guilty they are?
- try to find where they do itch, and approach them with Christ on that topic (a need for hope, meaning, peace of mind perhaps) with the assumption that God will put the 'sin and guilt thing' on the agenda in his time and in his way?

PART THREE

WHY WE SHOULD CALL OUT AND WHY WE DON'T

The previous chapters dealt with the 'what' of sharing your faith, this part covers the 'why' and the 'why not' of calling out.

Now I want to look, in Chapter 10, at the reasons for sharing our faith in Jesus. Then, in Chapter 11, I want to examine the other side of the coin: the reasons why we are unwilling to share the Good News.

FIVE REASONS FOR CALLING OUT

Introduction

Part of me feels that sharing the Good News of Jesus with other people is something that ought to be so natural that we should never need to ask why we do it. In fact some days I could be tempted to look at a chapter like this and say, 'if you need to read this then there is something wrong with your faith'. Yet only some days, because there are other days when I need a push, when I need encouragement.

I'm sure we are all like this, at least some of the time. We have some days when it is as if the sun is shining in our hearts and talking to people about Jesus is easy, especially if they are charming and interested. Then there are the other days. You know the sort: you are on the train; you are late. There is a black, moist cloud over your heart, your brain is fogged up and the person opposite you in the train looks as likely to be interested in Jesus as a claustrophobic would be in an offer of a week's caving. Do you really want to share the Good News? Or, you are looking at your mail. One letter offers you the possibility of going to work for Jesus in some distant part of the world. A place so remote that not only has *Titanic* the movie not made it there, but they have still not heard that the ship sank; the sort of place where when you ask about 'Windows' they tell you that they are not into new technology, so you have to start by explaining what glass is. *That* sort of a place. And as you sit there wondering what it must be like to have a disease unknown to science named after you, you open another letter that informs you of an interesting job vacancy where the salary and pension scheme is such that you can be retired before you have your mid-life crisis.

It's on those sorts of days that you need reasons.

Reason 1: We have a *compulsion* to tell people about Jesus

The resurrection of Jesus was not good news for everybody; especially for those that had been involved in making sure that the career of this troublesome prophet was ended publicly, finally and fatally. They were less than amused by the fact that, within a couple of months of his death, all Jerusalem knew the stories that he wasn't dead. Even worse, was the fact that thousands of people in Jerusalem had been persuaded by Jesus' followers that he was the Messiah. A number of miraculous healings in Jesus' name did not help matters, and once more, the city was in turmoil. Further action was needed.

The religious authorities had Peter and John, the leaders of Jesus' followers, brought before the council. It should have been easy, after all these two men were merely provincial fishermen and were without religious training. The authorities probably knew that early on the morning of the crucifixion, Peter had been challenged about being a follower of Jesus. Then, he had denied any knowledge of Jesus and had fled. He had broken once, and they must have assumed he could be broken again. There, for the sake of the old way of doing things, for the sake of the peace of Jerusalem, the council decided to order Peter and John not to speak any more about Jesus. They were in for a surprise. 'So they called the apostles back in and told them never again to speak or teach about Jesus. But Peter and John replied, "Do you think God wants us to obey you rather than him? We cannot stop telling about the wonderful things we have seen and heard"' (Acts 4:18-20).

I like that 'We cannot stop telling'. Repeatedly, the stories in the book of Acts tell of the driving compulsion that the first Christians had, to tell people about who Jesus was. The dictionary defines compulsion as 'an irresistible impulse to behave in a certain way'. That certainly describes what the early church had! Paul states it clearly; 'Since we know what it is to fear the Lord, we try to persuade people . . . For Christ's love compels us, because we are convinced that one died for all and therefore all died. And he died for all, that those who live should no longer live for themselves but for him who died for them and was raised for them.' (2 Corinthians 5:11,14, NIV). Paul was compelled to tell people about Jesus.

Have you ever met an avid football supporter when their team is on a roll? Has one of your friends ever fallen in love? Have you ever seen someone a day after their fantastic holiday ended? If you have, you will know that that is all they talk about it: the last match, their partner's beauty, or the beach!

When wonderful things happen to us we do not have to persuade ourselves to talk about them, we have to try to discipline ourselves *not* to talk about them for fear of boring the socks off everyone. When amazing things happen to us, we just can't keep them to ourselves. It is part of being human.

Now this is the first reason why we should witness for God: because of what he has done for us. If you are a follower of Jesus then think about this:

- You are loved, to an extent that you cannot imagine, by the one who made the whole universe and keeps it going.
- God loves you so much that he sent his Son to live and die for your sins and to provide a way whereby you can be forgiven and healed. He has done this to rescue you from yourself and the appalling fate that would have been yours after death.
- He has given you his Spirit to live within you so that you can

know his power and presence in your life.

- You are now part of God's family on this earth: a family that gives your life purpose and meaning.
- You have been guaranteed a life beyond death. Not just a mere existence, but a life of such a wonderful quality that the very best day that you have ever had is just the faintest reflection of what it will be like: and it will be yours forever.

Now if all this is true, then we ought to feel compelled to speak. Someone has said that many Christians are functional atheists; they live most of their lives as if God did not exist. Sadly, this is true. If you really do believe what I have written above (and they are all standard Christian beliefs), you ought to be expressing it in some way. Being a follower of Jesus is not simply about believing a set of facts or events, having a theory of history, or obeying a set of rules: it is something that changes our lives fundamentally. It is a revolutionary way of living, acting, thinking, hoping and risking. And it ought to be impossible to hide it.

If we never witness to the Good News of Jesus in words or actions, then we should be concerned: not because God will be angry with us, nor because the church will die, but, primarily, because it shows that the Good News has ceased to grab us and excite us.

Now if this is the case, and you realise that the reason you haven't shared the Good News is that you aren't excited about it yourself: then may I make a suggestion? You need to take appropriate action. That action is *not* to get out and tell people about Jesus: at least not yet. Witnessing about Jesus out of duty or guilt is not likely to be effective. Instead, may I suggest that you spend time asking God to reveal his love to you in a new way? Read again in the Bible – or in some good Christian book – what God has done for you and list the blessings that have been given to you in Jesus. Let God warm your heart. Then, freshly aware of his love to you, you will be better able to share it with others.

Reason 2: We have been *commanded* to tell people about Jesus

There are several places in the gospels where, when Jesus heals people, he does something that seems very strange. For instance, take this story from Mark:

> A man with leprosy came and knelt in front of Jesus, begging to be healed. 'If you want to, you can make me well again,' he said. Moved with pity, Jesus touched him. 'I want to,' he said. 'Be healed!' Instantly the leprosy disappeared – the man was healed. Then Jesus sent him on his way and told him sternly, 'Go right over to the priest and let him examine you. Don't talk to anyone along the way. Take along the offering required in the law of Moses for those who have been healed of leprosy, so everyone will have proof of your healing.'
>
> But as the man went on his way, he spread the news, telling everyone what had happened to him. As a result, such crowds soon surrounded Jesus that he couldn't enter a town anywhere publicly. He had to stay out in the secluded places, and people from everywhere came to him there.
>
> *Mark 1:40-45*

'Don't talk to anyone along the way.' What a strange order! In fact, we get a similar command elsewhere. In Mark 7, Jesus heals a deaf man with a speech impediment. Then we read 'Jesus told the crowd not to tell anyone, but the more he told them not to, the more they spread the news, for they were completely amazed' (Mark 7:36).

It often puzzled me that Jesus told people to keep quiet about him, but then I realised this was because at this stage in his ministry he was trying to keep out of trouble. After all if he had been arrested his ministry could have come to a premature end. That is why he seems to have dodged around the countryside, going from one administrative area to another, always moving on; now disappearing, now reappearing. But once Jesus had started his final trip towards Jerusalem, where he knew he was to be killed, he stopped telling people to be quiet. Now there was no hiding, he went public. The results – as he knew they would be – were inevitable.

The fascinating thing is that when Jesus told people not to tell anybody, they went out and did the opposite. They had such a compulsion that they couldn't help themselves. However, for us the reverse seems to be true – Jesus tells us to go and tell everyone, and we do the opposite – we keep it to ourselves. It seems that we would far prefer to have received the command not to tell anybody!

After the resurrection, Jesus gave new orders to his followers. We read that on the first Easter Sunday, 'the disciples were meeting behind locked doors because they were afraid of the Jewish leaders. Suddenly, Jesus was standing there among them! "Peace be with you," he said. As he spoke, he held out his hands for them to see, and he showed them his side. They were filled with joy when they saw their Lord! He spoke to them again and said, "Peace be with you. As the Father has sent me, so I send you"' (John 20:19-21).

With Jesus standing there with his wounded hands and gashed side and giving an order like that, I've always thought that if the doors hadn't been locked the disciples would have made a run for it. Imagine being sent to the world as Jesus was sent: after all, look what it cost him! But that is the charge he gives us. Go as I went; show everybody my Father's love for them, speak to them of his faithfulness and goodness, proclaim the Kingdom to them, show them what it means, challenge them about their selfish godless ways. And follow my example, even if it means the cross.

Jesus' example is particularly striking, as he himself lived for other people. Listen to the first words he spoke in public:

When he came to the village of Nazareth, his boyhood home, he went as usual to the synagogue on the Sabbath and stood up to read the Scriptures. The scroll containing the messages of Isaiah the prophet was handed to him, and he unrolled the scroll to the place where it says: 'The Spirit of the Lord is upon me, for he has appointed me to preach Good News to the poor. He has sent me to proclaim that captives will be released, that the blind will see, that the downtrodden will be freed from their oppressors, and that the time of the Lord's favour has come.'

Luke 4:16-19

Plainly, Jesus saw his ministry not as being to create a philosophy or a religion, but to reach out to others: to the poor, the captives, the blind and the downtrodden. Jesus was a man who lived, not for himself, but for others. He was someone who saw his ministry as centring on those who no one else bothered with. And the greatest privilege that we have is to continue this work in the world.

Matthew's gospel ends with the risen Jesus saying the following to the disciples: 'I have been given complete authority in heaven and on earth. Therefore, go and make disciples of all the nations, baptising them in the name of the Father and the Son and the Holy Spirit. Teach these new disciples to obey all the commands I have given you. And be sure of this: I am with you always, even to the end of the age' (Matthew 28:18-20).

Let me point out briefly, that this command has three important parts:

- Firstly, Jesus commands that his followers *make disciples*: that they do not just teach people about him, but they make them committed to Jesus.
- Secondly, Jesus commands that they *mark disciples*: they set them aside and identify them through baptism as part of the family of God.
- Thirdly, Jesus commands that they *mature disciples*: they teach them to follow Jesus by applying his words to their lives.

Now giving this command makes a lot of sense. Most movements or good ideas fail because, sooner or later, someone forgets what they are supposed to be doing. It is a particular problem with organisations formed by dynamic leaders: their successors frequently get lost in the wilderness or stuck in the mud. Jesus allowed the church no such uncertainty; he left his followers strict orders.

If we call Jesus Lord and we say to him that we love him, that means, at very least, that we must obey his commands. In fact Jesus said, 'If you love me, obey my commandments' (John 14:15).

Quite simply, therefore, we too are under orders.

Reason 3: We are *convinced* that people need to hear about Jesus

The first reason I gave for sharing the Good News of Jesus was instinctive: we share the gospel because of an inner compulsion. Responding to the second reason – because we had been commanded – lies in the area of our wills: we have to be obedient. A third reason is to do with our brains. It is simply that that we are logically convinced that we have to share the Good News.

At the heart of this lies a simple, but powerful, chain of logic, based on things that I discussed at various places in the first two parts of this book. The steps are as follows:

Step One: Everybody, everywhere, is a rebel against God and has sinned.

Step Two: Everybody, everywhere, deserves hell and unless forgiven by God, is destined to go there in due course.

Step Three: God will only save people through Jesus.

Step Four: Jesus can only save those who hear about him and accept him.

Therefore: We have an urgent duty to save people from hell by telling them about Jesus.

Now every step of this chain of logic has been ferociously attacked. The arguments come with various slogans: 'Not everyone is a sinner', 'there may not be a hell', 'there may be another route to heaven', 'it's all God's responsibility anyway', and so on. I have dealt with most of these objections already and won't do so again here. Despite the force of the attack, the logic of this argument has never been refuted.

One point that I do want to make is this: this sort of logical argument, although never spelt out exactly like this in the Bible, is very plainly what the early church believed. Paul puts forward all the steps plainly in his Letter to the Romans and clearly expresses the logic of the last few steps in Chapter 10:

> For if you confess with your mouth that Jesus is Lord and believe in your heart that God raised him from the dead, you will be saved. For it is by believing in your heart that you are made right with God, and it is by confessing with your mouth that you are saved. As the Scriptures tell us, 'Anyone who believes in him will not be disappointed.' Jew and Gentile are the same in this respect. They all have the same Lord, who generously gives his riches to all who ask for them. For 'Anyone who calls on the name of the Lord will be saved.' But how can they call on him to save them unless they believe in him? And how can they believe in him if they have never heard about him? And how can they hear about him unless someone tells them? And how will anyone go and tell them without being sent? That is what the Scriptures mean when they say, 'How beautiful are the feet of those who bring good news!'

Romans 10:9-15

This is not some late addition to Christian thinking; it lies at the core of the very earliest Christian message. It was one reason why the church grew so fast.

This conviction, that unless people hear of Jesus they are lost forever, lay at the heart of the modern missionary movement. From the eighteenth century onwards, thousands of men and women, frequently at the cost of their lives, spread the Good News from Europe and North America to every corner of the world. They were driven by the knowledge that God's desire was that the whole world had to hear. Peter's bold statement in Acts 4 about Jesus was burned into their hearts,'There is salvation in no one else! There is no other name in all of heaven for people to call on to save them.'

Reason 4: We have *compassion* for people who have not heard about Jesus

Another reason why we are called to be witnesses to Jesus is simply because of compassion. If the previous reasons I have listed have centred on our instincts, our wills and our minds, this one is firmly to do with our hearts. Although it is linked with the previous reason, it is a very different motive. You could be driven to be a missionary out of mental conviction alone, but I suspect successful missionaries are those who have compassion as well.

Certainly, Jesus' ministry was characterised by compassion. He loved people. In Mark 6:34 we read, 'A vast crowd was there as he stepped from the boat, and he had compassion on them because they were like sheep without a shepherd.' Elsewhere we see how he had compassion on the blind, the sick, the ritually unclean, children and despised people, whether tax collectors, pagans or prostitutes. He wept over a friend's grave and over his own capital city. Jesus was no ice-cold robot, he felt deeply and passionately. And we, who follow Jesus, need to be like that.

We need to be wary of what someone has called witnessing 'with dry eyes'. We need more compassion. Negatively, I believe we need less self-love. We need to hear again Jesus' warning about pursuing comfort and wealth, oblivious of the needs and life of others. Surely, the opposite should be the case? We should be actively concerned for those around us. And to be concerned necessarily involves being witnesses to the Good News.

Positively, we need more love. I have no idea what most

people who are not Christians make of 1 Corinthians 13, the passage (popular at funerals and weddings) about love that begins in the old Authorised Version: 'Though I speak with the tongues of men and of angels, and have not charity [love], I am become as sounding brass, or a tinkling cymbal.' Perhaps they think it 'sounds nice' or that Paul is somehow talking about 'falling in love'. Of course, if you read it seriously it is potent stuff. In fact, it was written as a real kick in the pants for a bunch of immature Christians on how they were to act. To me it is a sledgehammer that hits at the real danger of being a loveless witness for Christ. Consider the opening paragraph again in the New Living Translation:

> If I could speak in any language in heaven or on earth but didn't love others, I would only be making meaningless noise like a loud gong or a clanging cymbal. If I had the gift of prophecy, and if I knew all the mysteries of the future and knew everything about everything, but didn't love others, what good would I be? And if I had the gift of faith so that I could speak to a mountain and make it move, without love I would be no good to anybody. If I gave everything I have to the poor and even sacrificed my body, I could boast about it; but if I didn't love others, I would be of no value whatsoever.

Have you got it? Love isn't all you need – but if you don't have love, you have *nothing*.

Paul is the example of someone committed to sharing the Good News with others. He was compelled by the conviction that God had not brought people into the world just to condemn them. Paul lived out the compassion of Jesus for the salvation of others. Even when he was tired and despondent, his concern for other people drove him to share the Good News. Paul modelled himself on Jesus, for Jesus was the ultimate example of loving mission. And of course, when we see Jesus we see God. As Jesus loves, so God loves.

I believe that it is vital that we understand this. I was at pains to point out in Part One that all our sharing of the Good News of

Jesus came out of God's mission to this world. And behind that mission, the great calling out to humanity for men and women to come to him, beats God's passionate love.

So important is God's love in our mission that, very reluctantly, I want to tackle an issue that wiser people than me have skipped around. It is this: does God only love those who are going to be saved? It is probably easier if I look at this view, widely held in some church circles, in logical terms.

One: God is sovereign and all-powerful and his purposes cannot be defeated.

Two: If God loves someone then he will save them from hell.

Three: Some people go to hell

Therefore: God cannot love everybody.

Now, of course this seems to make perfect logic and I have to say has been held by many respectable Christians, some of whom have been great evangelists. But I believe that there are some strong arguments that suggest that it is either too simple or just plain wrong. Before I give them, I have to say that this is not simply rarefied theological nit picking. If we believe that God does not really love everybody, but only some people – the elect – it affects our witness consciously and subconsciously. Consciously, we are forced to accept that when we share the Good News we may be speaking to someone who is not a person that God loves. When we say to someone 'God loves you' there is a mental reservation; under our breath we are really adding '*but only* if you are one of his chosen elect'. Subconsciously, it gives us an excuse not to engage in persistent witness. Imagine someone does not respond to our invitation; we back off, justifying our actions by saying to ourselves that perhaps 'they are not part of God's chosen elect'.

My arguments against this view run along the following lines:

- There are just too many Bible texts that state that God's love is extended to all, and that it is God's desire that every single person be saved.

  - John 3:16 states this 'For God so loved the world that he gave his only Son, so that everyone who believes in him will not perish but have eternal life. God did not send his Son into the world to condemn it, but to save it.'
  - Paul says this in 1 Timothy 2:3-5: 'This is good and pleases God our Saviour, for he wants everyone to be saved and to understand the truth. For there is only one God and one Mediator who can reconcile God and people. He is the man Christ Jesus. He gave his life to purchase freedom for everyone.'
  - Paul again, in 2 Corinthians 5:14-15 seems to be plain: 'Whatever we do, it is because Christ's love controls us. Since we believe that Christ died for everyone, we also believe that we have all died to the old life we used to live. He died for everyone so that those who receive his new life will no longer live to please themselves. Instead, they will live to please Christ, who died and was raised for them.'

- There is no evidence of any sort of hesitant attitude towards non-believers in the account of witnessing that we have in the Acts of the Apostles. All the evidence suggests that the early church held out the Good News of Jesus without reservation to all who would listen.
- Practically, it makes talking about Jesus very difficult. We cannot say to someone 'God loves you' without at the same time crossing our fingers behind our back.

In short, I think we have to accept two statements. First, when someone is saved, their salvation is due to God's saving action alone; no one saves themselves and, without the Holy Spirit bringing repentance and faith, all would perish. Secondly, God loves everybody and the offer of salvation is for all. When, like Peter in the book of Acts, we announce that 'anyone who calls on the name of the Lord will be saved' (Acts 2:21) it is a genuine offer. I am not worried about the apparent contradiction. There are dangers in forcing logical arguments in matters that we do not understand. This is not just true for theology; it is true for other things. Scientists tell us that that light can be treated as both waves and particles and seem happy enough to live with that contradiction. I have no doubt that, in heaven, all will be made plain to us. In the meantime, let's get on with the job!

We desperately need to love those around us. I'm sure you are aware of the little catchphrase question on how we are to behave; 'What would Jesus do?' with its WWJD badges and wristbands. Now, as you talk to people, let me offer you another one: 'How Would Jesus See This Person?' We must learn the art of seeing people through Jesus' eyes of compassion.

Reason 5: The church was *created* to tell people about Jesus

Finally, let me give you another and very different reason for calling out: it is that the church exists to grow.

Let me remind you that a church is not a club or an organisation. It is an institution created by God and it thrives only when we follow his instructions. An essential part of the church is that it needs to grow. Churches are designed to do only three things: worship God, provide mutual support for other followers of Jesus and to reach out with the Good News to those who do not know him. If we neglect any of those three, then the church will decline and die.

The fact that preaching is at the heart of what the church is, can be clearly seen in the book of Acts. There, in the first few days, weeks and months of the church's history, we see remarkable evidence of growth.

Acts 1:15	The believers numbered around 120 on the morning of the first Pentecost.
Acts 2:41	By the end of that day 3,000 had been added to their number.
Acts 2:47	'The Lord added to their number daily' (that is at least 365 new believers each year; not bad for any church!)
Acts 3:4	'But many of the people who heard their message believed it, so that the number of believers totalled about five thousand men, not counting women and children.'
Acts 5:14	'And more and more people believed and were brought to the Lord – crowds of both men and women'. Had they given up counting at this point?
Acts 6:7	'God's message was preached in ever-widening circles. The number of believers greatly increased in Jerusalem, and many of the Jewish priests were converted too.'
Acts 12:24	'But God's Good News was spreading rapidly, and there were many new believers.'

Our churches must be outward looking. When we think of the church as having been given the gift of the Good News, then we need to realise that with this we either use it or lose it. A church that is not looking outwards, looks inwards. Navel-gazing churches will not last long.

Now this is more than business dynamics. Any organisational expert will tell you that corporations and charities have to grow to keep pace with natural decline, as people die off. This is not that sort of growth; it is something else. It is as if the church is an organism and in its genetic code is written the instructions to expand and grow.

Why then, do churches not grow? One answer is that growth ceases when a church starts looking inwards. The great church reformer Martin Luther once said that the definition of sin was 'a heart curved in on itself'. I think this is a great description of

what personal sin is: we become self-obsessed, and concerned
simply with ourselves, and what we want. You can even think
of sin as a sort of disease – a condition in which at the centre of
our hearts is me. Now, just as human lives can become
self-centred and introverted, so can churches. We can become
locked into ourselves; it is always a temptation. If a church is
going well, then we may become concerned about our
programmes, or our administration, or about new buildings; we
can even get obsessed with the business of doing worship. If a
church is in decline, we get preoccupied about the state of the
building, how we did things better in the past, and who is to
blame. The result is the same in both cases: a fatal case of
navel-gazing.

If the church is to be what it should be, it must be
outward-looking. But in every church I have been part of, there
has been a tendency to be at least partly inward-looking. That
isn't because the churches I have been part of have been
exceptionally bad and selfish places – I think it is because all
churches face the same temptations. Of course, if there is a
Devil, then this makes a lot of sense. After all, what better
strategy can you think up to neutralise the otherwise
unstoppable power of Spirit-filled Christians, than by getting
them to spend all their time in endless and heated discussions
about the seating, or whether the drums are too loud? As
someone once said, 'the church always seems to be arranging
the furniture when the house is on fire.'

Now if the church must look upward and outward – and it is
hard to call out when you are gazing at your navel – we need to
do something about it. May I make a suggestion here? If you
can look at people with the eyes of Jesus, then how about
looking at your service through the eyes of someone who is not
a believer in Christ? Invent personalities: Joe or Mary, Giles or
Felicity, Darren or Sharon, the sort of person who your church
would like to see become a Christian. Put yourself into their
mindset as far as you can, and go through a whole service
looking and listening to everything through that person's eyes

and ears. It's a hard, but rewarding, task. So much is off-putting; the little 'in' jokes, the hymns with their references to Jehovah or Zion, the endless and embarrassing songs about loving some mysterious 'you', this Bible that you can't find your way around, and the standing up and the sitting down.

Now don't get me wrong; I am not saying that we should make sure that everything we do is totally visitor-friendly. If you had to explain everything about, for example, a communion service, you would double the time you took. There are things that we will do as a church which are part of us being church: if we cease to do them, we cease to 'do church'. We just have to accept that increasingly in this culture, where so many people now have absolutely no previous church experience at all, it is going to be inevitable that there will be things that are going to make them wonder. Why sing and get excited about God? Why pray – what difference does it make? Why listen to some ancient words – most of them over 2,000 years old? Why say sorry for things you have done wrong? Why eat little bits of bread and sip wine? If those questions *are* raised, and the people concerned feel free to raise them, then great. If though, our visitors are embarrassed and feel out of place, then we have done something badly wrong.

I think that, regarding everything we do as a church, we have to ask two questions:

1. What is there that is alien and off-putting to outsiders?
2. What can we do – without reducing the significance of what we do – to make what happens less inaccessible to outsiders?

We need to give thought to explaining why we do what we do. We need to avoid using jargon and phrases. We need to be careful that we have not been snared in tradition (and it only takes a few months to create a tradition). Above all, we need to avoid creating a little club that outsiders feel alienated from. You see, if I am right in my reading of the priorities of the New

Testament church, then a prime concern – maybe the prime
concern – should be to get the Good News of Jesus over to
people. The problem is that much of the time its not the Good
News of Jesus that puts people off – it's the packaging that we
keep it in.

As you look around your church this Sunday, remember the
rule: *witness or die.*

Summary

I have listed five reasons why we should tell people about
Jesus.

- We have a *compulsion* to tell people about Jesus.
- We have been *commanded* to tell people about Jesus.
- We have been *convinced* that people need to hear about
  Jesus.
- We have *compassion* on people who have not heard about
  Jesus.
- The church was *created* to tell people about Jesus.

There are other reasons, but if you aren't convinced by these, I
don't see that 'pursuing the glory of God' or 'hastening his
coming' will convince you.

So, wherever you are and whatever you feel like remember
this: we need to witness about the Good News of Jesus to others
– for their sake and our sake.

Exercises

1. Do we take the Good News of Jesus for granted?

   ■ Read Ephesians 2:1-10. What, according to Paul, has God done for us; what is he doing for us now; and what will he do for us in the future
   ■ Read 1 Peter 3-9. What, according to Peter, have we received from God?
   ■ If we believe this, why are we so reluctant to share it?

2. Read Romans 9:1-5 and 10:1. Here, Paul tells of his desire for the conversion of his own Jewish people. Do we know anything of his passion for the lost? Now read Romans 10:14. To what practical conclusion does Paul's burden drive him?

3. Read 1 Corinthians 9:6-23. What do we learn about Paul's attitude to sharing the Good News?

Questions

1. Christians often use the term 'saved' to explain what Christ has done for them. What are we saved from? (It is more than a single one-word answer.) Do our lives reflect the importance of what we have been rescued from?

2. The picture that Scripture consistently gives is that all human beings are either God's sons and daughters through Christ or they are separated from him and live lives that are opposed to God.

   ■ Which category do you fit into? On what basis do you say that?
   ■ Do we see people in a similar perspective?
   ■ If we thought this way more often, wouldn't it help our calling out?

3. The cynical comment could be made that from the way most Christians evangelise you would think they had been sworn to secrecy.

  - In your experience, is this because they lack the compulsion, ignore the command, do not have the *conviction* or lack *compassion*?
  - What about you? What would it take you to become a better or more zealous witness for Jesus?

4. How could you encourage other people in your church or fellowship to share the Good News more effectively?

Chapter 11

OBSTACLES TO CALLING OUT – THE 'WHY NOT' OF MISSION

If the last chapter dealt with the reasons for sharing our faith, I want here to briefly look at reasons why we do not share the Good News with others. It seems to me that there are four main reasons why we might be reluctant to share Jesus with someone else. Three of these can be dealt with fairly quickly, whilst the fourth cannot be so easily dismissed.

Reason 1: I don't like sharing my faith

One common reason for not sharing our faith is that we simply do not feel like it. One of the problems here is that in our society 'liking something' has become the supreme test for everything. People break contracts with employers because they do not like their work and they break marriage oaths because they no longer like the person that they promised to love and be faithful to. Of course, a society based on 'liking' as a rule of how it lives, is in big trouble. Can you imagine a fireman refusing to rescue someone out of a burning building because he didn't *like* doing it? Or your boss not paying your salary for exactly the same reason? There are times in life when we have to do things, whether we like them, or not. I'm afraid to say that witnessing about Jesus is something where we have to say to our feelings,

'Tough, but this is what I have to do. And I'm going to do it.' Sorry, but that's the way it is! If it's any consolation, I don't suppose Jesus liked being crucified.

Reason 2: I'm worried I will turn people off Jesus

Every year there is a bizarre alternative counterpart to the film world's Oscars, the *Golden Raspberry Award Foundation* or *The Razzies*. Here prizes are given for the world's worst films: an area of human achievement for which there is never any shortage of candidates. Directors and actors dread them as much as they long for Oscars. In my darker moments, I think there ought to be a place for an equivalent award for witnessing about Jesus. I would suggest one, except for three things: it would be unkind, some day I might get one myself and, above all, God actually seems more tolerant than we are.

You see the odd thing is, sometimes people today *are* saved by pamphlets with titles like *Sinner, will ye not flee to Christ's bosom now*? Sometimes lives are changed by the almost totally incoherent bellowings from people with cheap megaphones in market places. Sometimes conversions occur at the sort of event that seems to be the unlovely offspring of an American political fundraising rally and a rock concert. But then that's God for you.

Now, of course I'm not defending tactless, insensitive or bungling evangelism. I think it needs to be done as well and as sensitively as we possibly can. But my point here is this: do the best you can and hand the rest over to God.

Let me tell you a story. There was once a man who had problems with the idea of getting married. His parents' marriage had been disastrous and he resolved not to repeat their mistakes. So, while he read book after book on marriage, he avoided getting into any sort of relationship that might have led to him getting married before he was ready. Yet, doubts remained in his own mind over his ability to be the perfect husband. Over the years, he worked further on the subject, probing ever more deeply the psychology of marriage, how to enhance marital relations and how to resolve conflict in marriage. The books he had read on marriage filled an entire shelf; he knew it all. He was finally close to being prepared to be the perfect partner. Then one day, still unmarried, he died. Lesson? Get out there while you can and do it.

I suspect God will reserve the real *Razzies* for those Christians who were too timid to do a thing. After all, *no witness* has got to be worse than *some witness*. And speaking personally I'd hate to be stuck with a *Razzie* – especially for eternity.

Reason 3: I won't be able to answer people's questions

So, you can't answer people's questions? Well, enlist in the J. John intensive reading, video and multi-media programme (all major credit cards accepted) and after only six month's training I will guarantee that you will have all the answers you will ever need.

Did you believe me? I hope not. For one thing, no one could ever know every answer to every question. For example, only last week I had a conversation that went like this:

Woman: 'So you claim that God made everyone, right?'
Me: 'Yes'
Woman: 'And although there are different races we are all one?'
Me: 'Yes.'
Woman: 'So why are there four blood groups?'
Me: 'Aaah . . .'

I had never been asked that question before. Actually, why we have blood groups is probably not a significant question (it's a bit like asking why some of us have blue eyes and others brown) but you take my point. There is always a new question.

For another thing, sharing the Good News about Jesus is not like surviving a round of Mastermind ('and your chosen topic J. John, is *Philosophical and Theological Problems of Christian Belief*). It is introducing one person, Jesus, to another person. Now to support that, let me suggest that you think about what happened when you became a Christian or, if that was too long ago, to talk to someone who has recently come to faith. Ask the following:

a) How important were intellectual questions in the process of your commitment to Christ?

b) Was the person who was responsible for leading you to Jesus able to answer all your questions?

c) Did they answer some of the questions wrongly?

My guess is that the answers were *a) Not very, b) No, c) Yes*. In other words, answering intellectual objections may not be quite as important as it seems. So be reassured: the lack of a Doctorate in Theology is no barrier to being a good witness for Jesus Christ. After all, the church started off using mainly fishermen, and we have been hard pushed to equal their achievements ever since.

Does this mean that you can say what you want? No, I think we need to fill in the gaps in our knowledge and to work at being able to give a reasoned defence for the Good News. The apostle Peter (one of the fishermen, remember) wrote the following: 'and if you are asked about your Christian hope, always be ready to explain it. But you must do this in a gentle and respectful way' (1 Peter 3:15). That rule has never changed. We do not simply make a request that people jump into the dark when they come to Christ. We try and illuminate the way for them as best we can.

Let me suggest some guidelines about trying to answer people's questions:

• Do not try to come up with an answer just to make yourself look good. Be honest: if you don't know, say so! The priority is to share Jesus not to win arguments.

- Think (and pray) before you answer. Be careful with coming up with half-remembered answers especially if they are from a source of unknown quality. Ignorance may be no sin, but stupidity (especially when it is coupled with arrogance) is certainly not a healthy advertisement for the Good News of Jesus. This is particularly the case in matters of science and faith. Here, it is common for people whose knowledge of science extends no further than being able to wire a plug properly, to say things like, 'of course you can't believe in Carbon-14 dating' or, 'the Big Bang is nonsense'. Are you prepared for the obvious follow-up question: 'Oh so you have an interest in isotope physics (or cosmology)? Splendid, can you justify your argument?' I have no objection to you making yourself look foolish, but can you try not to drag the Good News of Jesus down with you?
- Remember that there may be more than one answer to some questions. Bible-believing Christians from different backgrounds have come to differing answers on some controversial questions. There are, for example, probably at least six workable solutions to resolving the apparent conflict between Genesis 1 and science. It may not hurt to say, 'Well, personally I have always come to terms with this issue in this way ...'

In the Appendix, I will look very briefly at some of the main questions that are raised by people who are not yet followers of Jesus. Let me, however, give you three very useful answers when you are stuck with difficult questions. You might say:

a) 'I'm sorry, I don't know the answer to that. What I will do though, is read up on it and also ask someone who might know the answer. And I'll get back to you.' Of course when you say that, do what you promised. Wrong answers or ignorance may not put people off Christianity, but broken promises do.

b) 'I'm sorry, I don't know the answer to that. But does it mean a lot to you?' The advantage of this answer is that it continues the conversation and gets them to open up. You may actually find out that the real concern is not what they said but actually something else.

c) 'That's a good question and I'm sure it has an answer, but let me ask you one in return. If I *could* answer your question, would you become a follower of Jesus?' All too often they will look sheepish at this point because you have caught them out; the issue is not that of the mind, it is of the will. Mind you, it can be a bit heavy – use this one gently. Do remember to do this as Peter said 'in a gentle and respectful way.'

Finally, let me give you four pieces of advice that I hope are encouraging.

• You may feel that you are faced with an uphill struggle trying to change someone from 'common-sense thinking' to something special called 'belief' or 'faith'. We imagine people saying to us – in that triumphant '*got you!*' tone of voice – 'ah yes but can you *prove* God?' The fact is that everybody has faith at various levels; you have faith that the wheels will not fall off your car; you have faith you will be paid this month; you have faith your friend loves you. In fact, at one level, you need faith for everything, because there is nothing that you can ever prove completely. Nothing at all. I mean, can you prove that this book that you are now reading is not an illusion? Can you prove that you are not dreaming? We are seeking to convert someone not from 'common sense' to 'faith' but from one sort of faith to another. In fact, one of the most remarkable examples of faith is the atheist. For someone to confidently state that there is no God, from our standpoint as frail, short-lived creatures on a speck of cosmic dust, is astonishing. Believing in Jesus is nothing in comparison.

- I believe that there is a rather curious psychology to unbelief. It centres on this observation; people, especially educated people, disbelieve in the Good News of Jesus, not because of evidence in their own field of expertise, but because of the evidence in someone else's. The historian may consider that Christianity cannot be believed, not because history contradicts it (it doesn't) but because they think that *science* (about which he or she knows nothing) disproves it. The scientist, in turn, may consider that Christianity cannot be believed, not because science contradicts it (it doesn't), but because they imagine that psychology (about which he or she knows nothing) disproves it. And the psychologist considers that Christianity cannot be believed because philosophy ... and so on. You get the picture. It is almost as though someone has been spreading lies and I do not find it hard to think of a culprit. So it is highly unlikely that the archaeologist will say to you 'Ah yes but my knowledge of the Roman legal system makes it impossible for me to believe in the execution of Jesus as recorded in the gospels'. They are more likely to say 'but hasn't science disproved Christianity?' And they probably know very little more about that than you do.
- Most people chose to disbelieve not for intellectual reasons but for other, more basic reasons. It is sometimes easier to come up with pretend intellectual excuses for not believing in Christianity than to try to live with its moral demands. Immorality of life is often the cause, as much as the result of atheism. In other words, intellectual difficulties may be (but not always are) a smoke screen to cover other deeper problems. These are most likely to be our old acquaintances, guilt and sin. And in dealing with issues of the heart, your ability to answer questions of the head correctly is of little value.
- Personal testimony is vital. Ironically, it is one of the few areas of evidence that modern people are prepared to take seriously. They may have rejected the idea of an

all-embracing logical truth (they would say 'all truth is relative') but they will listen to a personal experience. You cannot convince them from it, but they may wonder if Jesus might work for them. A personal account of how you became a follower of Jesus is much less threatening too.

In conclusion, the fear of not being able to answer people's questions is over-rated. Do what you can to answer people but don't be paralysed with fear about having to have the answers to every question. You might, too, like to remember this: at the end of the day, very few people are ever argued into the kingdom.

Reason 4: I'm afraid of sharing my faith

The area of fear is a big and complex one and I want to say straight away that I am very sympathetic to those who get crippled by fear when they talk to people about Jesus. The first thing to say is that I believe that fear in this area is basically, a good emotion that has been allowed to get out of hand. Now let me explain what I mean.

Imagine you could create – by genetic modification if you wish – a super-evangelist. You might be inclined to remove entirely the circuitry that generates fear; after all what could be better than a fearless evangelist? Yet, the 'upside' of fear is understanding and sensitivity. What you would produce by removing fear would be a lethal monstrosity, a sort of gospel Terminator, a holy Lethal Weapon. Can you imagine the damage that such a charging evangelistic elephant could do? Such a person would be capable of talking about sin to the depressed, hope to the carefree and hell to the bereaved and of leaving a mile-wide trail of embarrassment and hurt behind them. In fact, such people exist, and rumour of their impending arrival can clear parties and entire rail carriages faster than a drunken football fan in a bad mood looking for trouble.

Those witnessing for Jesus in 'difficult countries' pray to be delivered from the visits of such fearless evangelists. There is reliable story that a good few years ago such a character somehow got himself into the presence of Syria's President Assad and with great boldness told him the good news of the Bible: prophecy demonstrated that the Israelis would destroy Damascus by nuclear weapons. No, I don't know that text either! Anyway, by the grace of God, either the jails were already full that month or Assad was in a good mood. The Syrian church survived with no more than heart palpitations, cold sweats and a strange aversion to answering night-time knocks at the door. You see there *are* worse things than being fearful!

So, if you are a sensitive soul, rejoice. You are exactly the sort of temperament that God uses. You are the kind of person that he can employ to bring comfort to the sorrowing, to get alongside the guilty and to help those who have problems. But you still have to deal with the downside of that sensitivity, fear.

To deal with that I want to look at the different sorts of fear that there are. My guess is that if I were to ask you to make up a list of what you were scared about in sharing your faith, it would include a number of things. Let me suggest the top two fears are:

- 'I'm afraid of appearing arrogant'
- 'I'm afraid of being rejected'

There may be more besides. Now I want to look at these fears and to try to help you through them if they are relevant to you. I must warn you that if you are expecting me to give you a few easy steps to get rid of all fear, you will be sadly disappointed. But before I look at these specific areas, let me make some general comments about fear first.

- We need to face our fears. Let me suggest that you try to analyse exactly what it is that you are afraid of. Fear is an emotion that prefers to exist as a vague oppressive cloud that hangs around and which casts a shadow on everything. Yet when you look at it carefully, you can often see that what it centres on is actually no real threat to you at all. Writing down your fears is often helpful.

- Remember that many fears are not rational. For example, many people are afraid of flying, yet all the statistics prove that this is one of the safest ways of travelling. Many people in Britain are afraid of snakes, yet there have been only one or two fatalities here due to snakebite in the last fifty years. Is your fear of talking about Jesus based on facts?

- In practice, if there is fear in a situation where someone is talking about Jesus, it is likely to be on the part of the hearer. They are almost always more scared of us than we are of them. After all, they know that in their hearts there is something missing. In what we are saying they may be getting the uncomfortable feeling that God wants to have a word with them, and praise is not on the agenda.

- Remember that we have an enemy who delights in using fear. Look at the situation from the Devil's point of view – we are well armed with the Spirit, we have the truth on our side and we have the final victory assured. One of the few weapons he has is to make us fearful and stay at home.

Now let me talk specifically about the two big problem areas.

'I'm afraid of appearing arrogant'

The fear that we may come over as being arrogant when we share the Good News is one that needs thinking about. Now of course, real arrogance does occur on the part of Christians, and we need to repent of that. In reality, we have no excuse for arrogance; after all God found us – we did not find him. And anyway, his verdict on us was hardly flattering; it was that we were sinners worthy of eternal separation from him. If we bear that in mind then there is very little basis for arrogance. As one great preacher said, evangelism is 'merely one beggar telling another beggar where there is bread'.

The one thing that does most effectively wither arrogance away is, of course, *love*. We need to always monitor what we are saying so that if we feel that we have stopped being loving we can either shut up (*good*) or concentrate on loving our hearer (*better*). We must remember that evangelism is not about winning arguments; it is about winning hearts. Ironically, you can win arguments and lose hearts and you can lose arguments and win hearts. I know what I want to do.

That said, the accusation that we are arrogant may still be made and I want to talk about it a bit further. You see, in our society, this charge of arrogance is probably inevitable. The feeling now is that there is no absolute truth and that everything is relative. For us to say that there is a God and that there is truth, right and wrong, and judgement, is like rubbing the fur of an ill-tempered cat the wrong way. You are likely to get scratched. Mind you, it is interesting that it is only Christians who get accused of arrogance. No one accuses a mechanic of arrogance when they say that our car needs a new gearbox or tells a doctor that they are arrogant for prescribing antibiotics.

In fact, an interesting answer to arguments that accuse Christians of being arrogant because we think there *is* an absolute truth is to respond is, 'I'm sorry but I think that for you to say that there *isn't* an absolute truth is very arrogant.' But it's hard to do it in a gentle and respectful way. And anyway, then you might be in the terribly dangerous position of winning an argument.

'I'm afraid of being rejected'

The fear of rejection, and of being laughed at and scorned, is a very real one. None of us likes the idea of being rejected. We all like to be part of some 'inner circle': accepted, welcomed and respected. This need to belong is built deep into our nature. Perhaps it is a survival mechanism going back to the days when the humans on the edge of the group were the ones the wolves got. We have to belong and preferably belong at the centre of things. Rejection is very hard to handle, and being laughed at or scorned is even worse. To be rejected is to be considered as merely unimportant; but to be laughed at is to be considered positively contemptible.

How are we to handle this fear? I think there are at least two answers. The first answer is, to say bluntly, that there always comes a point where we must chose between being accepted by people and being accepted by God. I wish I could point out to you some way of performing a delicate balancing act so that you (and I) could be respected by both the unbelieving world, and God. One book I will never write is *How to Witness About Jesus and Remain Socially Respectable*. God may give you the gift of being accepted in the best places, despite your anxiety to share your faith, but I wouldn't bank on it. Now I am not saying get rid of your non-Christian friends and adopt the drop-out-prophet routine, complete with hair shirt and 'Repent now!' placard. Over many things we can, and should, maintain good links with our friends who do not share our faith. We may even have their respect. But in many key matters (ambitions, morals) there will inevitably, sooner or later, be a parting of the ways. Especially when it comes to sharing our faith, we cannot have a foot in both camps. We will have to choose, and I need to warn you that the cost of choosing the right way may be very high indeed. I will deal with this cost in more depth at the end of this chapter, but it would not be fair to pretend that it is possible to avoid it.

The second answer is this, and it is related: we need a sense of perspective. God has not rejected us and will never reject us. He has not abandoned us, nor can he. Let me remind you of some verses in Chapter 8 of the letter to the Romans:

> Since God did not spare even his own Son but gave him up for us all, won't God, who gave us Christ, also give us everything else?...

Can anything ever separate us from Christ's love? Does it mean he no longer loves us if we have trouble or calamity, or are persecuted, or are hungry or cold or in danger or threatened with death? (Even the Scriptures say, 'For your sake we are killed every day; we are being slaughtered like sheep.') No, despite all these things, overwhelming victory is ours through Christ, who loved us. And I am convinced that nothing can ever separate us from his love. Death can't, and life can't. The angels can't, and the demons can't. Our fears for today, our worries about tomorrow, and even the powers of hell can't keep God's love away. Whether we are high above the sky or in the deepest ocean, nothing in all creation will ever be able to separate us from the love of God that is revealed in Christ Jesus our Lord.'

Romans 8:32, 35-39

If we have fixed in our mind the fact that we do belong in heaven with Jesus and that it is our eternal home, then we will find earthly rejection much easier to bear. It may also help to remind ourselves that human groups last no more than a few dozen years before death breaks up the party. With the eternal friendship of Jesus assured for me I can easily live with rejection of those in this world.

Fear: the final word

Before leaving the subject of fear, I want to encourage you to do two things.

First, be honest and realistic about your fears. Bring them to God and lay them before him. Try to work out how many of them are real and how many are simply in your mind. In prayer, ask God to deal with the ones that are most powerful for you.

Secondly, and very definitely before you continue reading any further, I want you to think about the reasons that I have just given for why we are afraid to be witnesses to Jesus. Which of them is the one that stops *you* from being faithful to his commandment? Not your church, not your friends, but *you*? Ask yourself, is it really valid? Can you really justify

your silence? Not to me, I am quite unimportant, but to him.
Ask yourself this: did Jesus die for me just so that I might
stay silent?

The bottom line

This chapter and the previous are linked. One said why you
should call out and the other said why you shouldn't stay silent.
If you are still inclined to back off from sharing your faith, let
me ask you to compare the reasons for speech and the reasons
for silence. Which are stronger: the reasons for calling out, or
the reasons for staying silent?

Before I end this chapter, there is something that I must say.
It may be that you have analysed the pluses and minuses for
speaking out and in the end you come down reluctantly on the
side of keeping quiet. But here I must remind you; sharing the
Good News is not a matter of choice, it is something that Jesus
has commanded us to do.

I must also spell out to you that the rejection and hostility
that Jesus received was not unique to him. One of Jesus'
promises that preachers rarely dwell upon (let alone tell us to
claim!) is that his followers were to share that rejection and
hostility. The Bible tells us clearly that Jesus had a very
negative response from the very people he was sent to save.
'But although the world was made through him, the world
didn't recognise him when he came. Even in his own land and
among his own people, he was not accepted' (John 1:10-11).
Jesus even received hostility from the citizens of his own town.
After speaking to them we read that 'the people in the
synagogue were furious. Jumping up, they mobbed him and
took him to the edge of the hill on which the city was built.
They intended to push him over the cliff, but he slipped away
through the crowd and left them' (Luke 4:29). And worst of all,
at the cross, when you think that he might at least deserve some
pity, the bystanders laughed and ridiculed him. 'The crowd
watched, and the leaders laughed and scoffed. "He saved

others," they said, "let him save himself if he is really God's Chosen One, the Messiah." The soldiers mocked him, too, by offering him a drink of sour wine. They called out to him, "If you are the King of the Jews, save yourself!"' (Luke 23:35-38).

The rest of the New Testament nowhere promises anything but that his followers could expect to go the same way as their master. I find no indication at all that they would have it easy. The apostle Paul could have written the textbook on suffering (probably with an absorbingly gruesome illustrated medical supplement entitled *My scars and how I got them*). Writing to Timothy, he said this: 'Yes, and everyone who wants to live a godly life in Christ Jesus will suffer persecution' (2 Timothy 3:12). Throughout Acts and the letters of the New Testament we get again and again the idea that the first Christians rejoiced that they were suffering rejection, because it showed they were going along the right lines.

Now I am no masochist, and am I very reluctant to say 'amen' when I hear people glibly pray for persecution in this country, but there is an uncomfortable link between the success of a church at spreading the Good News and its willingness to embrace ridicule, rejection and even persecution. This was the pattern of the Early Church and it has been repeated throughout history. Let me mention two illustrations of this from very different parts of the world, nineteenth century Madagascar and late twentieth century China. In the case of Madagascar, there were barely a thousand believers in Jesus Christ and seventy Bibles in 1837, when a brutal and unrelenting persecution began. When, twenty-five bloody years later, it ended, there were well over seven thousand believers. The Chinese story is better known. In 1949, there were no more than five million Christians but, after thirty years of ruthless persecution, there were at least sixty million.

That there is a real link between suffering and growth is strengthened by the fact that the opposite has been frequently demonstrated. Comfort and prosperity seem to be bad news for churches. Let me give you an illustration. In a certain Middle

Eastern country (to protect the innocent I name no names) there was a small poor Christian village that had been surrounded by Islamic neighbours since about 1000 AD. Despite centuries of hostility, they had survived. Twenty years ago, one of the villagers got the chance to emigrate to a prosperous western state and, as they were all by now pretty much interrelated, the whole village followed. Some years later, a westerner who had known the old community sought out the pastor to see how things were going. To his horror the man broke down and began weeping angry tears. 'Your culture,' he wailed bitterly, 'has done in a few years what nine centuries of Islam could not do. You have destroyed our faith.'

In the affluent West, the church seems to have a waning influence. An environment in which we desire comfort, publicity and social acceptance seems to be one in which church growth is rare. Wealth weakens, prosperity poisons, and status silences.

Let me, however, end on a more positive and challenging note. The power of our willingness to stand up for Jesus, despite our fears, can never be measured. Sometimes it can be an unspoken witness that makes a difference.

The story is told of how, in the middle of a very cold winter in the year AD 320, there were forty soldiers, all Christians, who were members of the famed Twelfth Legion of Rome's Imperial Army. One day their captain told them that Emperor Licinius had sent out an edict that all soldiers were to offer sacrifices to the pagan gods. Most of the army dutifully obeyed, but the Christians did not. Instead, their response was, 'You can have our armour and even our bodies, but our heart's allegiance belongs to Jesus Christ.' At this, the captain had them march onto a nearby frozen lake. He had them stripped of their clothes and said they must either die or renounce Christ. But they would not. Instead, these brave people sang Christian songs together throughout the night and, one by one, they fell to the ice as the temperature took its toll. At last, there was only one soldier left. Finally, this last person lost his courage and he stumbled to the shore where he did indeed, renounce Christ.

An officer of the guards had been watching all this and, unknown to the others, he had secretly come to believe in Christ. When he saw this last man break rank, he could keep his secret no longer. He walked out onto the ice, threw off his clothes and confessed he was a Christian. When the sun rose the next morning there were again forty bodies of soldiers who had fought to the death for Christ.

The bottom line is simply and bluntly this: we are under orders to call out the Good News of Jesus. And we need to know that there may well be a cost for doing so.

Exercises

1. Read Jeremiah 1:4-10, 17-19. Can you identify with Jeremiah's protest? How does God answer it? How does this passage encourage you?

2. Read Mark 14:66-72; Acts 2:13,14 and Acts 5:13. Was Peter naturally a bold person? What made the change? How does this transformation encourage you?

3. Read Matthew 10:18-20. What specific witnessing circumstances does this passage refer to? What promises does it make to the believer in these worst case situations? Does the principle of God helping us in our witness only apply there?

4. Read John 16:5-8. The Holy Spirit doesn't just strengthen us, he also works in those we want to reach. What do we learn of his work in this area here?

Questions

1. Do you need to be accepted by those around you? Why? Do you feel that preserving this acceptance is something that gets in the way of your witness?

2. If you were asked to talk to people in your street, what would you be most afraid of? Having savage dogs set upon you? Having doors slammed in your face? Being treated as a half-wit?

3. What would help you in sharing your faith? Would having Jesus with you help? Doesn't the Holy Spirit answer that need?

4. If someone was drowning, or trapped in a burning building, would you risk your life to rescue them? Why are we so reluctant to take risks for sharing Jesus with people who are lost without him?

PART FOUR

THE 'WHERE' OF MISSION

In the previous sections we have looked at what our message is, and why we should share our faith. In this section I want to discuss the 'where' of sharing the Good News of Jesus.

Chapter 12

SHARING OUR FAITH AT HOME AND ABROAD

Where do we begin?

Let me tell you what didn't happen in my conversion.

- I didn't walk past a notice board outside a church that said 'Seven days without Jesus makes one weak' and fall to my knees in acknowledgement of my need for God.
- I didn't stop to listen to the open-air preacher in the market place one Saturday morning and there on the street give my life to Jesus.
- I didn't come to a living faith because I was in a traffic jam behind a car with a sticker on its back window that said 'King Jesus has the victory'.
- I didn't get saved because late one night I was scanning the radio channels listening for music, when I heard a man telling me that I was a sinner going to hell.
- I didn't get converted on my way to a disco by seeing a tract lying on the ground telling me that 'now was the day of salvation'.

Now these things may have happened to you – but they didn't to me. I took Christianity seriously because of *people*; my friends and people I knew. I have a suspicion that, for well over ninety per cent of Christians, this is the case. Ask a dozen people who are followers of Jesus about their conversion and listen carefully. I am almost certain that you will hear something like this:

- 'Well, there was this girl I was working with, you see? In Accounts, she was. Now, I knew as she was religious like, because she'd never swear. So, one day we gets talking ...'
- 'It was a chap at the golf club. Old Dickie, been dead now many years. Fine fellow. Guards I think; been in Korea. Anyway, one day – must have been '82 or '83 – quite out of the blue, he catches up with me at the clubhouse. "There's a fellow speaking at the church tonight, I was wondering if you'd like to hear him ..." '
- 'It was my first week at college. To be honest I was feeling a bit lonely. My first time away from home and all that. Anyway, the guy opposite invited me over for coffee and we got talking ...'

Do you see it? *People* are involved.

If anecdotal evidence will not persuade you, will statistics? Look at these figures on the reasons why people come to church:

- 1% come because they have been visited by a church member. This figure varies a lot from area to area.
- 2% come because of the church programme – for example, a ministry for the deaf, a children's holiday club, meetings for senior citizens, lunch clubs etc.
- 3% come because of a special need – often because of a bereavement.
- 4% come because of children's work.
- 6% come because they see some publicity.
- 8% come because of some personal contact with ministers and other church staff, perhaps through hospital visiting, marriage preparation or pastoral help.
- 77% come because they were invited by friends or relatives.

Did that register? Over three-quarters of the people who go to church go because someone invited them. Of course, if becoming a Christian is more about getting to know a person – Jesus – than it is believing in a series of intellectual facts, then it ought not to be a surprise that people play such a prominent role in our coming to faith. People introduce people to other people. Isn't that how you and I meet ordinary people? Nine times out of ten, we are introduced. Even today with phones, faxes and advertisements, we still prefer to have someone introduce us. Haven't you made the sort of phone call where you begin by saying 'Now we haven't met, but I was given your name by John Smith and . . .'?

This truth explains why Jesus spent so much of his time with people. If you and I had planned things, I think we would have started off by going and sitting down in the Jerusalem Central Library with a big sheet of parchment and writing down something called a 'Ten Point Plan For A Better World' and then we would have got a committee or two going. But Jesus took people and made them do things with him, so that they in turn could do things for other people to show his love. I remember an Asian girl who became a follower of Jesus through a very timid and shy Christian. When she was baptised she gave her testimony and said, 'My friend built a bridge from her heart to mine and Jesus walked over it.' That's what happened to me, through my friend Andy Economides, when we were students in London in 1975. Only people can be bridge builders like that.

So at the heart of God's plan are people; and people, in this context, are you and I. But where do we begin? In fact, we have a clear strategy given to us by Jesus. In the opening chapter of Acts we read how, just outside Jerusalem, Jesus gave the final instructions to his followers before he ascended to heaven. 'But when the Holy Spirit has come upon you, you will receive power and will tell people about me everywhere – in Jerusalem, throughout Judea, in Samaria, and to the ends of the earth' (Acts 1:8).

There are lots of things to make us think in this fascinating verse, and I will be referring back to it again in the final section of this book. Here, though, I want to look at the example of strategy that it reveals. I want to do this not just out of a historical interest in what happened, but for very practical reasons. Christianity spread so fast from unpromising beginnings (assorted manual workers, fishermen and tax collectors and so on), that it is well worth looking at the strategy of the early Christians. They had obviously got something right.

The strategy that Jesus proposed: 'Jerusalem ... Judea ... Samaria . . . and to the ends of the earth' was hardly a comforting one, and I would like to know what the disciples thought about it. These were hardly seasoned globetrotters; they had made it into what we would today call southern Lebanon, and bits of western Jordan. And that was that. But there is more than an itinerary underlying Jesus' words here. There are implications for other aspects of mission.

Through these four steps, I want to trace out a way forward for our own witness.

1. To Jerusalem: Our inner circle

Jerusalem was the capital city of the Jewish people at the time of Jesus. But it would be misleading to see it as a sort of capital like London. It was far more important than that; it was the centre of worship, power and culture, and a site of pilgrimage. For the Jew, it was London, Rome, Florence and Mecca all rolled into one. No less a person than the great King David had established it a thousand years earlier, and it had been the focus of the nation's hopes ever since. David's son Solomon had built the temple and his palace there, and since then it had seen all the major events of the nation's life. The Babylonians had taken it, destroyed much of it and dragged many of its inhabitants off to exile. Yet when the exile was over, the people had returned to their beloved city and began the task of rebuilding it. For many

Jews, the high point of their year was the annual pilgrimage to Jerusalem to celebrate the festival of the Passover. As Jerusalem or as Zion (a synonym), its name occurred throughout the Psalms and every act of worship would have referred to it somewhere or other. In common thinking at least, Yahweh dwelt within the heart of the temple. For a Jew in the first decades of the first century, Jerusalem was not just the centre of the world; it was the centre of the universe.

Now most people who look at this instruction of Jesus tend to assume that Jesus was telling his followers to start in the easy bit – Jerusalem – before graduating on to the tough bits – Samaria etc. In one sense that is true, but it also overlooks the fact that, for the disciples, Jerusalem would, as we say, carry 'a lot of baggage'. Think about it:

- Jerusalem had been the site of their greatest expectations as they had gone there in the days leading up to Good Friday. Despite their leader's sombre warnings, they had expected that here Jesus would become king, and the kingdom would finally be restored to Israel. They had got that very badly wrong. Instead, Jerusalem had been the site of the dreadful events of the trial and crucifixion.

- They were known in Jerusalem. It was not a large town; there were possibly only 25,000 inhabitants in the main part of the city, and as country boys from up north they would have been easy to spot. Ever since rumours of the resurrection and the empty tomb had begun to circulate, they must have been the subjects of speculation and interest. They had left Jerusalem shortly after the first resurrection appearances to go back to Galilee, but they had now returned. And as they walked along the streets, it was probable that, already, heads turned as they passed.

- Jerusalem wasn't exactly a healthy place for new religious movements. Because it was so central to everything, the Romans knew that if there was going to be trouble, it would be here. And because it was so central, the Jewish religious authorities knew that they had better keep it under tight control. It must have crossed the disciples' minds that, from entering Jerusalem on a donkey in triumph, to exiting it under a cross in shame, had taken Jesus a mere five days.

- Above all, not only had Jesus' death in Jerusalem been traumatic, the disciples had hardly covered themselves in glory there. Judas had been bought and had betrayed Jesus; and he may not have been the only one to have doubts about Jesus' management of things. Among the others, there had been misunderstanding, cowardice and fear. They had fled and Peter had made a devastating and public denial that was probably well known. Only the women had come out of it with any credit: a fact that must have added insult to injury.

You see, for the disciples, Jerusalem was not only the centre of their national and cultural identity, it was dangerous, and it was the location of their biggest shame. So, by sending them to Jerusalem, Jesus was not setting his disciples an easy task. It's not as if they had a good reputation and were building on a strong public image; if there was a place where that applied, it was probably Galilee. Instead, Jesus was sending them to start off in the place where they had messed up. He was explicitly instructing them to begin their mission for him in the place of greatest failure, in the one place that they would have preferred to avoid.

Now the question is this: where is our Jerusalem?

Essentially, 'Jerusalem' is that area of our lives that is local and immediate to us. I think it is helpful to think about our 'Jerusalem' under the three natural divisions:

- Kinship – it is our family and closest friends: those with whom we share the closest of bonds.
- Community – it is people we meet regularly and those who we share common ground with. These might include those we see on an almost daily basis at school, college, or in our workplace.
- Common Interest – it is people with whom we share the

same concerns and likes; hobbies and leisure activities. They are the people we know from the sports club, the evening class, or the music band.

I like to think of 'Jerusalem' as being that circle of our lives where we are on first name terms with people and where they know us fairly well. If I was writing your biography, it is these people that, above all, I would want to interview.

Now our 'Jerusalem' might be centred geographically on where we live: in the past, it certainly would have been. But nowadays, as distance is less of an issue, the geography side of things has changed. For instance, you might live in Swindon and commute to London every day: for you, both the office and home might be your Jerusalem. There might even be someone who is on the other side of the world, but with whom you communicate so regularly over the Web, that he or she fits within the scope of your Jerusalem.

I suggest you spend a moment or two thinking about these people; or if you have the time, writing down their names. Now think about how you have shared the Good News of Jesus with them. Now if you do this, a variety of feelings will almost certainly emerge: guilt, scepticism, and perhaps even hope!

- *Guilt* will be there because, if you are anything like me, you will realise that you haven't really begun to make inroads with many of these people, some of whom are very close to you.
- *Unease* will be present because these people know you, warts and all. You can hardly pretend about who you are with people like this. They have seen you under stress!
- You will have f*ear*, because you are, frankly, scared about what your colleagues, peers, friends or relatives will think of you when you seem to be, as they will call it, 'trying to convert them'.
- There will be *disbelief*, because at this point in time it is quite difficult to picture them becoming Christians. It is curious

how we can accept that God converted us, but find the idea of him converting others hard to believe.

- And, all being well, there is *hope*, because you might even have got a whiff of optimism about how wonderful it would be if they came to faith in Jesus.

Difficult eh? Well, let me encourage you. Remember what I have been saying all the way through, that conversion is something that God does. It is at the heart of his mission. You want your friends and colleagues to become converted? Well, so does he! God wants to see your kinship group, your community and those you know from your common interests, as part of his family, far more than you do. You are not on your own.

Remember too, that, in calling the disciples to witness first in Jerusalem, Jesus knew he was asking them to go to the hardest place. He was asking them to go to the place where they had really messed up, where their credibility was shot through, where they felt most vulnerable. The chances are, your Jerusalem will be similar. Jesus himself knew the heartache and complexities of going against the grain in this inner circle. One of the most illuminating stories in the gospels about Jesus' own inner circle occurs when he had caused a stir by performing healings and exorcisms. We read that 'when Jesus returned to the house where he was staying, the crowds began to gather again, and soon he and his disciples couldn't even find time to eat. When his family heard what was happening, they tried to take him home with them. "He's out of his mind," they said' (Mark 3: 20-21).

So, if you are considered a religious loony, rejoice! You are in good company. Interestingly enough, soon after the resurrection, Jesus' brother James became a leading member of the Christian community. We do not know what happened, but there is an intriguing statement by Paul in 1 Corinthians 15:7 that the risen Jesus appeared to his brother James. I find the fact that Jesus cared for his family encouraging.

I want to also say here, that Jesus' command that they start in the place that they had messed up in, is wise psychology. If they had skipped this part of their world, they would have left themselves vulnerable. You can almost hear the accusations can't you. 'They went to the Samaritans and the Gentiles because they couldn't handle their own kith and kin.' 'Of course, the people who knew them would have nothing of them.' And lurking in the back of their minds might have been that haunting feeling that they could not hack it with their own people.

What is interesting is that it is this sphere of witness that we are all to be involved in. Let me share with you two current situations where I am witnessing in my own 'Jerusalem'.

- I am sharing my faith with my hairdresser – he's fascinated and intrigued. On my last visit, he said that he couldn't wait for me to go and get my hair cut again!
- I am having great conversations with the cleaner at my local gym, who is a political refugee. He was choked with emotion when I said that I would pray for his wife who he hasn't seen for seven years.

Now these, of course, involve me in witnessing as a private person, not as a 'professional evangelist'. I see no reason why any ordinary Christian could not do something similar.

Yet, I have to say that, in many ways, the inner circle of our lives is the toughest area to witness in. After all, mess up in Outer Mongolia and you can get on the plane and never look back. Mess up at home and you have to stare at your failures across the breakfast table. Yet God can achieve amazing things in this area. Look what happened when the disciples, empowered by the Holy Spirit, did witness in Jerusalem. The story is there in Acts chapters 2-5. In my Bible the word 'amazed' crops up a lot! It seems that what they did caused quite a stir; some of the inhabitants of Jerusalem wanted to hear more, some believed, and some made fun of them.

But then that is the key point about witnessing in your inner circle: they cannot ignore you. You are going to get acceptance, or rejection, but at least you won't get apathy.

2. To Judea: The neighbourly neighbours

Judea was the territory around Jerusalem – it was the wider area outside the inner circle of their immediate life. It was a step out from the inner circle, but not an enormous one. There was the same language, the same culture and the same values as Jerusalem, but it was a bigger and more diverse area. And critically, for good or ill, the disciples would not have been known there.

So where is our Judea? I suppose our Judea would be those people that we occasionally come into contact with. I see it as representing those people who we count as acquaintances or distant friends, but who we don't very often see. I tend to think of it as being the people who you meet so infrequently that the first thing you do when you meet them is to desperately try and remember their names and details. They are the sort of people where the conversation includes such things as 'Now, hadn't you just moved house when we last met?' 'You're in Accounts aren't you? 'Oh, remind me how old your children are now?'

It's worth thinking about who these people are. It may be some distant relatives or old friends. It might be those people in the office on the floor below, or those you tend to bump into occasionally. It is hard to be certain who is in this group; after all, by definition, you may never see them again. The number of people in this category, though, will run into very large figures; think of all those school friends, fellow students, colleagues and neighbours who have featured in your life.

Now these are people that we can still reach. The bad news is that they don't really know us well so that it is often quite hard to move quickly into the deep and personal 'conversation mode'. The good news is that they aren't likely to know us well enough to call us hypocrites! We should never dismiss the effectiveness of our witness with those we don't know so well.

Let me give you two examples of people who I think fit into the Judea sphere of my life:

- I am currently corresponding on e-mail, with someone who I have never met, about the Christian faith.
- On Easter Monday I was in the steam room of my local gym with a Christian friend and met a devout Hindu. I commented on how good the steam room was and he replied, 'Yes – it gets rid of the sins.' We got talking and very soon, it emerged that he and his family had been talking about the death of Jesus over the weekend. My friend and I shared our own testimony and he said that he wanted to talk more.
- It is easy to overlook this area of our lives, but there can be great results in it. A friend of mine is excellent at remembering people's names and God has used that gift to good effect. Years ago he was very involved in summer camps put on for young people, both Christians and those who had not yet begun to follow Christ. One year as the coach arrived at the camp he recognised a young man from the previous year who had been in his small group. My friend was pleased to see him, as he hadn't been a Christian the year before. Remembering his name, he called out to him, 'Alex! It's great to see you again.' Later on in the week, there was a time for testimonies, when the young people could share what God had done in their lives. In the middle of this Alex stood up, 'I came last year and didn't think anyone noticed that I was around. But this year when I got off the coach my old leader called out my name. This week I have given my life to Jesus, because I thought, if someone cared enough to remember my name, then what they believe in must be true.' We never know when the smallest act of kindness, the tiniest gesture, the most casual remark, may have an impact far beyond what we could imagine.

3. To Samaria: The not so neighbourly neighbours

In terms of geography, Samaria was as close as most of Judea. Yet, there was a lot of hostility between the Samaritans and Jews.

- There were *racial differences*. Because of inter-marriage in the past with Gentiles, Jews considered the Samaritans to be 'half-breeds'.
- There were *religious differences*. The Samaritans only believed in the first five books of the Old Testament. Strict Jews felt they were, effectively, pagans.
- There were *cultural differences*. The Samaritans did not worship in Jerusalem and had their own way of doing things.
- There were *political differences*. The Samaritans kept out of involvement in Jewish politics and often denied that they were Jews, especially if the people asking the question looked bloodthirsty and had armies standing behind them.
- There was a long *history* of hatred. When the Jews returned from exile and tried to rebuild their temple in 537 BC, Samaritan opposition blocked all significant progress for nearly sixteen years. The Jews returned the favour in 128 BC by destroying the Samaritan temple. The Samaritans desecrated the Jewish temple around AD 6 by scattering bones in it. And so on ...

Even though they were next-door neighbours and had much in common, they were sworn enemies. The Jews looked down on the Samaritans and at the time of Jesus, a Jewish person would avoid going through their country; they would not speak to, come into contact with, or share anything in common with Samaritans. So the disciples being told to go to Samaria was a tall order.

Interestingly, Jesus had set the example of bridging the divide between the two peoples. Choosing to take a route through Samaria, Jesus had talked to a Samaritan woman, claimed to be the Messiah and offered her the 'living water' (see John 4). This raises again the principle that Jesus asked the disciples to do nothing that he had not done already. The same is still true; whatever he asks us to do today, we may be sure that he has already set the example.

So where is our Samaria? It is anywhere where there are people with whom we feel uncomfortable. It is where there are people with whom we have racial, political, cultural, or religious differences; or where there is a history of bitterness. It may be simply be that they come from the wrong side of the street, go the 'other' school, support the wrong football team, or like the wrong music. Or it may be far worse. It may be that between their family and ours, their community and ours, lies centuries of bitterness and bloodshed. And you don't have to go beyond the British Isles to find examples of that sort of thing. In this situation Jesus orders us to go and talk to the people who naturally we might prefer not even to see. And I think we can extend Samaria to those cultures and lifestyles that we find totally at odds with ours. For us today's Samaritans may include those unlovely youngsters with their dead-end lifestyles on the run-down estate, Joey the stinking alcoholic who sleeps rough round the back of the church, and the man doing time for sexual abuse in your local jail. And talking about Jesus means caring for them all.

It is an interesting and challenging exercise to list those groups of people in your immediate neighbourhood who you really would prefer *not* to talk to: not about the weather, not about the state of the roads and *most of all* not about Jesus. We might protest that we are very ill suited to talking to these people and that there are others who are much better suited to working 'in Samaria'. Now this is what might say, yet God of course knows what he is doing. In fact, in the Bible, we see that God uses very surprising people to reach others. So the ex-Pharisee, Paul, is sent to the non-Jews; Moses, who has been raised by Egyptians, is sent to free the Israelites from Egypt; fishermen are sent to educated teachers. God seems to repeatedly make the point that our divisions do not matter to

him. Actually, sometimes I think they do; I think he looks out
for them and likes to trample all over them. I suspect that God
gets great pleasure (and Satan exquisite agony) from seeing
churches where people from once warring factions are now
reconciled in Christ.

Samaria is tough, but I have to say that there is nowhere
where the Christian testimony is so remarkable. You see, as I
hinted in the history of the Samaritans and Jews, there is no part
of human existence that is more deep-seated and irremovable
than hatred between peoples. Political systems come and go,
empires rise and fall, but hatred remains. Arab and Israeli,
Ulster Protestant and Catholic Nationalist, Hutu and Tutsi,
Turk and Armenian; the list goes on and only gets shorter when
one group is wiped off the map. Someone once said that
tribalism was the curse of Africa. They were wrong; it is the
curse of the world.

Jesus has given us orders to go to Samaria and we need to
obey. The world is watching.

4. To the ends of the earth: No one is excluded.

There is much that Christianity and its 'mother', Judaism, have
in common. For instance, they share the same Old Testament
and have many common beliefs in God. There are, though,
differences, the most basic being that Christians believe that
the Messiah has come. However, one of the most major
changes is how the two faiths relate to outsiders. Judaism is
essentially a closed family of faith, looking inwards towards
Jerusalem. While outsiders are allowed to become Jews,
generally there is no active recruitment or evangelism.
Christianity is, however, extraordinarily different. It is open,
and looks outwards, away from Jerusalem and has only the
ends of the world as its limits. This switch in perspective, which
clearly took place right at the very start of Christianity, was one
of the most significant events in history. The Christian faith –
unless severely distorted – has a built-in outward urge: locked

into the deepest level of our faith is the need to go and tell.

In our age of global holidays and instant worldwide communication, we can lose the awesome and terrifying impact that this phrase 'to the ends of the earth' must have had to the Jews of Jesus' day. There were Jewish communities elsewhere, but they were not an exploring, adventurous race. The only Jewish sailor of note in their history had been Jonah and his fate was hardly an encouragement!

Yet, with the odd hefty push now and then from the Holy Spirit, the Acts of the Apostles recounts how, against all odds, these men (and later, women) took the Good News out beyond their own country. The account in Acts increasingly follows only a single strand of Christian mission, that of Peter, and then Paul towards Rome, the centre of the known world. Of most of the other twelve disciples, we have only sketchy rumours. There is strong evidence for Thomas having founded churches in India, and tales that Matthew may have been martyred in Ethiopia.

The spread of the Good News is remarkable. In little less than a quarter of a century, without armies, tape recorders, television, or the printing press, the gospel of Jesus had spread to the capital city of the most powerful nation in the world. It had overcome every barrier of race and language and was now being lived out in front of Caesar's palace.

Do I need to spell where – or who – the ends of the earth are for us? As there are, of course, no literal ends of the earth, this is an unlimited command. What Jesus is saying is this: 'Go, and preach to whoever you meet'. Of course, this is not just a commandment about *where*; it is about *who*. No one is to be exempt. The message of God's love, the proclamation of the kingdom of God in word and deed, is not simply relevant for one social group, one nation of the world, one specific race or continent. In this command is the great mandate for the extension of Christianity to all the nations of the world. This command includes in its scope, the tribes of New Guinea, the slum dwellers of Brazil, and the refugees from the Balkan wars.

There are simply no limits, except those we add, to the Good News. Now, as we think about this outermost circle of spreading the Good News, I want to make one important and heartfelt plea. It is this: can we be sure that we spread the Good News of Jesus and *nothing else*? Because the people of this outer circle, especially those in the far off countries, are so different to us, it is easy to accidentally smuggle something else into the message; we want them to become like us. Along with Christianity, we sometimes add our culture, and that isn't right.

We can easily dismiss the complaint that Christianity is just a western religion. Christianity began in the Middle East, and the majority of the world's Christians today actually live in the Southern Hemisphere. Actually, it is only in the West that Christianity is in any sort of decline. We can less easily deny the criticism that the culture of western Christianity has imposed itself on the global church, and in doing so, it has swamped and suppressed any local culture.

In some of my trips to southern Africa I have been embarrassed to find that some of the Anglican churches in the townships have had imposed on them, probably with the best of intentions, a certain very English way of doing their worship. This has involved using the *English Hymnal*, a Psalter for chanting the Psalms, and the *1662 Book of Common Prayer*. Even more curious, is that fact that an only slightly modified form of this service (with its roots in Tudor England!) can still be heard today in the churches in Israel and Palestine – the heartland of Christianity. And it isn't just English Anglicans who do this; churches founded by German Lutherans tend to sing Lutheran hymns, even if it is 30 °C outside. Fellowships planted by American Southern Baptists often seem to believe in the values of the southern United States, even if, in the streets outside they are burning the 'Stars and Stripes'.

My advice to Christians in Africa and elsewhere would be the same: distinguish between the message of the Good News and the packaging of the message. While the message cannot – and must not – be changed, the packaging is totally disposable.

Ironically, in the case of the Anglican example I have quoted above, the service pattern that has become so permanent was actually created to make the gospel and worship meaningful to ordinary people who were confused by the old Latin mass. In a modern phrase, they were trying to be 'culturally sensitive'. I'm sure they would be horrified at the way the structures they created to spread the Good News have become barriers to impede it.

No, going to the ends of the earth isn't about making everyone like our society, or making them imitate our way of doing things. God does not belong to any one racial group, culture, or church. He is no one's possession; it is we who are his possessions. Thankfully, this is being changed and there is something of a growing exchange of ideas between the different branches of the worldwide church. This is very helpful and we need more of it; I would love to have the input from Brazilian pastors who have worked successfully in shantytowns, on how we deal with some of our inner-city estates. So mission, as always, can help us stay fresh. We gain as much as we give by getting involved in mission.

Let me conclude: the God who loved the whole world so much that he sent his son, that whoever believes in him should have eternal life, has not changed. The gospel is for the entire world; Jesus is for everyone. The original hearers of the command to go to the ends of the earth are long since dead, and are now alive in heaven. Yet, time has not changed that order. Jesus commands us to go today in exactly the same way as he did two thousand years ago.

Summary

Jesus said 'you will receive power and will tell people about me everywhere in Jerusalem, throughout Judea, in Samaria'. That order has never been annulled. It still stands. So what are we going to do about it?

Let me make some points. The first thing to say is that I do not think that our witnessing for Jesus is to be in only one of the categories that I have discussed above. I'm fairly certain that you cannot say 'oh I'm just a Jerusalem person myself' and leave Judea, Samaria and the ends of the earth to others. We are all called, in different ways, to all of them, and I think our churches need to be doing what we can in all of these areas. None of us is exempt from active personal involvement in our 'Jerusalems' and 'Judeas'. Most of us will have the chance for some bridge- building for whoever the Samaritans are in our neighbourhood. The ends of the earth may seem far away. Of course, they are not. There is barely a village in the United Kingdom that does not have someone from an immigrant family, whether from China, Korea or Kosovo. Some towns are full of overseas students, many of whom are lonely and ill at ease in what they often find is an unfriendly culture. I am sometimes tempted to think that God is so exasperated by our failure to go out to the peoples at the ends of the earth, that he has brought them here to make it a bit easier for us!

Secondly, can you (yes, *you*) get involved in working in the mission to the ends of the earth? This is not the book to talk about full time service abroad, and there are others better qualified than I am to talk about it. But Jesus still sends and people still cry out in need. Now in some ways, working abroad for Jesus is easier than it has ever been. Few places on earth are more than thirty hours away from your home. Most places now have phone or e-mail links and modern medicines have reduced the risk of many diseases. Yet, in some way it is as tough as it has ever been. If you have learnt anything from this book, I hope it is that God is not the God of the quick fix. If he were, he would have opted out of the whole bloody business of the cross. In some places, to be effective will require you to face up to a lifetime's labour. As God became incarnate and became one of us, you and I too must become 'incarnate' and one of those that we want to reach. After all, to really effectively communicate the Good News, you need to know the language and the culture, and you don't do that straight off the plane. You also ought to realise that some of the most needy areas, like Central Asia, are those with the toughest languages. And unless you are very gifted, learning them will take time. For example, to master Arabic to the extent that you can read and write it and engage in deep and serious conversations will take at least two years of solid work. Chinese and other languages would take longer. But then if that is what God is calling you to do, you will only be happy doing it and you will be unfulfilled doing anything else.

Now you may say that it's too late and that time has passed you by. Not necessarily: there are even growing opportunities for early retirees. Go on, shock them at work; take early retirement and instead of growing roses go to Tashkent or Nepal instead. I'll be surprised if you regret it. Of course you may miss the intensely heart-stopping excitement of competing for the 'Rose of the Year Contest' at the local fete, but I've no doubt you will be recompensed!

Now even if you cannot personally get involved in going to these places, can you please get involved by supporting the people who are? It is a costly work, in every sense. Does your church have people working abroad for Jesus? They may even still be called missionaries. How can you support them? They will need finance and someone to keep an eye on their house (and maybe their prize roses). And when they come back, they will need somewhere to stay and somewhere where they can just unwind. Above all, they will need prayer; that vital work where we get alongside God and plead with him to open hearts and save souls. In short, there is a lot that we can do as individuals.

Thirdly, I believe that all of us should have what we might call a portfolio of mission interests that we support. There are so many different ways to be involved in the mission to the ends of the earth. I am forever amazed and moved by the commitment of many Christian organisations to work for relief and elimination of poverty, for education and medicine, for translation and education in some of the most desperately poor and needy parts of the world. All of these ways show God's love in Jesus to a world that needs to know it. In your portfolio of interests you might wish to include one mission that works within the UK, one that works abroad, and another that works in relief and development work. And for each, give and pray. How do you choose one? Well, I wish I could give a list but there are so many societies to choose from that to give a list of names would be very selective and it would inevitably result in a stream of letters where people asked for their favourites to be listed next time. But you might like to look at the issues or needs that interest you. Have you been somewhere exotic on holiday? Why not find out what is happening there? Is there one particular country that God has laid on your heart? What are the global issues you feel strongly about? Ask around about Christians working in that area. Your church leader should be able to help and the Christian press always has articles and advertisements. A very useful resource, overflowing with facts and addresses is the book *Operation World* by Patrick Johnstone, the sixth edition of which is due out late in 2001. Another resource, pitched at a younger age group is *You Can Change the World* by Jill Johnstone, published by OM publishing. In my experience, your local Christian bookshop is often a very valuable source of useful information. Above all, pray.

Finally, encourage your church to be involved. Jesus gives us the wonderful vision of the ends of the earth, but the devil loves to change the focus so that we become preoccupied with the state of the organ (or the music group), or whether we ought to change the layout of the pews (or the seats). We must do all we can to make sure that our churches look outwards. And not just to look but also to pray, give and send.

Exercises

1. Read the whole of Jonah (it isn't long!)

   - Why do you think that, when commanded to go to Nineveh, the capital of the brutal Assyrians, Jonah fled in the opposite direction?
   - What annoyed Jonah (see 4:1) about the outcome of his preaching to Nineveh?
   - What was God's attitude to Nineveh (see 4:11)?
   - What can we learn from this for our own calling out?

2. In contrast to Jonah's attitude read Isaiah 2:2-5. In this poetic prophecy, Isaiah looks forward to the glorious day of the Messiah. What will be the position of the nations then? How is our witness fulfilling this ancient prophecy?

3. Read the story of Namaan in 1 Kings 5:1-19, noticing the role of the unnamed slave girl. Notice that a) she was isolated, b) she was in a hostile and alien culture, c) she was at the very bottom of the social ladder, d) she actually said very little but, e) she had more faith than the King of Israel (verse 7) did. What lessons and encouragement can you draw from this for your witness?

4. Compare Luke 9:51-54 with Acts 5:25. How do you feel John, in particular, must have felt at sharing the Good News in Samaria, in view of his past attitudes?

Questions

1. Were people involved in your coming to Christ? What was the role of ordinary believers and evangelists in your coming to faith?

2. List five specific people who belong to your inner 'Jerusalem' zone.

- What strengths have you got in sharing Jesus with these people?
- What obstacles have you got to overcome in sharing Jesus with these people?
- Do you pray specifically for opportunities to share in this area?

3. Think of the sort of people who might fit into your 'Judea' zone.

- Do you have much opportunity to share the Good News with them?
- How could you get to know them better?
- In what ways could you increase the possibility of having good conversations with them?
- Do you pray for opportunities in this area?

4. Who (or where) is your Samaria?

- What divides you from them?
- Have you ever seriously thought of these people becoming Christians?
- In what way could you get more involved with these people? Are you praying for these people?

5. What are you contributing (your prayer? your money? your life?) to the Good News going out to the ends of the earth?

- Who do you know who is doing this?
- Have *you* ever thought that God might want you to get seriously involved in spreading the Good News to the ends of the earth? Why not?

PART FIVE

THE SEVEN PILLARS OF MISSION

THE 'HOW' OF CALLING OUT

We have looked at the basics of mission; we have considered what we call out, why we do so and where we do so. Now we look at the whole area of how we call out.

The subject of how we call out is so vast that all I can do here is to give you some general pointers. I do hope, however that it will stimulate you into thinking, acting and praying.

In the collected sayings of the book of Proverbs we find the following, 'Wisdom has built her spacious house with seven pillars' (Proverbs 9:1). In the seven chapters that make up this part, I want to look at what I see as being the key components of how to witness. I like to think of these components as being pillars. In building a house you cannot pick and choose which pillars you are going to erect; they all have to be put up. I believe the same is true with these principles of mission.

Now right at the start of discussing how to do mission I want to say that there is no rigid formula or magic recipe for sharing our faith in Jesus. Because talking about Jesus is all about sharing one person with another, then naturally the shape and form of how it is done varies. There can be no hard and fast rules; how you do it will be different from how I might do it. Nevertheless, there are some biblical principles that we would do well to look at and in outlining the seven pillars below, I have tried to be faithful to what I see in the Bible. These biblical principles have been tested and proved effective by faithful Christians and churches throughout many centuries and across many differing cultures. We would do well to learn from their experience.

The seven pillars (and I'm sure others might want to change their names and the order) are the following:

1. **Prayer:** All that we do must be rooted in God's will and power.
2. **Presence:** We can only speak to people about Jesus if we are there with them
3. **Proclamation:** We must speak out about Jesus.
4. **Persuasion:** We need to speak with people to help them understand the truth of the Good News.
5. **Power:** We need to allow the Holy Spirit to work in whatever way he chooses.
6. **Praise:** In all that we do we must honour God and make

sure that all the glory goes to him.

7. **Patterning:** When people do become Christians, then we need to do more than simply welcome them, we need to encourage and help them on their way. Above all, we need to model new patterns of living for them.

Chapter 13

THE FIRST PILLAR: PRAYER

PRAY!

Let me start by saying that prayer is not so much a pillar as a foundation. It underlies all that we do. There are lots of things in mission that I could say are optional. This is not one of them.

Prayer lies at the heart, not just of calling out, but also of what we are as Christians. In fact it seems that a habit of crying out to some higher power is something that is common to all humans, however sceptical they may be. There is a lot that I could say about prayer but here I want to focus on its role in mission. I think there are three problems that we commonly have in prayer.

For a start, I believe that we do far too little prayer for our witnessing. For one thing, too much of our praying is for ourselves. Sometimes I think if we taped our prayers – both silent and spoken – and then listened to them, we would be embarrassed at how much of the time we prayed for ourselves. Assuming that you are a Christian yourself (the first require- ment for witnessing to others!), this sort of self-centred praying converts no one. The foundation for being a fruitful witness to Jesus is to make the salvation of others the focus of prayer. For another thing, I think that in this lack of prayer for conversions there sometimes lies an extraordinary self-confidence. What we are saying by not praying is that we believe that we can convert people to Jesus without God being involved at all. We are saying, in effect, 'No problem God, you keep out of this. I can do it myself.' Now this is very serious. No one can be converted without the Holy Spirit, so by us pretending that we can convert people on our own, we are making ourselves little gods! This is extraordinarily foolish and, of course, under such circumstances, God is hardly likely to give us success; that would merely confirm our arrogant self-confidence. We need to be much more dependent on God. And when we do pray for people's conversions I'm afraid that much of our prayer is distorted. We have somehow caught the idea that praying is twisting God's arm. 'Go on God,' we say, 'there's Charlie. I want you to make him a Christian.' What we are doing wrong here is giving God orders. I'm really not sure that that is a good idea; he is our Lord, not our butler. No, quite simply, we need to pray because we are inadequate to do this work ourselves. At the heart of all true prayer is the recognition that God is far greater than we are. True prayer – and I wish I knew more of it myself – should cause us to look away from ourselves and to make us recognise that we have needs. However self-sufficient, talented or competent we may be, (or these days, however advanced we are technologically), we still need help. To pray properly is to say, in effect, all my own clever plans count for nothing, I need God to work. Prayer is the acknowledgement of that need. It comes from an awareness that we are not actually able to achieve anything worth achieving, do anything worth doing, say anything worth saying, without the help of God.

This dependency is the essence of prayer. Consider one of the stories Jesus told: 'Then, teaching them more about prayer, he used this illustration: "Suppose you went to a friend's house at midnight, wanting to borrow three loaves of bread. You would say to him, 'A friend of mine has just arrived for a visit, and I have nothing for him to eat.' He would call out from his bedroom, 'Don't bother me. The door is locked for the night, and we are all in bed. I can't help you this time.' But I tell you this – though he won't do it as a friend, if you keep knocking long enough, he will get up and give you what you want so his reputation won't be damaged" '(Luke 11:5-8). According to the customs of Jesus' time, whatever hour of the day or night visitors arrived, they must be given food. Here, the friend who has received the surprise guest has nothing to set before him; embarrassingly his cupboards are bare. So, in desperation he goes to his next-door neighbour to ask for help in his need. Eventually, the neighbour gives in to his persistence and supplies him the bread. I draw three helpful lessons from this for our mission.

- Firstly, this story reminds us that prayer is about knowing that your cupboards are bare; it is realising that you do not have the resources yourself. Of course, this is true in sharing our faith; we can't argue or persuade people into the kingdom and we certainly cannot give anybody spiritual food. Only God can do that.
- Secondly, this story shows us the right attitude to God. The man does not go to his neighbour and order that he be given bread. Instead, he goes to him humbly and pleads for bread. In the same way, we are to go to God believing that he will supply us with what we need.
- Thirdly, this story encourages us to pray persistently. If we keep praying, Jesus says, God will answer us. The man in the parable does not knock once and then, with a sad shrug of the shoulders, go away empty handed. Instead, we read that he keeps knocking for a long time so that eventually his neighbour gives him what he wants. God, Jesus says, is like that. We are to keep praying.

So, mindful that we have nothing, where do we start in praying for others?

The priority is that we need to start praying that those who do not know God's love will know it. I do not believe that anyone can find Jesus on their own. No one can come to faith simply because they have worked it out for themselves and they think that Jesus is a good idea. That's not the way that faith works. Our friends, our neighbours and even those we don't know, can only say yes to God because of his powerful work in their lives. Listen to what Jesus says, 'For people can't come to me unless the Father who sent me draws them to me, and at the last day I will raise them from the dead' (John 6:44). Only God draws people to Jesus.

The reason why it is God who has to do this is clearly given in the Bible. 'Satan, the god of this evil world, has blinded the minds of those who don't believe, so they are unable to see the glorious light of the Good News that is shining upon them. They don't understand the message we preach about the glory of Christ, who is the exact likeness of God (2 Corinthians 4:4-5). Satan has blinded minds and only the Spirit of God can open people's eyes to see the goodness, the truth and the reality of the love of God.

We must pray for people! Listen to what Paul says to Timothy: 'I urge you, first of all, to pray for all people. As you make your requests, plead for God's mercy upon them, and give thanks. Pray this way for kings and all others who are in authority, so that we can live in peace and quietness, in godliness and dignity. This is good and pleases God our Savior, for he wants everyone to be saved and to understand the truth' (1 Timothy 2:1-4). We need to pray for those who don't know God, because it is only God who can help them see. We need him to work in their hearts and minds and lives to draw them to himself.

Here we come to a great paradox that I find hard to understand and I know I am in good company. While it would seem that people have the ability to refuse God and turn their backs on him, it does seem that our prayers can make a difference. Somehow, when we pray to God for people, he is able to change their minds so that they turn to him in repentance and faith. I do not claim to understand how this works. The facts are simply this: when we pray – and pray persistently – people are converted and when we do not pray, people are not converted. I am inclined to suggest we put the theological and philosophical questions involved into the mental file marked 'To be asked in heaven' and get on with the task of sharing the Good News.

So much for the theory; now to the practice. Now if you remember the image I used in the last chapter, it would be a good idea here to think about the people who fall into the 'Jerusalem circle' of your lives. Here there are people who you ought to pray for regularly. If you have made a list of them, now is the time to look over it and consider realistically how often you might be able to pray for each one of them. I suggest that a good rule would be to pray for those people we are closest to at least twice a week. And if you have made a 'Judea list', perhaps you could pray for each one on this list once a week. The people or groups in your Samaria and 'ends of the earth' sections could perhaps be prayed for each fortnight. This actually is not very much, and if you are able to pray for them more than this, fantastic! But I would urge you to get into a routine or pattern where you can regularly lift up to God those who don't yet know his saving love.

Finally, and with great trepidation, may I make four brief suggestions regarding prayer? The first suggestion is that we follow Jesus. Jesus is our model in everything, and in the case of prayer, we would do well to copy his example of prayer. Time and time again we see him making space to pray, even if it meant getting up before everyone one else, or even not going to bed. 'The next morning Jesus awoke long before daybreak and went out alone into the wilderness to pray' (Mark 1:35). 'One day soon afterwards Jesus went to a mountain to pray, and he prayed to God all night.' (Luke 6:12). For Jesus prayer was vital. It is interesting that the prayer life of Jesus so impressed the disciples that they asked him to teach them how to pray (Luke 11:1). We ought to be sure that it is the same for us.

The second suggestion is to remember that prayer is work. Some people seem to think that prayer is all about rapturous experiences of fellowship with God, and they are disappointed when these feelings do not happen to them all the time. Such experiences may occur, but much prayer – and for some people, most prayer – is hard work. The reason for this of course is that there is an enemy, the Devil, who desperately wants to obstruct our praying. You don't need very much experience of prayer to know how, when you decide to pray, yesterday's newspaper now becomes extraordinarily attractive. Suddenly, finding lost socks or cleaning fingerprints off windows acquires a burning urgency. That, I have no doubt, is the Devil's strategy. We need to remind ourselves that our praying here on earth is always done 'against the flow'; it is a struggle. I wish I could give you a simple solution to successful prayer – perhaps four easily memorable techniques that would turn you, overnight, into a prayer warrior, whose name was feared in hell. There are *no* easy answers and I am suspicious of those who claim that there are. As far as I can see, the only answer is one that seems dull and unattractive: it is to be disciplined, and to recognise that we face opposition. We need to get into good habits and that is one reason why regular times of prayer are helpful. I think it is very significant that the New Testament uses the images of warfare and soldiering. We need to prepare for prayer in the same way that a soldier would prepare for battle. There is a lot to be said for making prayer lists, meeting with others for prayer and of being accountable to each other for the way we pray. All these things will help us to be able to pray regularly, consistently and seriously for those who don't know God's love.

The third suggestion is that we be bold in prayer. You see it is the God of the universe that we deal with, and he is the one who holds the nations in his hands. Cautious requests may represent modesty and caution on our part, but they may also represent a lack of faith. The passage from 1 Timothy that I quoted earlier included the reference to praying for 'kings and all others who are in authority.' Of course, in Paul's day the highest king was the Roman Emperor himself and here Paul is saying, 'pray for him'. History is full of remarkable turns of events that appear to have no logical human explanation. Let me give you two that have occurred in the last ten or so years. An event on the largest scale was the collapse in the late eighties of the Communist systems of Europe one after another. People had been praying for the breakdown of Communism for years, but few, I think, believed it could happen. On a smaller scale there has been a remarkable, but largely unmentioned, religious revival within the gypsy communities of Britain with a turning to Christ of large numbers of men, women and children. I have no doubt that prayer lay behind that too. So can I encourage you to be bold enough to pray for whole streets, suburbs and cities? Pray for breakthroughs in the tight-knit Islamic communities, from within the cults and in the deprived urban areas.

My fourth suggestion is that we should aim to become people of prayer. If I was to ask you what your ambitions were for the next twelve months, what would you say? Would you really say 'I want to become better at prayer'? Frankly, most of us would probably say something along the lines of how we would like to have greater contentment, peace and joy. We might, I hope, say that we wanted to see our friends converted, or that we wanted to know our Bibles better. These are all good things, yet surely prayer comes before all of them. In fact, without prayer, we are unlikely to make any progress at all in any area of the Christian life. Can I ask you to make prayer a priority in your life? And, if you have any influence at all in the matter, in the life of your church? If nothing else, set an example: little things can help. For instance when you have fellow believers around for a meal, or even coffee, why not make a habit of closing the evening by praying briefly?

One of the most vital things for our witness, is for our praying to become as natural as breathing. I have been greatly helped by realising that you can pray anywhere. When we are waiting for a bus or train we can pray: when we brush our teeth, stand at the checkout at the supermarket, or wait at the pedestrian crossing, we can also pray. Who said you have to close your eyes? And there is no shortage of things or people to pray for. God made everyone and everything. Often looking around us can inspire us to pray. You can pray silently or out loud, you can sing or whisper. All forms of prayer are acceptable to God when it comes from our deep need of him. The worst prayer of all is no prayer at all.

You could, of course, move on to the next chapter now. But why not pray instead?

Exercises

1. What things are prayed for in the following passages?

   - Ephesians 1:18-19
   - Ephesians 3:16-19
   - Colossians 1:9-12
   - 1 Timothy 2:-2
   - 2 Thessalonians 3:5

Do we pray for these things in the way that these people did?

2. Almost all the references to prayer in the Book of Acts are highly significant. What can we learn from the following? Acts 1:14; 2:42; 3:1; 4:24; 4:31; 6:4; 12:12.

Questions

1. If, as Christians we really believed that our prayers changed things, would it make a difference to the way we prayed?

2. What are the obstacles to prayer in your life? What action could you take to overcome them?

3. How can we help each other pray for others to come to faith?

Chapter 14

THE SECOND PILLAR: PRESENCE

GET OUT THERE!

I hope you have gathered by now that, underlying all that this book is about, is the belief that it is God himself who calls us to witness. He wants us to be part of his mission to save and redeem this damaged world. We have just thought about the part that prayer plays in this and how God calls us to ask him through prayer to intervene in the hearts of individuals, culture, communities and countries. What I want to say in this chapter is straightforward, but nonetheless important. It is that, to share our faith, we need to have a presence with people.

This is of course obvious, particularly if you have been following one of the themes of this book; that 'calling out' is something that people do to other people. Men and women are not, on the whole, converted by texts pushed under their doors, messages on the Internet, or even 'Jesus Saves' banners trailed across the sky; they are converted by others who share the Good News with them. And of course, for sharing to take place, means that there has to be a presence. If we don't know anybody, we cannot share with them.

The most amazing truth of the Christian message is that God loved us so much, he became flesh. In 1996, Joan Osborne recorded a song called 'One of Us' in which she pondered what it would be like if God had been one of us. The Christian response is that God has been one of us; indeed, that he *is* one of us. The extraordinary and awesome news of Christianity is that in Jesus, God chose to be born into humanity. He became in every way what we are; he passed through all that we have passed through and will pass through; he was breast fed, had his nappy changed, his body washed and learned how to speak, walk, play and pray. He grew up through adolescence and maturity; he related to others and made friends, took on work, knew hunger, thirst and tiredness. Finally, he knew hatred, injustice and death. As one of us, someone who faced all the temptations that we do, Jesus is able to understand and sympathise with us; a point made in Hebrews 4:15. In order to reach us, God became one of us.

In the account of the trial in John's gospel, Pilate led Jesus out in front of the crowd and announced 'here is the man!' Thoughtful readers of the Bible have always seen in this a wonderful irony (and as John delights in double meanings it may be intentional); this, Pilate is saying, is not only a man, he is *the* man. Here truly, is what we were meant to be.

I find that helpful. There have always been people who have wanted to deny the messy side of being human. Today there are, for example, a whole class of people (mostly men) who, in the interests of pursuing their business careers, have turned away from family, friends and social involvement. From the moment they wake, to the moment they sleep, they are dedicated to their work and their careers: nothing else matters. Now as most of these people are not followers of Jesus Christ, I can understand why they have let their profession take over them. Some gods demand sacrifices, and 'My Career' is one of the cruellest of all deities. But what I do not understand is why there are so many Christians who are less human than Jesus was. I often meet believers in Christ who apparently desire to be different from ordinary people; they seem to breathe an air of unreality. They seem to want to be superior, aloof and totally uncontaminated by the world. With them, you get the feeling that if only life could be nothing more than being with Christians and worshipping with them all day and every day, everything would be wonderful. I'm sure it would be. One day, in heaven it will be what we do forever. Yet down here it is not what we are about; here we are to get involved in a dirty and untidy world. Those are orders.

There have always been temptations for Christians to escape out of the world; I suppose it was part of the attraction of the monastery system. I think the reason people fall for this sort of thing, is that we easily adopt a false view of what Christians are here on earth for. We imagine that God is best pleased when we stand up in our fellowships in neat rows of families, singing beautifully in harmony over the immaculate sounds of our music group or organ, with the sun shining on our scrubbed faces and neat, pressed clothes. That, we tell ourselves, is the goal of all that we do; this is what church is for, that is what true religion is all about. But is it?

Isn't worship also helping the poor and the needy, dealing with dysfunctional families, ministering to drunks and drug addicts, counselling the bereaved? In the New Testament, James says that 'Pure and lasting religion in the sight of God our Father means that we must care for orphans and widows in their troubles . . .' (James 1:27).

Let me give you an illustration. Suppose that I was the designer of a lifeboat. If, one sunny day, I went down to the lifeboat station and there was the boat laid out for my inspection, polished and shining, and without a cable out of place, I would doubtless be pleased. But suppose I went on another day, with wild seas and driving rain and I saw my boat ploughing its way back into harbour after successfully rescuing people from a sinking ship. Its paintwork might be scratched, its hull might be dented and there might be torn cables hanging loose, but I know I would have a far greater joy at seeing it. That, I would say, is what I built it for! Now I think God feels the same way about his people. He takes more pleasure in us when we are out there serving him, than when we are on display.

I am sure of this, because God, very literally, got his hands dirty. The whole point of God becoming flesh – *the* incarnation – was that he came and lived with us and was one of us. It is this principle that we need to carry with us as we go out to witness for Jesus Christ. Jesus' 'mission strategy' was not to stand aloof, borne hither and thither by a chariot, and being served by men and women; it was to breathe our air and walk our paths, to share food from our plates and drink from our cups. He was one of us and amongst us: not as a superman, or as a pretend human being, but as a real one. In fact, Jesus was the only really real person who has ever lived on this planet.

Reflecting on the incarnation, John Drane says in his excellent book *Evangelism for a New Age*: 'The incarnation is not about transcendence and power . . . at the centre of the gospel is the fact that God became a child. Weakness, vulnerability and powerlessness are central to Christian belief – and to the extent that Christians fail to model that in both lifestyle and evangelistic communication they are bringing the very gospel into disrepute.' (p. 53)

You see if Jesus' incarnation means anything to us in our life, it means something very significant about our presence in the world. Missionaries and aid workers talk dismissively about high profile visitors who turn up at the sites of famines or trouble spots. Surrounded by security men and camera crews, they briefly talk to selected victims and make the appropriate noises of sympathy or outrage, and then retreat rapidly by helicopter or air-conditioned four-wheel drive to the nearest five star hotel. That was not God's way in Jesus. This was no hit and run operation: no arriving in a place for a night, holding a rally and nipping off the next morning. Jesus took the time that was needed to build friendships and trust with the people who were around him. He calls us to live as he did among those he came to save.

In the Acts of the Apostles, we find that Paul's missionary strategy is the same as Jesus. We read that:

- In *Iconium*, Paul and Barnabas 'stayed there a long time, preaching boldly about the grace of the Lord' (Acts 14:3).
- In *Antioch*, 'upon arriving they called the church together and reported about their trip, telling all that God had done and how he had opened the door of faith to the Gentiles, too. And they stayed there with the believers in Antioch for a long time' (Acts 14:27-28).
- In *Corinth*, 'Paul became acquainted with a Jew named Aquila, born in Pontus, who had recently arrived from Italy with his wife, Priscilla. They had been expelled from Italy as a result of Claudius Caesar's order to deport all Jews from Rome. Paul lived and worked with them, for they were tentmakers just as he was.' A few verses later we read that 'Paul stayed in Corinth for some time after that' (Acts 18:1-3, 18).
- In *Ephesus*, 'Paul went to the synagogue and preached boldly for the next three months, arguing persuasively about the Kingdom of God. But some rejected his message and publicly spoke against the Way, so Paul left the synagogue and took the believers with him. Then he began preaching daily at the lecture hall of Tyrannus. This went on for the next two years, so that people throughout the province of Asia – both Jews and Greeks – heard the Lord's message.' (Acts 19:8-10).

The pattern is hard to miss. Usually Paul stayed in a place until he had caused a riot or been thrown out by the authorities. Until that happened, he stayed in the area, generally locating himself in one place. As he made relationships in the city, he seems to have worked for his living as a tentmaker. The case of Ephesus is very interesting, because in Acts 20, as the apostle left the area for what he knew would be the last time, Paul summarised his ministry:

When they arrived he declared, 'You know that from the day I set foot in the province of Asia until now I have done the Lord's work humbly – yes, and with tears. I have endured the trials that came to me from the plots of the Jews. Yet I never shrank from telling you the truth, either publicly or in your homes. I have had one message for Jews and Gentiles alike – the necessity of turning from sin and turning to God, and of faith in our Lord Jesus. Watch out! Remember the three years I was with you – my constant watch and care over you night and day, and my many tears for you . . . I have never coveted anyone's money or fine clothing. You know that these hands of mine have worked to pay my own way, and I have even supplied the needs of those who were with me. And I have been a constant example of how you can help the poor by working hard. You should remember the words of the Lord Jesus: "It is more blessed to give than to receive."'

Acts 20:18-21, 31, 33-35

We see from this how Paul gave everything he had to the witness and mission and how he held nothing back from the Ephesians. That was how he did mission and in making such a strategy, we can easily guess who it was that he imitated.

One of the reasons we find mission so hard these days is because we know so few people who are not Christians. We might live among them but we do not come into regular contact with them. There are several reasons for this. One reason is that we may have chosen to withdraw. Many new Christians, relieved to find a new set of friends who care for them and who do not expect either sexual intimacy or nights of boozing, are only too happy to give up their old lifestyle. I sympathise, but the danger is that we form inward-looking Christian ghettos that are almost impossible to witness from.

Another reason is the way that we all live now. Most British people now no longer live in communities and most of our non-working life is spent either inside our own homes, or in cars (which are effectively mobile extensions of our houses). Courtesy of the video, television and Internet we now even get our entertainment in our own homes. In fact, if people work at home and arrange their shopping efficiently, they can easily achieve total social isolation for days at a time. And when we do take our pleasures, because of the car, we can often spend the time many miles away, rather than in the amenities of our local community.

A useful, but often unsettling, exercise is to take a single sheet of A4 paper and on it draw a sketch map of where you live with the nearest dozen houses. Now on that sketch map write down against the relevant house everything that you know about the occupants. For many of us today, we would not completely fill the single sheet of paper. If this is the case, then in what sense do we have a presence in our community?

I believe that we have to work hard to build networks of relationships with people who aren't part of our churches. Let me, here, talk about a problem that I am sure affects many of you reading this book. You are committed Christians. You are involved in church. In fact you are so involved in church that you have very little time for anything else; you are out night after night on church committees. My question is this: where are you meeting those who are not believers in Jesus? I have to say that if you are like this, you are not just a committed Christian; you are an over-committed Christian! I think it is a very good rule that, with very few exceptions, we should try to have as many free evenings as possible. Not so that we can put our feet up and overdose on television, but so that we can be involved in our community and have a presence in it. It is a criticism of British universities that they take people who are good at research or teaching and promote them, making them into bad administrators. Churches tend to do the same thing with people who are gifted at sharing their faith. They are soon mysteriously taken from the place where there are most badly needed, and turned into people who keep the church going. Some people should be banned for life from church committees, not because of their weaknesses, but because of their strengths! We need presence more than we need organisers.

Partly to combat this sort of thing in my own life, I decided a few years ago to do a course at college. Because I was only free in the afternoons, my options were limited. The only choices I had were gardening, interior decoration, cross-stitch or cordon bleu cookery. I had no skill or interest in the first three, and I could see how the last could be of great practical benefit, so I plumped for developing my culinary skills. I arrived at the kitchens to find I was the only male there, I was ten years younger than most of my fellow course members, and I didn't have blue- rinsed hair. Sooner rather than later, we all got talking and there was stunned silence when I said I was a minister. Over the following weeks it was amazing how people treated me. Some tried to convince me they were part of a church, but then when I asked them who their vicar was, they hadn't got a clue. But on the whole, time and time again they would come to me on the quiet and share with me their problems, their anxieties and their longing to believe. It gave me an insight and a whole set of opportunities that I would never have had, and I got them, not because I said something remarkable or did something of note, but just because I was there.

Now there is a danger here that I must briefly address. Although I am intensely committed to calling out for Jesus (so you noticed eh?), I believe that our evangelism must be ethical. Now as that may seem a strange thing to say, let me explain what I mean. You see I think there is a danger that we give sharing the Good News such a supreme priority, that honesty and sensitivity can be brushed aside. In particular, there is the danger of a loveless evangelism, where we treat people as nothing more than 'potential converts'. This is both wrong and stupid. It is *wrong* because it denies the fact that all men and women are made in God's image and should be treated with respect and love as human beings. It is *stupid* because people are not fools; they will soon realise what you are really after and that behind the apparent deep concern is nothing more than a convert hunt. This is the sort of thing the cults do: it should not be our way. Incidentally, it is also psychologically self-destructive, as you are always putting a mask on and living a lie. That way mental disaster lies. No, a better way is to seek out situations in which you can be entirely yourself, in which you can enjoy what you are doing, and ask God to give you there, people who you can love.

That said, let me return to the big problem, how do we have an authentic presence in our world today? I have, I'm afraid, no simple answers. I would, however, ask you to think about where you live and how you interact with people. Let me make some suggestions:

- If you haven't already, I would urge you to lay before God the area where you live. If you are looking to move, make this a priority as much as house price and schooling. Beware of moving into a Christian 'ghetto' already well served by Bible study groups and churches. If you are settled somewhere with a good Christian witness, have you ever though that God might want you to move somewhere where you can be of more use?
- Do you know your neighbourhood? Who runs the various shops? What are the community needs and problems? What church groups are working in your area? Find out. Why not talk to your councillor about the area? Walk around it, praying for it. Make time to talk to people doing their gardens or fixing their cars. Get to know your area and pray for its schools, shops and social services.
- Are you involved in your neighbourhood? Shouldn't you be more so? What can you do? What opportunities are there for service? What annual events are there
- Do they need help? My guess is they will leap at any offer of assistance.
- What societies are there locally? Why not sign up with one? Activities that give chances for conversation are especially good for getting to know people.
- Get involved properly. It is dishonouring to God to simply run out from the safe enclave of Church life, grab a few people and then try to drag them back into the church with

you. Get involved and stay involved. Our witness is not just about one conversation, or about one opportunity: it is about the whole of our lives.

- Avoid making Christian sub-groups. If you are in say, a dramatic society with other Christians, try not to spend all your time with them. Remember, the idea of getting out into the outside world is to get people out there to come into church, not to take the church out into the world for change of scenery.

- Try to be human. There are two errors often made when we get out of church: to fall into sin or to be 'holier than thou'. Carefully, reverently, and prayerfully, try to steer a middle line between the two. It is not easy, but the third error – of doing nothing – is even worse.

- Put on L-plates. The L stands for *Love*, *Listen* and *Learn*. In the past, Christians had a right to be heard; after all, we were the heart of the community and pretty much sole dispensers of decent funerals or weddings. In terms of religion, we were the only show in town. Not any more. We now have to earn the right to be heard; we have no automatic right to a platform. When the world is (at least in these things) hard-headed and pragmatic, people won't just listen to us because we open our mouths. We need to acquire a deep, caring feeling for where people are. Incidentally, do remember that most non-Christians can easily feel threatened by people who are on a 'mission from God'. Press too hard and they may move as fast as a fox does when faced by men in red coats, and for the same reason. Evangelism as a blood sport is a nasty business. Eventually, if we pray about it, I'm sure God will grant us a chance to speak. But of course, our actual presence may speak louder than any words that we will ever use. It was St Francis of Assisi who said, 'Preach Christ on all occasions; only when necessary use words.' When we speak, the way we have acted should be such that our hearers feel that there is a consistency between what we say and what we do. A true Christian is neither ashamed of the gospel or a shame to the gospel.

- Be prepared for the long, hard haul. We live in an instant society and there is a naive belief that witness is easy and that if its not, you are a failure. For many years, religion has been a private matter to the average Briton; it is now ever more so. Religion for many people, especially those who know that they should be doing something about it, is now something more private than their sex lives. In other words, they are more likely to admit to impotence than they are to being troubled by their conscience. And of course be prepared for the ultimate indignity of having them 'get converted' by someone else, after you have done all the hard work!

- Be prepared for rejection. Every witness for Jesus knows what it is like to have, either metaphorically or literally, a door slammed in your face. Psychologically or physically these are bruising encounters, and for sensitive people (and as I said earlier, they are the best sort of evangelist) the immediate reaction can often be, '*Ow*! I'll never do that again'. Can I assure you that such a reaction is exactly what the Devil wants? I am sure some potentially able evangelists have been pushed into a lifetime of silence as a result of some such encounter. When it happens – and it will – find a Christian with more experience and confide in them what happened. If together you decide that there are lessons to be learned, then decide to learn them. Then pray together about it, get on and put it behind you. Remember, if you had stopped trying to walk when you fell over as a toddler, you'd be looking pretty stupid now.

Finally, can I remind you not to be lured into trying to target the high and mighty? The way some people act and talk, you might think the church was like some stately home with conversions mounted along the walls like stuffed hunting trophies. May I remind you that there no prizes for 'The Most Prestigious Conversion of the Year'!

In fact, the contrary is true. We are, it seems to have a special ministry towards those people who society doesn't really value. This is hard: it is easier to talk to those we enjoy being with and with whom we share things in common, than to those who live in alien worlds to us. Once again here, we look to our great missionary leader, example, and model – Jesus. As we read the gospels, we find again and again that he mixed with those who no one else bothered with: those who were looked down upon or shunned by society. In fact, some of the finest examples of modern missionaries are those who have done just that. In India, for example, the church has made great in-roads among the much-despised low-caste Hindus and there have been some amazing examples of churches formed in deprived urban areas across the world.

Frankly, going for the poor and dispossessed makes no practical sense at all. Everybody knows that the best long-term strategic action would be to go for the media and the universities, but not to bother with those at the bottom of the pile! Yet God has his own logic and we would be well advised to obey his orders. Sometimes, the most important witness we have is not by speaking, it is in the things that we do for others; especially when it is loving and caring for those who are unlike ourselves. Marie Elizabeth Dyer, a hospital chaplain, wrote of her experience: 'I already knew I was not an evangelist. I did not feel called upon to baptise all nations, nor peoples. I learned to love more deeply and to hold this commandment primary in my life. One day I was reading Matthew 25:35-36, "For I was hungry and you fed me. I was thirsty and you gave me a drink, I was a stranger and you invited me into your home. I was naked and you gave me clothing, I was sick and you cared for me. I was in prison and you visited me."'

Marie began to interpret these verses in a new way because she knew the hunger, thirst, nakedness and imprisonment of her patients. So she wrote:

I was hungry . . .

for a new life away from the pressure of an alcoholic husband –
you did not give me a life away, but new ways to live with my man;
for lack of breath that would make me gasp – I continued to gasp
but you stayed, I knew that you cared; for company; for I am the
only one in this room without visitors – you brought me a flower,
laughed at my jokes and read Scripture to me.

I was thirsty . . .

for the knowledge of a diagnosis – you helped me to face whatever
I heard; for righteousness, a sense of forgiveness in life – I knew
that you believed and I began to believe too; for hope that a loved
one indeed would not die – you left me with hope and promised to
stay by my side;

I was a stranger . . .

for I did not speak English – thank you, you tried to communicate
and did not just smile and walk away; for I had never been in
hospital before, I felt not only strange, but terrified – you believed
my fear and stayed with me;

I was naked . . .

for I was a doctor, my inability to express feelings was exposed by
your words – and you put your hand on my shoulder to tell me you
knew that I cared; for I was old, my veins and even my bones stuck
out – you clothed my skin with loving caress; for my grief showed
all over my face – you did not avoid me, but sat to talk.

I was sick . . .

and you visited me;

I was in prison ...

in the loneliness of being unmarried –you told me you remembered the hardness of such days; in a room with no windows – together we shared.

Let me end with some words from my mentor Dr Leighton Ford. 'Jesus was born in a borrowed manger. He preached from a borrowed boat. He entered Jerusalem on a borrowed donkey. He ate the Last Supper in a borrowed upper room and he was buried in a borrowed tomb. Now he asks to borrow the lives of Christians to reach the rest of the world.'

Are you and I willing to lend him our lives that he might have a presence in our part of the world?

Exercises

1. Read John 13:1-17. What point do you think Jesus was trying to make here about how we should live? What bearing does this have on how we relate to our community?

2. Read Philippians 2:5-11. What cost did Jesus have to pay in order to become 'involved' in the world? How does this set an example for us?

3. Read 2 Thessalonians 3:7-10. What rights did Paul give up in order to be an effective witness in Thessalonica?

4. Read Romans 1:1; James 1:1; 2 Peter 1:1 and Jude 1. What do Paul, Peter, James and Jude all describe themselves as?

Questions

1. Supposing there was a street or a village near you that was entirely – or almost entirely – Christian. What would attract you to live there? Could you resist the temptation?

2. Think of the people who live in the area around your church but, who are not believers in Jesus. What do they think about what your church does and what it represents? Are there any points of contact at all? What would it cost you to establish points of contact?

3. Imagine that a local community hall is planned in your town that will, amongst many worthwhile things, serve as a Bingo Hall, a centre for evening classes on New Age Spirituality, and a contact point for people on drug addiction programmes. Should your church:

   ■ Offer to help with building it.
   ■ Do nothing, but hope that your minister will be allowed to pray publicly at the opening.

- Pray against it.

What other strategies might you adopt?

NOTES:

John Drane, *Evangelism for a New Age* (0-551-02843-2, Marshall Pickering, 1994)

Marie Elizabeth Dyer, source unknown

Chapter 15

THE THIRD PILLAR: PROCLAMATION

SPEAK OUT AND LIVE OUT THE GOOD NEWS!

The message of the last two chapters was that, in order to call out, we need to pray and get out there. In this chapter, I want to talk about the task of proclaiming the Good News. In Part Two, I talked about exactly what the Good News was in terms of its content, and I do not want to go over that again. What I want to talk about here is how the Good News is proclaimed, who proclaims it and where and when.

First, I want to look at the popular view of how the Good News is to be proclaimed, and then to present an alternative.

Three popular beliefs about proclaiming the Good News

If we were to analyse what the average Christian in Britain thinks about sharing the Good News of Jesus we would, I imagine, eventually come up with something like the following three statements:

1. Most evangelism is done by specialists (pastors, vicars, ministers, evangelists) in special settings.

2. Ordinary people are only involved in evangelism on extraordinary occasions.
3. Evangelism is the sharing, in words, the truth about Jesus with non-Christians.

Now before reading any further ask yourself whether you agree with these statements of belief. Take your time!

I suspect you agreed with them; most Christians would. Well, let me annoy you. I think that all three statements are very misleading. They are either incorrect, or at best half-truths, and they are certainly damaging to the spread of the Good News of Jesus. Taken together they represent one of the most astounding achievements of the Devil. Nothing like being controversial is there!

Let me deal with these beliefs one by one.

Belief 1. Most evangelism is done by specialists (pastors, vicars, ministers, evangelists) in special settings

The commonest version of this is that proclaiming the Good News can only take place in church and that it is only really a proper 'proclamation of the gospel' when it is done by a trained man in the pulpit over at least thirty minutes. Under pressure, exceptions to this rule may be allowed for visiting evangelists (who are allowed to use sports halls or theatres), and study groups like Alpha who can use homes. Some Christians (if you twist their arms) will also allow especially gifted women to preach. But you get the point. Sharing Jesus is a professional's job; it is more like rewiring a house than replacing a light bulb.

Now this view is not entirely wrong. There is something particularly powerful about someone who knows what he (or she) is talking about; having people's undivided attention for a substantial period of time on the subject of the Christian message. And of course, there are some issues where an untrained person could make a real mess of things, if there was a hostile audience. There is also an atmosphere or dynamic amongst large numbers of people that you do not get when you talk to individuals.

We must acknowledge that the Bible clearly recognises people with special gifts of evangelism. Take, for example, this statement: 'He [God] is the one who gave these gifts to the church: the apostles, the prophets, the evangelists, and the pastors and teachers. Their responsibility is to equip God's people to do his work and build up the church, the body of Christ' (Ephesians 4:11-12). Plainly, God gives to some people in the church a specific gift of evangelism; the combination of passion, confidence, communication skills, wisdom, drive, vision, and joy, to communicate the message of the Good News of Jesus. Those people will usually know who they are and, more importantly, the church they belong to will see the anointing of God on their lives and provide opportunities for them. If the church can afford to, then it should set them free to use their gift. The gift of evangelism is, of course, just one among many giftings in the church and, as an evangelist myself, I am not convinced that it is the greatest of the gifts. But it should not be despised either.

Yet, there are real problems with believing that evangelism can only be done by specialists in special settings. The main problem is that it allows people to say '*I* don't have to do evangelism' or 'oh that's the evangelist's job. After all it's what we pay them for'. You can even get a belief that there can be no evangelism outside church. Sometimes when I come across a view like this I wonder how the church survives, let alone grows!

Belief 2. Ordinary people are only involved in evangelism on extraordinary occasions

The second belief says that ordinary people live lives that are outside of that mysterious circle in which effective about sharing Jesus takes place. Evangelistic encounters (like seeing angels or getting vast bequests from unknown aunts) are things that only happen to other people – not to them. Over their lives, God seems to have stamped 'Grade B Christian: Not to be used in evangelism.' Of course, every so often they hear of people who have been brought to Jesus by an ordinary person: a nurse, a teacher or a shop assistant. Then they are inclined to look heavenwards, smile gently and point out that, well, miracles can happen but that they shouldn't be relied on: at least not with them.

Now when I spell it out like that you see the problem immediately. It is a self-fulfilling prophecy constructed exactly along the same lines as the 'I'm ugly and dull so no one will talk to me' viewpoint that ruins life for so many adolescents. If you believe – as an article of faith – that you will not get opportunities for sharing the Good News then, surprise, surprise, you will find that you do not get them. In Acts 8, there is the wonderful story about how Philip encounters an Ethiopian who is reading a key chunk of Isaiah's prophecies of Christ and who asks him 'who is he talking about?' Some Christians today have so firmly fixed in their minds the idea that they do not get involved in evangelism that if the equivalent happened to them they'd probably shrug their shoulders and say 'Sorry, I think there's been a mistake'.

We human beings have an extraordinary ability to take firm hold of a truth and spectacularly misapply it. So in this area of sharing our faith, people are capable of recognising that there is a gift of evangelism but all too often, they then say, 'Ah yes, but I do not have it.' They are then freed from the burden of having to witness for Jesus at all. 'Sorry,' they mutter under their breath as they walk by the lonely person sitting alone in the works canteen, 'it's not my gift'. Yet, strange to say, they still feel guilty about it.

Belief 3. Evangelism is the sharing in words of the truth about Jesus with non-Christians

This third statement is effectively the icing on the cake of the argument of the last two beliefs. Sharing the Good News is, it says, basically a 'word thing'. It is, to coin a phrase, 'up-close and verbal'. Evangelism belongs in the same category of human endeavour as debating in parliament, giving a seminar at a university, or playing Hamlet at Stratford. To do it well you need a golden tongue, a razor-sharp wit, an infallible memory, degrees in logic and theology, a vast IQ, and unlimited self-confidence. And if, of course, you do not possess these gifts (and, I hasten to add, I don't) the irresistible temptation is to say, well *that* isn't me. Therefore I can't do evangelism.

Now I could batter this belief all day. For a start, the Holy Spirit is more than able to compensate for any inadequacies we may have. After all, think of the early church; nowhere in my Bible do I read that Jesus sought out Honours Graduates in Oratory from the Jerusalem College of Advanced Religious Studies to be members of his team. He picked out working-class people with thick regional accents, whose Greek was probably just about up to haggling over fish prices.

But my main argument is this – and it is something that I have been saying repeatedly in this book – there is more to sharing the faith than using words. We are to call out, yes, but there is more to calling out than a specific evangelistic formula. Our mission is our life, not just our words. How we live, how we relate to people, how we respond to good news or bad news, is all part of our sharing. Some people who are very effective at sharing Jesus' love are often quite unable to express in logical steps what the Good News really is. But they can radiate God's love in a way that is far more effective than any number of slick slogans. This is something that is so important that I will return to it later.

Getting it utterly wrong

I have already said strongly that I believe that each of these three beliefs is harmful. I want to now go further and say that taken together these beliefs are utterly and terribly wrong. But before I explain why I think these views are so wrong, let me say that I understand why these beliefs have grown up.

For one thing, these beliefs conveniently give ordinary Christians an excuse not to get involved with sharing the Good News of Jesus. It's not our job, they can say; it is the job of expert-evangelists, and with a more or less clear conscience, they are now able to duck difficult conversations about their faith. And after all, removing evangelism from having any sort of priority in your life has its plus points; you can ignore people you don't like and do what you want to do with your time. Of course, put like that it does sound rather selfish doesn't it?

For another, these views justify the existence of those who can be called 'professional ministers'. Beliefs like this keep pastors, vicars and evangelists in business; they are the only ones accredited to do evangelism. Now in saying this, I realise that I am in danger of shooting myself here, but speaking personally, if everybody in the church started doing evangelism and put me out of a job, I'd be delighted. This view, though, has had an interesting effect. You see throughout history that there has always been the temptation in Christianity to have priests; a group of special people who can do something that ordinary people cannot do. The temptation to have a priestly elite even occurs in branches of the church where the word 'priest' is never *used* of their ministers. And by making only a few people authorised to perform evangelism, what we have done is created a new priesthood, that of evangelists.

This is not the real danger. The really serious problem is something else. It is that, if we hold to these beliefs we are restricted in witnessing to Jesus Christ in time, place, and manner. What we are saying is this:

- The good news about Jesus can only be proclaimed for two hours on Sunday.
- The good news about Jesus can only be proclaimed in an authorised place.
- The good news about Jesus can only be proclaimed by accredited specialists.
- The good news about Jesus can only be proclaimed using a specific way of words.

The implications for the people who do not know Jesus are staggering. Unless they are foolish enough to stray into a church on a Sunday, they are safe from ever having to hear the Good News again.

Now do you see what I am getting at? If a totalitarian regime had imposed these rules on Christians in the UK, we would march on London in protest. Yet, the truly stunning thing is that we have done all this ourselves. We have marched into the prison cell, locked the door behind us and thrown the key out of the window.

Somehow we have restricted the proclamation of the Good News of Jesus; we have let ourselves be squeezed out to one place, one time and one way. What a marvellous triumph for the Devil! And we have done it ourselves.

A Radical Alternative

Now this restriction of the gospel is, of course, totally wrong. What I want to offer is an alternative. The formula I propose is this, *All Christians are to proclaim Jesus all the time in all that they do*. It has three parts, which correspond to the three popular beliefs that I have so heavily criticised above. Let me look at these in turn.

1. Evangelism is to be done by all Christians

Although there were 'specialist' evangelists in the early church, there is absolutely no basis for assuming that only they spread the Good News. For example, in Acts 8, we read how a deacon was involved in the conversion of the Ethiopian, and if 'deacon' sounds spiritual to you, remember that he was really a church administrator.

There is much practical evidence all around us that ordinary people can do evangelism. If you talk to people who have recently become Christians you will find that, in a surprising number of cases, what stuck in their minds and haunted them before they were converted were not things from sermons, but simple statements made by Christians, often during ordinary conversations. Sometimes these people had never been in church and were still converted.

Now once again I am not seeking to give the impression that we all have the same role in proclaiming or persuading. I like to think that evangelism is a bit like a court of law where you have both witnesses and lawyers. The witnesses are asked to bear testimony to what they know, while it is the lawyers who take the facts and arguments and urge for a decision to be made. I feel that the role of the evangelist is like that of the lawyer. We are not all called to this role but we *are* all called to be witnesses. In fact, the courtroom image is very helpful in another area of how we are all to proclaim Jesus. Imagine a trial in which there is a string of witnesses. The most compelling witness, the one who decides the case, may not be the one who speaks the most or who is the most fluent. It may just be that they were at the right place at the right time and their few simple words may make all the difference. In fact, a simple unvarnished testimony may be more convincing than a polished virtuoso performance. Do you get the lesson?

Thankfully, God doesn't leave the work of witnessing to Jesus, just to evangelists – it's far too important just to be left to them – he calls every follower of his to join in his mission to win this lost world.

2. Evangelism is to be done by all Christians all of the time

If you remember, I said that the second misleading statement that people made was that 'ordinary people are only involved in evangelism on extraordinary occasions'. Behind that, lay the idea that, once in a lifetime, if you were really good, someone might ask you about becoming a Christian.

Sorry. That is wrong. We can do evangelism all the time, we should do evangelism all the time and in fact, we *do* do evangelism all time. Let me spell it out.

- We can *do* evangelism all the time. If you know when an evangelistic opportunity is going to come up, then you are better than me. Phone calls, visits, meaningful conversations, can occur at any time. You bump into someone at the gym or at a train station and suddenly, there you are talking about the meaning of life or hope. Frequently, it is not at a convenient time; you may have a train to catch, a meeting to make, shopping to do. But it can happen at any time. In fact, God gives us opportunities at the strangest times. Perhaps he likes to keep us on our toes. More probably, it is that he wants to remind us that he is Lord.

- We *should do* evangelism all the time. If evangelistic opportunities can be given to us, then we should also do what we can to make them happen. It's no good sitting behind closed doors waiting for some searching souls to knock. Get out there, make friends, get involved. Become known as someone who can help, someone with a sympathetic ear, someone who is always there. Look at your lifestyle critically. As Jesus' representative in your part of the world, ask how you can make a better impact.

- Finally, we *do do* evangelism all the time. Now a better way of saying this is that, if you are a Christian you have no choice about whether or not you are going to be a witness for Jesus Christ. You are one. You decided to be one when you became a Christian. The only issue is, whether you are a good one or not. I suppose it might be possible to be a Christian without it slipping out, but it's hard to keep the light hidden. Sooner or later your family or work colleagues will find out. And from that moment, you are a marked person; everything you do and say will be weighed against what they think a Christian should be like. Now you may protest that you never say anything but that is of little use. Psychologists and others increasingly point out the value of non-verbal communication. The genuineness of our Christian profession may be demonstrated in subtle ways that we are not even aware of; perhaps in the gentle way we deal with a problem, or the way we stoop to an old person so that we can hear them speak. There are a thousand ways of touch, eye contact, body language and gesture that can convey a silent message: I care, I am concerned, I am listening. But it can also send out clear signals to people that indicate that we are insincere and uncaring, or even that we do not really believe in what we say we do. I do not think you need me to tell you how utterly disastrous it can be for our mouths to say one thing and our actions to say another. So it's not so much 'Mission Impossible' as 'Mission Inescapable'. We *do do* evangelism all the time; we are already witnesses, whether we like it or not. So we may as well try and do a decent job of it.

3. *Evangelism is to be done by all Christians all of the time in all they do*

I said that the third popular belief on evangelism was that it was the sharing in words with non-Christians of the truth about Jesus. It is true, but it is not the whole truth; in fact, it is another dangerously misleading half-truth. We are all called to bear witness, but (and let me say it again) witness isn't *just* about the words we speak or the answers we give. For me that is too narrow, too exclusive and above all it's too small.

Witness is done with our words, our actions and attitudes; it is done with our tongues and our bodies, it is done in our driving, our eating and our spending. It is more what we are than what we say. Listen to what the apostle Peter, the great pioneer of evangelism, wrote to the early church:

Don't repay evil for evil. Don't retaliate when people say unkind things about you. Instead, pay them back with a blessing. That is what God wants you to do, and he will bless you for it ... Now, who will want to harm you if you are eager to do good? But even if you suffer for doing what is right, God will reward you for it. So don't be afraid and don't worry. Instead, you must worship Christ

as Lord of your life. And if you are asked about your Christian
hope, always be ready to explain it. But you must do this in a gentle
and respectful way. Keep your conscience clear. Then, if people
speak evil against you, they will be ashamed when they see what a
good life you live because you belong to Christ.

1 Peter 3:9, 13-16

Now the temptation is to just take one verse, 'And if you are
asked about your Christian hope' as being relevant to our
witness. But I would suggest that we take the whole passage,
because I see all the ingredients of witness as being here:
kindness rather than revenge; being a blessing to people rather
than a curse; being eager to do good; being prepared to go
through a hard time for the sake of right; living a life which is
not defined by fear and worry; speaking when asked about the
hope Jesus brings, not harshly or arrogantly but gently and with
respect; being men and women of integrity; and, whatever the
reception to our words or lives, to continue to live as examples
to all.

If our mission is about the mission of God; to create, save,
love and redeem this world; if it is really about everything that
God is and everything that God does; it must be about
everything that we do and everything that we are too. Mission
can't be reduced to stating a few cool religious phrases, some
sanctified sound bites. We have to *be* the gospel, not just say it.
It is not just about speaking to non-Christians about Jesus. It is
all about every word we speak to every person. It's not just
about supporting overseas mission organisations – it's about
the way we use all our money. It's not just about what we do
with the short time we might spend with our non-church friends
– it's about what we do with every hour of the day. It's not
about whose door we should knock on – it's about who we open
our homes to. It's about how we treat the poor, the refugee, the
hungry, the lonely, the sad, the desperate, the arrogant, the
self-assured. Mission is not just speaking – it's about living.
Listen to Peter again: 'Be careful how you live among your

unbelieving neighbours. Even if they accuse you of doing wrong, they will see your honourable behavior, and they will believe and give honor to God when he comes to judge the world' (1 Peter 2:12). Our whole lives must speak to the world about the God who has created us, saved us and promised us eternity in his presence.

This, incidentally, has a great deal of relevance to the issue of whether we get involved in social action such as working with the homeless, the poor, the environment and so on. A few years ago it used to be said that social action was needed in order to provide a platform for the Good News of Jesus to be understood. Behind that, lay the thinking that people would only give time to hear what we said, if we had cared for their needs. Now on the one hand, this is true; people will care about what we know, when they know we care. Yet on the other, it could look as if we were buying people's attention. In fact, the better way is to do these things simply because we know they are what we ought to do; they are works of the kingdom. Actually, Jesus didn't do any of his miracles in order to get in the good books of his hearers, or to earn their attention. Rather, he seems to have done them either out of simple compassion, or because they were signs of the Kingdom of God. So it should be with us; we serve people, not because we want them to come and listen, but because Jesus has made us people who want to serve.

There is no contradiction: word, action and proclamation, all go hand in hand. Let me repeat my radical alternative. Evangelism is to be done:

1. by all Christians
2. all of the time
3. in all they do

Got it? Good, now sit down and think about how you apply it in your life.

A plea to the professionals

Before leaving this topic, I feel obliged to insert a plea here to those of you who are preachers, teachers, ministers and evangelists. I also want to address any of you reading this who are thinking of becoming full-time workers in proclaiming the Good News of Christ. In many ways, it would be easier to omit this, or make some brief comment to Paul's wisdom on these topics in the letters to Timothy and Titus and then move on. Yet I think I need to say something more. But please remember that what I say, I say in weakness and in genuine humility.

a) Watch your life

Do I really need to point out that moral failings in an evangelist are catastrophic? Of course, we are still sinners, but the visibility that we have sought for the Good News has also made us visible and we stand exposed to public scrutiny. Because of this, we stand a far greater chance of any financial or marital sins being brought to light. That would be bad enough, but in our case things are worse because we are so linked with the Good News. Although we might hope that people could distinguish between a person and his message, for many we represent the gospel. It is a dreadful thing to tarnish its reputation.

We must be wise here. We must never ever assume that we are above risk. We must keep a close watch on our lives and we must surround ourselves with those to whom we are totally accountable. We all need to have one or two praying friends to whom we can be totally open. We must be those who have, as far as possible, mapped out those areas in our lives where we are vulnerable and have taken precautions. We need to constantly check ourselves before God and his word. How is our prayer life? Are we making progress in holiness? Are we reading challenging books? Are we growing in grace and knowledge of Christ?

Of course, all this is obvious and rudimentary but I am afraid that it needs repeating.

b) Watch your doctrine

If watching our lives is obvious, watching what we teach is perhaps less so. Yet we need to take care. If a moral disaster will destroy our ministry, then a failure in our teaching will soon cripple it. It seems to me that there are two dangers here that are always before us. One is the error of watering down what we preach. History is full of men and women of God who started off with a vibrant, dynamic faith in the cross of Christ, but who ended up quite unsure of almost anything. Errors that have been evicted out of the front door have a nasty way of sneaking around and coming in through the back door. A second peril is that of the diversion, the emphasis on a novelty belief that distracts a ministry from its great task of preaching Jesus Christ. Church history is full of people whose energies for Christ got diverted into schemes, systems and innovations.

Here too, we need to take a constant check on ourselves. It is worth examining what we believe now against what we did when we were called to the ministry. What have we subtracted from the things that we received as being of first importance? Are there, perhaps, doctrines or even elements of the creed over which we now have doubts? And what have we added to the things that we received?

c) Watch the world

This may seem like strange advice, but I think it is valid. I feel that if we are those who are called to share the Good News of Jesus with our world, then we need to understand it. For us to be effective communicators presupposes that we understand the language, idioms and culture of our hearers. The trouble is, that the world we are living in is changing at a ferocious pace. It is important that, as we continue in ministry, we need to maintain knowledge of where people around us are at. There is a danger, over time, that we slowly drift away from our culture and so become increasingly ineffective. We need to maintain our roots in our culture and talk to people about what they are reading, seeing and hearing.

A failure here is unspectacular: it is neither the sudden destruction of moral collapse, nor the deviation into the heretical or the peripheral. It is just that, slowly and imperceptibly, we become irrelevant.

d) Watch your spiritual life

I need no excuse for mentioning this. We need to be spiritual men and women who are constantly seeking God and his blessing on us and our ministry. We may be morally pure, we may be orthodox in every way, and we may have a total familiarity with our culture, but if we have not got spiritual power or anointing we – and our ministries – are nothing.

This seems so obvious a matter, that I feel that it is impossible to overlook. Yet it is a real threat. We get overworked and our relationship with God suffers. Very soon, we are trying to maintain a ministry with the fuel gauge close to empty. We lose zeal, we lose conviction, and slowly the joy of sharing the Good News becomes a burden. We must take measures – sometimes drastic ones – to ensure that we stay sharp and filled with a knowledge of God and the power of his Spirit.

There is, of course, far more that I could say, but we must move on. But there may be a question in your mind about these warnings I have just given. As you read them, you may have wondered whether I was warning anyone in particular. The answer, I'm afraid is yes: I was warning myself.

My vision for proclamation

Let me conclude by repeating my belief that the Devil wants the Good News locked up. If needs be, he will use oppression and a secret police force but I'm sure he is far happier (it is much less fuss), when, as in modern Britain, we have done his job for him. He would, of course, prefer to see the Good News silenced altogether, but he will happily settle for it being restricted to a tiny portion of our world. He can live with a bit of preaching from a pulpit on a Sunday, if it means the rest of the world is his for the rest of the week.

My dream is to reverse that. My vision is for Christians to take the gospel out in all that they say, all that they do and all that they are, so that no part of this world is free from our influence. I want to make the whole world, whether it is the office, pub or the supermarket, a dangerous place for the unbeliever. I want to see a society in which you cannot go into a shop or a in taxi, have a meal or watch the TV, without there being the real risk that in some way or another the Good News of Jesus will challenge you. Of course I'm not talking here of some goal of putting a gospel message on every car bumper, or something shallow like that. I want to see a situation where people are exposed to the Good News in a thousand ways, from quiet acts of kindness, through high quality service by believers in shops, to good Christian drama on the television, and care from their Christian neighbours.

I want to release the Good News out of the prison cell that we have locked it in. I want to let it loose.

Exercises

1. Read Acts 6:1-7. What were the Twelve to be freed up for? What were the seven to do? What, in verse 8-10, do we see Stephen doing? What, in chapter 7, was the result? What lessons do you learn from this?

2. Read Acts 8:1-5. What happened as a result of the persecution under Saul? Who did the sharing of the Good News? Why do you think they did this when silence must have seemed the best policy? Was Philip an evangelist? (see Acts 6:5). So what was he doing inaugurating a mission to the Samaritans? Read Acts 8:26-40. Philip now starts a ministry to Africans. What lessons are there here for us about how the Good News is proclaimed?

3. Read Acts 11:19-26. What innovation did the 'ordinary' Christians in Antioch start? Was this part of deliberate church policy, or was it just something that the Spirit led them to do? What was the reaction of the church leaders in Jerusalem? How did Barnabas strengthen what was going on? What further lessons can we learn from this about evangelism and how our church structures should handle it?

4. Read Acts 17:13-17. We have at Paul's important speech in Athens earlier. Why, according to this passage, was Paul in Athens anyway? Did he have to evangelise there? What does that tell us about Paul's vision for evangelism? Are there lessons for us about when we evangelise?

5. Read 2 Timothy 4:1-5. Although Paul is specifically addressing Timothy here, what lessons can we learn about the where, when and how of the sharing of the Good News? Incidentally, from 2 Timothy 1:5, who appears to have brought Timothy to faith?

Questions

1. Before you read this chapter, what sort of activities and situations did you think of when you thought of evangelism?

2. Is the best way of doing evangelism in churches to set up an evangelism committee and evangelistic programmes? If not, how do we do it?

3. How can those who are not in the full-time evangelistic ministry best help those that are?

4. How can those who are in full-time evangelistic ministry best help those that are not?

Chapter 16

THE FOURTH PILLAR: PERSUASION

CONVINCE!

We have looked at the importance of engaging with people in word and action; here I want to look more at this. What I want to say is very simple: we need to do all we can to persuade people of the truth of the Christian message. Now that might seem an obvious thing to say, but it is not.

There are, for example, some people who have got themselves into the mind-set where proclaiming the Good News is something that they *have* to do, like walking the dog. They do it, not to confront people with the truth of Jesus but simply to discharge their responsibility to proclaim the Good News. 'Well I did my bit for the week' they say as they collapse in the armchair and put on the TV.

Equally, there are people who seem to have given up any real hope that God will actually work. There are evangelistic sermons where you feel certain that the preacher *knows* that no one will respond; there are pamphlets that might as well have written on the front of them 'Please throw me away before reading'; and there are meetings that seem almost deliberately designed to put people off. Sometimes, behind this lies the view that the world is going to get worse and worse before Jesus comes, so that the more people reject the gospel, the sooner he will come. Or something like that. I can't get my head around the logic.

Now can we *please* have nothing of this? When we talk about Jesus, let's do it seriously. Let's get involved in sharing the Good News with the expectation that people will hear and respond. Of course, we cannot guarantee that, and of course when people are converted, it is because of God's gracious dealing with them. But the fact is, that if you play football expecting to lose, that is almost certainly what will happen. If you go out expecting not to change anybody, then that will almost certainly be the case. I am not, of course, saying 'just believe it and it will happen'. What I am attacking is the opposite: a fatal defeatism or apathy.

Let me be blunt: sharing the Good News is actively preaching for a verdict; it is seeking to sway an opinion, to change a mind. It is to seek to persuade. In this chapter, I want to look at how we can do all we can to persuade people to let Jesus Christ be their Saviour.

A pattern for persuasive witness

I am not going to give you techniques or a formula to employ in order to persuade people to become believers in Jesus. I am not a techniques person, and I don't think that God is either. Now that is not to say that I am against programmes such as Alpha: in fact, I warmly commend such things. Their strength lies precisely in the fact that, unlike techniques, they allow interaction and questioning. What I would like to offer you here though are some general guidelines for persuasive witnessing. I think that these apply whether your sharing of Jesus is in a quiet one-to-one over a cup of tea, or a talk at church.

a) Persuasive witnessing is natural

It is important that when you speak it is *you* that is speaking. People today are very wary of hypocrisy, or of anything that does not appear genuine. In today's culture, that you believe in something is critical. People will happily accept what is plain nonsense from someone if they seem sincere, and reject obvious truth if does not come over sincerely. One fatal mistake is to have a special evangelistic tone of voice and look, into which you switch when the need arises. I think that very few things put people off more than when their friends suddenly go into evangelism mode. It confirms their suspicion, that to become a Christian is to have an alien eat your brains.

No, I believe that the most convincing witnessing is where you demonstrate that deep in your heart is a real and genuine conviction that Jesus loves you, that your sins are forgiven, and that when you die you will go to heaven. If, by what you do and say you can show that this conviction is as real for you as the belief that you woke up this morning and you will go to bed this evening, you may keep your hearers listening. Remember that in the non-Christian mind, the word *religious* is often associated with the word *fanatic*. Of course, all of us have days when we do not really feel like talking about spiritual things: maybe you face problems; maybe you have a cold; maybe your dog died. But if it is usual for you to find talking about Jesus difficult and something that is never natural for you, then I suggest that there might be a problem. It might be a good idea for you to explore where that lies, find some experienced Christian and talk about it to them.

Let's be plain about it: the most persuasive witnessing is natural witnessing.

b) Persuasive witnessing is appropriate

What I mean here is that persuasive witnessing takes into account where other people are. I believe that the Good News has to be communicated intelligently and understandably, and to do that means to identify with our hearers as far as possible.

To do this we need to use *appropriate language* for our listeners. This is one of the problems of having a rigid evangelistic formula, because I think it is vital to use the images and idioms that people are familiar with. There is not a lot of point in using the language of *The Times* with someone who only ever reads *The Sun*. Equally, there is not a lot of point in using images from *Radio One* to explain something, if our friend only listens to opera. There is also more to language than words. Some people respond well to logical arguments. Others (now perhaps the majority of people in this country?) seem to think with their hearts; they are unaffected by logical arguments.

In our use of language there is a particular problem for people who have been Christians for many years. When they come to speak of religious things, they tend to use a special language and vocabulary that is not understood outside church circles. Every culture and special interest group, whether that of horse racing, painting, football or Christianity, has its own language and jargon and it sometimes comes as a surprise to people in those groups to realise that people outside do not understand them. It is far too easy for Christians to slip into using old-fashioned language, clichés, and illustrations that do not connect with people today. Now if you are someone who has been a Christian for years please do not misunderstand me; we desperately need people like you with all your knowledge, to get involved with sharing the gospel. But ironically, the language we use in church is often not the best language to communicate what we believe to those outside. We need to speak about Jesus in a way that the world can understand: not just in the old clichés or in a religious jargon. We need to use images and illustrations that are recognisable and accessible today, whilst not compromising the gospel truth.

Now what I am saying here is not a modern heresy. If you read any of the great evangelistic preachers of the past (try C H

Spurgeon, J C Ryle or John Wesley) you may find that their words sound old-fashioned to you. But if you compare their language, especially allowing for the fact that it was doubtless tidied up for the printed sermons, with that of their contemporaries, you find that it was often almost daringly fresh and blunt. In their day, these people were sharp, punchy and – above all – relevant. In our day, we need to be the same.

Furthermore, our witnessing needs to be *culturally appropriate* for our listeners. Do they understand anything at all of the basics of the Christian message? There is very little point, for example, in referring to Old Testament stories in sharing the faith, if our hearers know nothing of it. Equally, we can misjudge them. We could, for instance, spend a lot of time defending the idea of the miraculous to someone only, to find that they actually have no problems with that concept. In short, ask yourself where they are, and then translate the message accordingly.

Part of our problem is that the language of Christianity is still familiar enough to be part of our cultural baggage. Tabloid headline writers, TV programme makers, authors and advertising companies, employ all sorts of religious language and symbols: sin, hell, heaven, God, angels, priests, churches. Sins, for example, are certain types of food that you are allowed if you are being good with your diet. Diamond crosses adorn the necks of the rich and famous on the pages of *Hello*; rosary beads hang from the mirrors of taxicabs; football players cross themselves before a game. TV presenters end phone conversations with young people saying 'bless you', and eighty per cent of the population say that they pray. But what any of these words, symbols or practices mean to anybody, is anyone's guess. There are two problems here. One is that people feel that they know very well what these words mean; and in this case, familiarity has bred both contempt and boredom. 'Been there and done it' is the reaction. The other problem is that our key words, concepts and symbols no longer mean what we think they mean. Our talk of love and sin for example is now mistranslated into something very different. We have to learn to proclaim the Good News to our culture in a new, fresh, authentic way, which somehow gets round these barriers to communication.

What we say needs to be *psychologically appropriate* for our listeners. Many people, for instance, feel trapped by life and want freedom; to push the idea that Christianity involves taking Jesus as Lord may not be the best opening gambit. Equally, if they are struggling with particular sexual issues, it might not be the wisest tactic to start by going on about how God hates immorality. Now don't get me wrong, these things must come up at some point and we cannot hide the fact that the gospel makes hard demands. But there are ways of portraying these things sensitively and it is much easier to tackle hard issues if we have already built some bridges. Confrontation may occur when we share Jesus, but I do not see it as being the best place to start.

We need to remember too that everyone starts at a different level. There is a way of looking at this, which represents people as being on a numerical scale that goes from 100–0 (openly hostile to the Good News of Jesus to ready to become a Christian). It is quite helpful and you can find details of it in some of the books I have listed at the end. It does make the point well, that people start at varying distances away from being converted. Let me expand on that by giving you some examples:

- Andy is a young man who was brought up in a very strict Christian home without much joy or celebration, where the emphasis was on right behaviour and observance. Recently, his father was exposed as having had a secret affair for ten years, and has since run off with the woman involved.
- Mary is a woman from a non-Christian home. She has wonderful Christian neighbours, who helped the family when they were hard up financially and she is now working for a relief organisation. Her new flat-mate has just become a Christian and she is amazed at the change.
- Wallace is a middle-aged businessman whose wife became a

Christian around five years ago, with the result that she is a completely different person. He is very interested, except that he doesn't feel he has the time.

- Melanie is young woman who studied comparative religions at university and has travelled extensively around India and the Far East. Whenever she thinks of Christianity, she always remembers an acrimonious exchange with a member of the Christian Union, who told her that anybody who isn't 'washed in the blood of Jesus' is destined for hell.
- Dave sang in a local church choir when he was a boy and was later confirmed. However, a growing sense of homosexual orientation has made him feel distanced from the church. The media's portrayal of the church's views on homosexuality has made him feel unable to even think of going inside a church building again.

Now I have made all those characters up, but they could easily have been real case studies. But do you see how each of them will start at a different place? Some have a past knowledge that is actually good and can be built on, while for some people, the past has done more harm than good. They may have hurts and wounds that have been inflicted on them in the name of Christianity and these may need to be appropriately addressed.

As an aside though, can I add a word of caution? Although many of these accounts of hurts at the hand of Christianity may, sadly, be true, it is possible that what we are hearing is exaggerated. It is not uncommon, for example, for people who have rejected their parents' Christian faith to paint their upbringing as being totally negative. There are a number of cases of this in literature where, later, impartial investigation has shown that the family situation was by no means as terrible as depicted. But then, 'I was *not* abused by my Vicar dad' neither sells papers, nor gets you sympathy, and anyone who has ever heard two divorcees talk of their marriage will realise that memory can be selective.

But the point is this: what we say has to be appropriate to our hearers. On the one hand, hurts and wounds have to be considered, misunderstandings and misconceptions have to be addressed, and errors put right. On the other hand, any healthy positive experiences can be built on. It is particularly helpful if people have seen positive changes in friends who have become Christians. This partly explains why churches where conversions have occurred are churches where more conversions are likely. There is a snowball effect.

I could say more about this, but I'm sure you get my point; it is not enough to simply take the facts of the gospel (perhaps as I have laid them out in Part Two of this book) and declare them. They must be presented in a way that is appropriate for our hearers. Now some people might say that this is marketing, the packaging of a product, and that it is not appropriate for the Good News of the gospel. I would a take a different view; I would say that to do anything less than to put together our words appropriately is to be arrogant and to presume upon the power of the Holy Spirit to cover over our incompetence. You don't believe me? Look at the way that the Good News of Jesus Christ is presented in the Acts of the Apostles. Notice how the speeches, whether they are to Cornelius the Roman (Acts 10), to the Jews in Pisidian Antioch (Acts 13), or to the intellectuals of Athens (Acts 17) present the Good News. In every case, the gospel is preached, but in each case, it is sensitively adjusted to the hearers, whether they are an individual or a crowd. We need to have the same sense of what is appropriate.

c) Persuasive witnessing engages

A point about persuasive witnessing is that it must engage with our hearers. It is not enough to simply present facts, however well we do it: what we say must interact with our hearers. I'm not saying that every time we speak it should have our hearers sitting on the edge of their seats. But what we say should be said in such a way that the person listening to us is involved.

Talking to people in a way that is engaging is, I think, more difficult today than it has ever been. For instance, there was a time when our politicians used to feel happy about giving us straight ten-minute speeches on television. Now if you watch party political broadcasts you find that there are short snatches of words (the 'sound bite') with background music and images to hold the attention. Now of course we cannot match that, nor should we try to, but it is what our hearers are used to and we need to bear that in mind.

How then, can we speak in a way that engages our hearers? One way, that I have already touched on, is to be sincere. Another way is to be genuinely enthusiastic. There is something about enthusiasm that is exciting and attractive. I have to say I have come across Christians who are more enthusiastic about their gardens than they are about what the eternal God has done for them in Jesus. I think something is wrong there.

We also need to talk *to* – and *with* – the other person rather than *at* them. To involve them, we need to tailor what we say to them. To use a cooking illustration, there are two extreme ways of making a friend a meal. One way is to simply go to the cupboard, open a can of something, put it in the microwave and then slap it on the table. The other way is to spend some time with recipe books finding a meal that your friend would like, to go to the shops and buy just the right ingredients, then to carefully prepare them and serve them with all the trimmings. The results are both food but your guest is far more likely to be engaged by the second, caring and thoughtful meal, than they are by the first. Equally, you can talk to people about Jesus in a way that is almost dismissive of them; there is nothing special about what you are saying. In a way, this is like saying that they do not really matter. Now the other way, speaking to people about Jesus as if they matter enormously to you, is hard work. And, of course, it is very difficult to do if you have to speak on the spur of the moment. But if we want people to come to faith in Jesus, letting them know that we care about them is a good start.

The need to engage with people is one reason why a personal

testimony can be particularly effective. After all, if you cannot speak with sincerity and enthusiasm about what has happened to you, you're in trouble! Furthermore in today's world, people are far more interested in personal stories than they are in cold, abstract facts. You only have to look at newspaper headlines to see that they want a personal aspect on every story, whether it is a crisis in the NHS or some war abroad. It's what is called the human interest factor. A good honest testimony can do wonders in this area and it doesn't require a degree in theology to do it. What you are trying to do in a testimony is to raise the question in your friend's mind 'why couldn't I too, become a follower of Jesus Christ?'

Now the business of engaging with people raises the subject of answering their questions. Real questions (as opposed to the 'Question as a Diversionary Tactic') are good, precisely because they show we are engaging with our friends. In the Appendix, I have taken some of the most asked questions and attempted to illustrate where I would begin in answering them. But I believe that it is more important that we give such people an authentic response, than a right answer that crushes them. One of the most attractive responses a Christian can give to a seeking unbeliever is, 'I don't know, but I'd be really willing to think through that question for you.' Sometimes our desire to have all the answers for everything can be quite off-putting. But to be involved in a questioning dialogue is good news.

If we are not engaging, everything that we are saying is simply bouncing off our hearers. People may be polite and they may listen patiently, but can I remind you that witnessing for Jesus Christ is far more than having a polite conversation. It is making people sit up and take notice; it is breaking through possibly decades of disinterest and apathy; it is engaging with them so that, perhaps for the first time in their lives, they begin to wonder whether there might indeed be a God and whether that God might want to know them.

I once heard the story of a son who moved away from the firm Christian faith of his parents. When his father asked him why, he got the following answer. 'Dad, the reason I gave up on church was that the preacher said all the right things, but he wasn't saying them to anybody. He didn't know where or who I was, and *it would never occur to him to ask*' (italics mine).

Do you understand? We have to engage. To share about Jesus without engaging with your hearers, is like talking to an empty room. If you keep talking without engaging, you will soon have no hearers to talk to.

d) Persuasive witnessing looks for a response

We're not simply presenting facts when we talk about Jesus; we are looking for a decision. It is all too easy to share the message and then to just let our hearers decide what to do about it. We need to do what we can to push for them to make a decision. Now you may feel uneasy about this. After all, it sounds very un-British to try to persuade people; I mean shouldn't we let them make up their own minds?

In answering, can I remind you of the law court situation that I used as an image earlier? What you are doing when you have a chance to speak for Jesus Christ is that you are trying to change people's verdict about him. The case is this: is Jesus Christ the Son of God and the Saviour of the World? Our job as evangelists and witnesses is to persuade our hearers that this is, in fact, the case. It is to win the verdict of hearers that Jesus Christ is who he claimed to be.

As you are talking to someone it is not a bad thing to be trying to think about where you going. What do you want them to do? Do you want them to come to church; to read a book about Jesus Christ; to join a Bible study; to let you pray with them? These are all possible things that we might want people to do after talking to us. It is all too easy to just leave things up in the air by ending our conversation with something like 'well I hope you've enjoyed our little chat'. We need to push for something more.

Sometimes hard-directed questions can do the trick. Of

course, you have to know your hearers and you have to have earned their trust in order to do this. You can ask such questions as: 'What stops you from becoming a Christian?' 'What are the things that are standing in the way of you following Jesus?' or 'So who do you think Jesus is?' These are hard questions and our friends may very well try and dodge them, but the point is that we are pushing for a decision. Some people might say that this is coercion or 'pressuring', but in fact, what we are doing is no more than any decent teacher would do in any subject. We are challenging our friends to examine their own beliefs and to come up with reasoned answers. The fact is that we all suffer from mental laziness; we prefer to believe what we have always believed.

The claims of Christianity regarding Jesus are so enormous that there are only two options:

- Jesus was mistaken in thinking he was the Son of God and simply suffered from extraordinary delusions of grandeur. In this case he is, to put it bluntly, no more than number one in the list of 'Great and Sad Loonies of the World'.
- Jesus is indeed the one who he claimed to be; he can forgive sins and one day all human beings who have ever lived will be summoned before him to be judged. In this case, we'd better make peace with him pretty quickly.

There are really no other options. Our job, as witnesses to Jesus Christ, is to make people break out of their apathy or ignorance and think through those claims, to decide for themselves who Jesus Christ is and to act upon that decision.

We cannot force people into faith; it would be wrong even to try. But we are to force them to think about their faith and come to a decision. It is this need to get a response from people that lies behind the fact that many evangelists encourage people to show, either by standing up or by coming up to the front, that they have made a decision. Now this practice has been much criticised. It is certainly misleading, if people think that by coming forward or standing up, they have actually become Christians. In fact, I see it as meaning nothing more than people are showing that they have been convinced by the message to the point that they need to know more. The positive thing about getting people to do this, though, is that it makes the point that I have been trying to make in the previous few paragraphs: a decision is required. You cannot keep going away and saying 'I must think about this some more' for ever. Sooner or later, you have to make a decision.

Yes, of course this can be abused. But so can almost everything else. Whether you, or your church, use this method may not ultimately be important. But it is important that we all realise that what we are about, is persuading people to making a decision.

e) Persuasive witnessing is patient

What I want to say here is, in some ways, a balance to what I have just said. While we are to do all we can to encourage people to make a decision for Jesus Christ, we must also learn to be patient.

The key thing here is to recognise what conversion is all about. It is not about a change in lifestyle, so that, instead of lying in bed on a Sunday morning, we start attending a religious meeting instead. It is not about moving from one social circle to another; it is about a wholesale life-changing action of going from being (as we think) our own master, to coming under the authority of Jesus Christ. Let me give you an example of what it is like. Imagine someone who was fanatically French (or English) and who had a passionate attachment to his or her own culture, language and history, and contempt for anybody else's. Imagine that, one day, this person suddenly decides to cross the Channel and to adopt the nationality of his or her ancient enemy. They put behind them their past life, language and culture and start a new life based on their new culture and values. That sort of stunning, total shift in everything that we are is really what conversion is all about. It is this sort of a change that we (or God through us) are asking people for when they come to Jesus. Is it surprising that people take a long time and hesitate about becoming Christians?

We are often impatient to see our friends converted. It is important to realise that people have a long journey to make, and I want to say here that it is becoming harder and harder for people to become Christians. An image that is often used is that of two lands separated by a sheer-sided deep valley: on one side is the world of the non-Christian, on the other is the Kingdom of God. To become a Christian is, we say, to cross over this gulf from Satan's territory to that of Jesus. I think this is a very helpful picture, especially when you use the idea of the cross as the bridge. The point, though, is this: although there has always been a deep gap between the two territories, over the last century, in Britain, the chasm has become wider. There is an ever-growing divergence between the Christian and the non-Christian world. This is apparent in terms of language, morals and culture, and to become a Christian now is to make a major shift in everything you are. The gap between those that know Jesus and those that do not, is now an enormous one. The difficulties that people face in crossing from unbelief to faith should not be exaggerated.

I don't think I am alone in the disappointment that I have felt over the fact that I have non-Christian friends who have not yet come to faith. Some of them I have now known for over twenty years and they still seem a long way from reaching the point of commitment. I am sure that our expectations for our friends who are outside Jesus are so unrealistic, precisely because we do not realise how much of a shift in mindset, lifestyle or understanding they need to go through to respond to the gospel.

I also think that we have some curious ideas of how conversion works that we need to look at, and I want to examine those. But in thinking about conversion, can I remind you that this is God's work from first to last. Faith is something God brings to birth in us, and it is God that makes conversion happen. There must be, even to those who feel they had a gradual conversion, a specific point in time when they became a Christian and the Holy Spirit came to dwell in them. But my experience is that we can get ourselves into trouble when we think of conversion as an event when it is, in fact, a process.

I believe that, on the whole, conversions occur as a result of God working in people very gently and over a long period of time. It is common to talk of people having a 'Damascus Road' experience; the sort of blinding flash of illumination that struck Saul, in Acts 9, and we can pray for it to happen to our friends. Yet, we forget that in Saul's life there were things that must have played a major part in his sudden conversion. For one thing, Paul had had a rigorous upbringing in the Jewish faith, he had had a lot of contact with Christians (even if it was as a persecutor), and he had seen Stephen being martyred. His conversion was not actually quite so 'out of the blue' as it might seem at first sight.

Now I think a long and slow preparation for becoming a Christian is quite common. Jesus himself uses the image of being born, in John 3, as a picture of becoming a Christian, and that picture of the birth of new baby is one that I find very helpful. The birth itself happens in a short period of time (although my wife tells me the pain seems to go on forever!), but babies don't just appear. There is a slow and largely hidden process of growth in the womb from conception through incubation to birth. Not only that, but the period of pregnancy and gestation varies. For some animals, it is merely days while for others it is longer; in elephants, it is eighteen months! Now I believe that each person who becomes a Christian will have a different gestation period (I guess this means that some of my friends are elephants). The problem is that we often want people out of the womb before they are ready. Now I find this analogy helpful, not just because it is one Jesus used, but also because I see my job as an evangelist as being like that of an obstetrician or midwife. I simply assist at a spiritual birth. I am rarely responsible for the conception and certainly not for the development; I merely help the birth to happen. Incidentally, do remember that this is all an evangelist does! The subsequent spiritual growth and development of the child is the responsibility of the church.

I mention this because I find, when I do an evangelistic meeting for a church or a group of churches, that there are two problems to do with those who are not yet Christians.

- One problem occurs when non-Christians are not there. The reason for that is because Christians have not actually brought their friends who are not believers. This is either because they haven't really got any, or because they are too scared to invite them. Exactly *what* they are afraid of is something I would like to know, but that is another matter. The fact is they are not there, and to ask an evangelist to preach Jesus to people who are already converted is about as useful as giving flying lessons to birds.
- The other problem occurs when non-Christians are there. What happens here is that some people bring their friends along and expect them to be up at the front at the end of the meeting, praying a prayer of commitment. The problem is that these people are often still in the early stages of development: they are not ready to be born again. God still has work to do in them.

Part of the problem is that we live in such an instant society. Our demand to have things now (or preferably ten minutes ago) lies behind such modern inventions as instant loans, instant coffee, microwave meals, mobile phones, e-mail, pagers, faxes and pot noodles. Most of these are good things, but the problem is that the 'I want it right now' attitude cannot be transferred to relationships. Patience here, is still a virtue.

In fact, an extreme impatience to see your friends converted can be unfortunate. It can be based on two misconceptions. First, it assumes people are products and that conversion is just a process that can automatically be applied to them. In fact a conversion is the creation of a personal relationship with God and that, as with all relationships may take time; after all there may be a lot to discuss. Secondly, it assumes that God can be given orders. It is treating him as little more than a cosmic conjuror who, when asked, can produce born-again rabbits out of hats.

In fact as almighty God, he knows not only what is best for his children, but also, when it is best. Interestingly, when you read the Bible, there is what we might feel is a rather leisurely pace to many of the relationships people have with God. God takes his time dealing with people and, as the stories of Abraham, Moses and David illustrate, progress in faith may take decades. As any cook knows, there are some things that cannot be microwaved; there is no alternative to the long slow bake. Relationships with God are like that.

Let me use another illustration. Imagine buying an old, tumbledown house in order to do it up and live in it. There are two basic strategies. In one, you move in straight away and, living amid the dust and rubble, rebuild it around you. In the other, you get it rebuilt first and then move in. Now conversion is similar to restoring ruins, and God has a lot of work to do in all of us. I think he uses both strategies. If someone is converted quickly, then God will have a lot of hard work to do afterwards. A delayed conversion may be because God has decided that the floorboards must be ripped up first.

So when people bring a friend who is not a Christian along to an evangelistic meeting and expect everything to happen right then and there, and it doesn't, they should not be downhearted. Conversion is a process and it is of the most vital importance that we help that process along and do not hinder it.

Sometimes this is a hard thing to remember. Imagine this situation. You have been praying for your friend to become a Christian. Suddenly he splits up with his girlfriend and she moves out. Cast into gloom, he starts to consider who he is and what he is doing in life; he listens to you when you talk about Christian things. Silently you rejoice; God is working! Surely, you tell yourself, his conversion cannot be far away. Suddenly, however a new woman appears in his life; his gloom and seriousness is blown away by the surge of hormones. Now, at this point, a temptation may occur to you. 'Perhaps', says a little voice in your mind, 'your friend is resistant to the gospel; perhaps, he has missed his chance. You might as well stop praying now.' Let me give a single word of advice. *Don't*! Remember, we do not know the real psychology and spiritual state of our friends and we do not know what God has planned for them and when he has planned it. We need to be humble and we need to pray. Persuasive witnessing is patient: it doesn't give up at delays. Keep praying!

A plea for persuasive proclamation

Frankly, persuasive proclamation is hard work. It involves everything that I have talked about above. It also involves a constant and often painful self-criticism. Are we relating? Are we connecting? Is there anything in what we say, do, or are, that is putting people off? The problem is that our culture is changing at an incredible rate. What was effective at reaching people ten years ago may not be today; it will not be tomorrow.

Recently at an event for young people, I heard the Radio One DJ, Simon Mayo, ask George Carey, the Archbishop of Canterbury, a question about communicating the gospel that seemed to me to sum up the problem. In his question, Simon Mayo used the illustration of two buildings on the A1 in London. There, he said, is a church that has a big sign outside it saying 'Jesus is Lord' and a picture of a cross and right next door is a car mechanic with an equally big sign saying 'Mr Clutch'. Simon Mayo pointed out that we have reached the stage in this country where people who drive past those two buildings know exactly what Mr Clutch is about, what it is offering, why they need to go there and what they will get when they go in. On the other hand, they have no idea what 'Jesus is Lord' means, why they need Jesus, and aren't in the slightest way interested in finding out. That illustration has stuck with me, because I think it shows the size of the task that we have in proclaiming and persuading of the Good News today.

Interestingly enough, all the evidence of the book of Acts suggests that the early church was very serious about grappling with these issues of communication and culture. Paul, in Athens, for example, seems to have done a masterly job in setting the Good News into a framework of philosophy, culture and literature that his hearers could identify with. Yet, when he was with Jewish people he was one of them. The gospel remained the same, but the way he proclaimed it was fresh.

Let me close this section by giving you some lessons I have learned myself: not because I think I have all the right answers, but because these are personal things that I have worked through myself. I have been a full-time evangelist now for twenty years and in this time I have preached thousands of times and have conducted more missions than I can remember. In evaluating what I have done, I think the most effective on-going mission themes that I have preached on are those that have dealt with issues that affect people's lives. Over the last couple of years, I have been preaching through the Ten Commandments, in ten mission nights on the same night of the week, in the same location, for ten weeks. These have been evenings that were not primarily for church members, but to reach those outside of the church. My reasoning in doing these was that the Ten Commandments represented one of the few remaining points of cultural contact between the church and the world.

The response has been overwhelming and I believe that this is largely because the series addressed men and women through practical issues that are real in everyone's life. I also made an interesting and deliberate decision about giving the series titles. As you probably know, all but one of the commandments are negative ('thou shalt not'). Now there are good reasons for this, and I touch on them in my book *Ten*. But in our culture today we do not respond positively to negative statements. So, rather than bill them in the traditional terms (no coveting, no lying, no stealing, etc) I use the following titles:

- How to find true contentment – *coveting*
- How to hold to the truth – *false witness*
- How to prosper with a clear conscience – *stealing*
- How to affair-proof your relationships – *adultery*
- How to tame your temper – *murder*
- How to keep the peace with your parents – *honouring father and mother*
- How to stop driving yourself crazy – *the Sabbath*
- How to take God seriously – *the name of God*
- How to know the real God – *idols*
- How to live by priorities – *have no gods before God*

Now in fact, as you can see from the book, the content was fairly traditional and I broke no new ground in what I said. The big difference was that I tried to apply it to where my hearers were, rather than where they weren't.

Another thing I did was to reverse the order in which I talked about the commandments. Now there was a method in this too. You see, in the Bible, the commandments are given to a nation that already knows who God is; so it is perfectly logical to start from God and to work out from there to morality. For our culture, I felt it was more reasonable to start where people were. So I began the ten weeks with issues which concern everyone, whether they went to church or not and whether they believed in God or not; contentment, respect, good relationships. I brought God in at every turn, but did it in a way that allowed people to see that God was concerned with helping them live their day-to-day lives. By the time we got to Week Eight I felt they were finally ready to hear a talk about taking God seriously.

Well that's how I did it. Can I remind you that the issue is not whether I was right or wrong (I am responsible to someone else over that), but how you try to persuasively proclaim the message in this culture.

Yes, persuasive proclamation is hard work. We need to think through all that we are doing as churches and Christians. The bad news is, that there may be things that we will have to start doing to reach people. The even worse news is, that there may be things that we will have to stop doing to reach people. We may have to undertake the messy and painful execution of some of our sacred cows.

Let me end on a sober note. Rather than do persuasive proclamation, it is actually far easier to pretend to do it. Of course, we would never dream of calling it that. But in reality, by what we say and how we say it, we are not really engaging with the very real and very lost world around us. Do we really want to see people converted? A friend of mine, who is a lay-preacher, went to preach in a rural church. He found the congregation rather elderly and asked the church secretary whether they were trying to get new people in. There was a moment's pause as the old man considered the evidently radical suggestion. 'Oh no,' came the blunt answer, 'we are quite happy as we are.' That honest opinion could, I fear, be echoed in many other churches and in many Christian lives: 'we are quite happy as we are.'

Be very careful if this is you. If you do not spread the Good News then you will have it taken from you. As with so many things, the rule is the same: use it or lose it. The church must proclaim the Good News of Jesus Christ; or else, the church is not the church of Jesus Christ, it is a social club in decline, whose closure is imminent.

Exercises

1. Read Acts 19:8-10. What do we learn about Paul's style of evangelism in Ephesus? Assuming he only preached for an hour a day and only (!) six days a week in the lecture hall of Tyrannus, how many hours did Paul spend in total sharing the Good News this way? Do you think Paul's persuasiveness was the result of his sharp mind, divine strength through the Spirit, or sheer hard work? Are these mutually exclusive?

2. Read Acts 26:1-29. Paul is pleading for justice for himself. What does he turn his defence plea into? What does this reveal about the extent to which sharing the Good News had become his chief priority? How persuasive do you think he was?

3. Read 1 Corinthians 5:9-11. What does he reveal here a) about how seriously he views persuading people, and b) why he treats it so seriously?

Questions

1. Find my illustrations of Andy, Mary, Wallace, Melanie and Dave. Imagine you are sitting down with each of them. How might you start off a conversation with each of them about their faith? What goal might you aim for in each conversation?

2. Think of some of the people you actually do meet. What things are there in their lives that you can build on to lead them towards Christ? What things are there in their lives that are obstacles to faith?

3. Why is it important to really want to convince people that they need Jesus?

4. How do you become someone who can share Jesus with total integrity?

Chapter 17

THE FIFTH PILLAR: POWER

LET THE SPIRIT WORK!

I have already talked about the Holy Spirit. In Chapter 5, I discussed who the Holy Spirit was and in Chapter 9, I talked about how the Holy Spirit was essential to our witness. Just to remind you, there, I pointed out that we need the Spirit to help us love people; we have to be sensitive to the Spirit's leading; we need to have faith in the Spirit; and we should be open to extraordinary workings of the Spirit.

What I want to do here is to emphasise again the importance of the power of Holy Spirit in our calling out. The work of the Holy Spirit is a key pillar in the work of evangelism. Indeed, I cannot stress enough the fact that, unless we rely on the power of the Holy Spirit, all our efforts at calling out are likely to be totally ineffective.

I wish I could leave it at that. However, precisely because it is so important, the area of the Holy Spirit's ministry in evangelism is one that is fraught with dangers and difficulties, and I feel that I need to try and address these.

Three temptations

First, I want to point out that three temptations can occur in the area of the Spirit's power and evangelism.

The first temptation: to disbelieve in the Spirit's power

For much of the last two hundred and fifty years, there has been a trend, in Western Europe and America, of playing down the supernatural element in Christianity. Under the influence of an over-optimistic belief in the power of reason and science, the supernatural has been slowly eased out. People were told confidently that humankind had now 'come of age' and that the miracles and manifestations of the Spirit described in the Bible and recorded in the history of the church could not now be believed. Such accounts were, it was said, the product of naive and credulous minds that were unaware of scientific laws and rules. The effects on Christianity were drastic. Instead of God being someone who was involved in every aspect of his creation, he came to be seen as a remote character watching as the universe kept going under the rules that he had written. Finally, God was reduced to little more than a concept or principle, reducing Christianity to merely a series of moral beliefs centering on the idea that there had once been a good man called Jesus. One of the first casualties of this dilution of the Good News (which is generally termed liberal Christianity) was the Holy Spirit. He was soon reduced from being seen as having any real influence, and finally, became eliminated all together.

Of course, this was catastrophic in evangelism: sins didn't really exist, God was either too distant or too powerless to act, there was no Saviour to save people and there was no Spirit to change lives. In short, there was no message to preach. That did not stop people still trying to preach, but results in every way were disastrous; the almost universal response to such a watered-down Christianity was simply a big yawn, why bother? Significantly, liberal Christianity found little support in Africa, Asia and South America, and it is probably not surprising that it is in these areas that the church has grown so dramatically over the last hundred years. However, in the last century this liberal view has began to wane in the West, and almost all lively churches today have a new faith and confidence in what, historically, Christianity has always claimed: God has spoken and acted in history and can do so today. They would also believe, in varying degrees, in the powerful working of the Holy Spirit today.

Yet, I believe that it may be dangerous to assume that such sceptical views have gone forever. For a start, they have a long tradition. The first words of the Devil, in Genesis 3, to humanity were an encouragement to doubt God. "Really?" he asked the woman. "Did God really say you must not eat any of the fruit in the garden?'" Even in Jesus' day there was an entire group within Judaism (the Sadducees) who were sceptical over such basic things as the existence of an afterlife. In other words, I believe that there is always a temptation to rule out the possibility of the Holy Spirit working.

Now this doubt may not be stated openly. Very few people in Church circles are going to say 'Oh, I don't believe in the Holy Spirit'. Rather, what we are in danger of doing, as we talk to people and we plan our evangelistic ventures, is just quietly assuming that the Spirit cannot work. We may say that we believe in God's power working today, but we may say it with so many qualifications that what is left is little more than a philosophy. We have lost the belief that God can work in the lives of those people around us. We need to believe that the Spirit can convert people, that he can change lives and that he can send people out on mission.

Although I would rather duck the issue and get on with talking about something else, I feel I must say something here about the debate about 'power evangelism' and charismatic signs and wonders. If you are not aware of it, a range of views exists within Bible-believing Christianity. There are two extreme positions. One sees the miraculous gifts, such as those recorded in the book of Acts, as having come to an end as the New Testament was completed and the first generation of the apostles passed away. Such signs and wonders, they say, do not occur today. On the other extreme are those who say, equally strongly, that the pattern given in the book of Acts should be the pattern for our evangelism today; we should expect to see the lame healed, the blind given sight and even, on occasions, the dead raised. So basically, one group expects no miraculous signs and the other expects them all the time. Now theologically, there are arguments that point both ways and this is not the place to discuss them. Personally, I have to say that there are far too many miracles of healing today for the first view to be correct. But I also have to say that there are not enough – and not enough of the quality that were seen in Jesus' ministry – for the second view to be entirely correct either.

Having said that, there are two extremes, I feel that this is actually rather artificial. In my experience, very few people hold to either extreme position. Most Christians are somewhere in the middle and tend to swing backwards and forwards a bit. Even those who believe that the age of miracles has ended pray when someone is sick, and even those who believe that miracles should be more common do not go into hospitals and try to empty the intensive care wards.

In fact, I believe that there may be no hard and fast universal rule on the extent to which signs and wonders occur today. For instance, there is a good deal of evidence to suggest that the way that the Spirit works varies from place to place and time to time. For example, many cool-headed missionaries have reported awesome workings of the Holy Spirit in areas where demonic activity and witchcraft are widespread. These workings appear to be different in scale to those seen in Western Europe and North America. However, if occult activity continues to increase here in the West, then it may be that we will see more openly miraculous confrontations occurring in these regions.

Let me try to list some things that I am certain of, and that I think most Christians would agree with.

- All authentic Christianity is supernatural. The very basis of our faith centres on a God who intervened in the world and who, through the power of the Spirit raised Jesus from the dead. If you do not believe in a God who acts, then what you have is not Christianity, it is a philosophy: and a rather feeble one at that. The God of authentic Christianity can easily do miracles today if he chooses.
- God's power shows itself in all sorts of ways. Sometimes, he works in a way that is awesomely visible and obviously miraculous. At other times, he works in a way that is low key. We ought to give thanks for both.
- God has his own agenda about performing miracles; he chooses to do them in his time, in his way. Getting publicity is not, I think, on his agenda. On earth, Jesus did not always perform miracles and often shunned public attention. He plainly rejected the opportunity of getting attention by doing stunts (Luke 4:9-12). Miracles are more than just a spiritual firework display.
- Miracles are signs or indicators of the coming kingdom of Jesus. They are not simply 'curiosities' or 'unexplained phenomena' of the X-Files type; they foreshadow Jesus' final triumph over evil. Perhaps I am being trivial, but I think of them as being like the cinema trailers for a forthcoming film. They encourage us to look forward to the glorious future. That is why we should want to see signs and wonders, not because we like supernatural special effects, but because they remind us of what lies ahead.
- There is both a danger of presumption ('God will heal') and a danger of scepticism ('God will not heal'). I do not think it is a wise policy to give God orders as to what he will, or will not, do. We need a reverent and prayerful balance.
- The Devil would love nothing more than to see Christians getting annoyed and irritated with each other over our attitudes

to how the Holy Spirit works. Even if he cannot persuade us to go that far, I'm sure he is delighted if we can become distracted from the business of proclaiming God's kingdom.

- God can use suffering for his glory as the glorious testimonies of many crippled and disabled people proclaim. In the light of God's mysterious purposes, healing and prosperity may not always be the best thing for us. I know that this may sound cold comfort to you if you are actually suffering but it is true.

- All our views on healing need to bear in mind that this is not some abstract, theoretical area of theology in which we can happily play around with ideas. It is an area filled with anxious people who are desperately concerned to have either themselves or their loved ones healed. We need a great deal of sensitivity here, in order not to dash hopes of healing or to build up false expectations.

Anyway, the debate continues, and as long as it is done in love and charity, this is probably a good thing. We always need to examine – and re-examine – what God's word says and how it applies to us today. But as this is a book on evangelism, can I remind you here that we must not overlook the fact that conversions themselves are miraculous? For lives to be changed requires a direct supernatural intervention in the very heart of a human being. No one is converted by arguments or reason. Only the Holy Spirit of God can turn someone into a new creation. Every conversion is a miracle.

And it is here, rather than on healing, that I want to challenge you practically. Do you really believe that the Holy Spirit can help you share your faith with your friends? Now some of us need the assurance of the presence of the Holy Spirit to help us witness more than others. I am very fortunate in that I worship in a large and growing church where encouraging things are happening. But I am aware that many of you reading this will be part of churches where things are not so happy. You may well be part of some echoing, empty church or chapel where the bare seats seem to stretch on forever and where, every year, the number that attend are fewer. Your church may not have seen a conversion in years. Now if this is you, let me say that it is precisely to people like you that this belief in a powerful, Holy Spirit applies. God wants to help you. His resources are available to you. You are not on your own!

I also want to speak to those of you who find the idea of sharing your faith difficult. Perhaps you read some of the comments I made in his book earlier about sharing Jesus with the people you work with, or with your family, and your reaction was to shake your head in disbelief. 'How can my witness affect my boss/my secretary/my husband?' Now if, indeed, it was just your witness, you would be right. But the power of the Holy Spirit, who is given to all who are believers in Jesus Christ, can witness through you. And that is another matter all together. Don't ever be tempted to think that the Spirit cannot work – he can.

The second temptation: to try and manipulate the Spirit's power

The first temptation denies the power of the Holy Spirit. The second temptation that I want to talk about is very different. It recognises that power, but wants to use it in the wrong way. The classic case of this is to be found in the book of Acts, where, in chapter 8, we read of a magician called Simon who had a ministry in Samaria. As we read the story, we see how he makes a profession of faith and then, just as we think it to be another of the successful conversions recorded in Acts, we come across the following:

> When Simon saw that the Holy Spirit was given when the apostles placed their hands upon people's heads, he offered money to buy this power. 'Let me have this power, too,' he exclaimed, 'so that when I lay my hands on people, they will receive the Holy Spirit!' But Peter replied, 'May your money perish with you for thinking

God's gift can be bought! You can have no part in this, for your heart is not right before God. Turn from your wickedness and pray to the Lord. Perhaps he will forgive your evil thoughts, for I can see that you are full of bitterness and held captive by sin.' 'Pray to the Lord for me,' Simon exclaimed, 'that these terrible things won't happen to me!'

Simon had recognised that God was at work and, being familiar with occult powers, thought that the Holy Spirit was something similar. He wanted to be able to use the Spirit for his own purposes. Sadly, I have to tell you that the temptation that Simon faced has not gone away in twenty centuries. We still face the temptation of using the Spirit's power to proclaim Jesus Christ, not for the benefit of the kingdom, but for our own benefit.

This temptation is not confined to spectacular signs and wonders ministries where there is healing and some of the more dramatic works of the Holy Spirit, it has also happened throughout history when there have been successful preachers or evangelists. Whenever crowds flood into the churches or stadiums to hear a Spirit-anointed preacher, evangelist or healer, there is always someone to whom the tempting thought comes: wouldn't it be splendid if this could be controlled or managed? 'How wonderful,' they say, 'if this could continue on a regular basis: we could have an extension, take on more staff, and have better publicity. We could do so much.' And all too soon, the work of the Spirit has become something that we seek to control.

Expressed like this, you can, I hope, see the danger. The Spirit is the one who was present at the creation and who was involved in the making of the universe. Do you really want to mess around trying to manipulate him? Personally, I'd feel safer publicly insulting the latest heavyweight boxing champion of the world. Can I remind you too, that the great title *Lord* is not only given to God the Father and God the Son, but also to God the Holy Spirit? And behind that word 'Lord' is the idea of rule, authority and independence. That, after all is the whole point of saying 'Jesus is Lord'. By saying that, we are admitting that Jesus is in charge and we are not. We need to remember that there is only one name that the Spirit will magnify and that is the name of Jesus.

The problem is that we tend to think that it is a case of us using the Spirit. If you have that idea, or even a trace of it, in your thinking, please get rid of it now and make sure it never returns. *We* do not use the Spirit; we let *him* use us. The difference between the two, as far as witness goes, is total failure, or success.

Attempts to use or manipulate the Spirit are almost always disastrous. Quite simply, under such circumstances, the Spirit exercises his royal prerogative and leaves. And as he goes, the signs and wonders, or the anointed preaching, just end. Hopefully, those that are involved see their error and repent, and the Spirit's presence and power can be restored. There are, however, rare but horrid situations where, instead of repenting, other means are sought to try and make up for the excitement and power the Holy Spirit brought. Skills in crowd manipulation, or speaking, are used to replace the power of the Spirit. But it is not the real thing and soon everybody knows it.

Can I plead with you that if you are ever in a ministry – whether of preaching, evangelism, or whatever – that was once Spirit-anointed and the Spirit leaves, seek God in humble repentance? Do not to try to find a substitute power supply.

The third temptation: to find substitutes for the Spirit's power

There is a third temptation that I want to draw your attention to and this is perhaps the most subtle. In this, we do not deny the Spirit, nor do we try to manipulate him; instead we somehow just let him get edged out. Ironically, books and courses on evangelism can actually make this temptation more compelling. What happens is people learn techniques and skills, they pick up bits of psychology, master Bible arguments and learn the flaws in the way people think today. Soon the skills have replaced the Spirit. Where once the Holy Spirit alone was involved in calling out, now we have something very different. It was once purely spiritual; it is now technological or psychological instead.

If the first temptation is to be an atheist, the second temptation is to be a magician, this is the temptation to be a technologist. The problem is that the Spirit is untameable and we find that frustrating. What we would really like, in this modern age, is a Spirit who is freeze-dried ('just open the pack and add water') or digitally processed ('just plug in and switch on'). But he refuses to play ball; he cannot be switched on at will. He comes and goes at his command, not ours.

Frustrated, we find it is easier to try alternatives: techniques, programmes, technology. They may not be quite as effective as the real thing but they are easier to control and more reliable. You don't have to pray and wait. Now when I say it like that, you realise (I hope) just how terrible and stupid an idea it is. There are simply no substitutes for the Spirit in sharing our faith. Even if we have learned a thousand texts of the Bible, have memorised a dozen evangelistic outlines and know a hundred appropriate responses to difficult questions, it is all totally useless unless the Spirit works with us.

Now I'm not, of course, encouraging you to do evangelism badly. As I hope I have made clear, I believe that we should share Jesus as well as we can. As far as public evangelism goes, I think good seating and good organisation are very helpful. Whenever you have a chance to speak, I think it is a good idea to do your preparation, research your material and know what you are talking about. And the same goes for personal evangelism too; if you are meeting someone who is a Muslim to talk about spiritual things, it makes sense to do your homework. But we must all be wary in case we create such a smooth and slick sermon, event, or conversation, that there is very little scope for the Holy Spirit to actually work.

The Holy Spirit is not like the stabilisers on the child's

bicycle: something that we need initially but which we are subsequently able to discard and never use again. We always need him and always will.

I suspect this is the real danger for the professional or regular evangelist. We do it so often that there is the danger that we slip into automatic pilot mode: we let our skills and habits take over. If you are involved with anyone who is doing regular evangelism, do pray for them that they stay fresh by relying upon God's power and not upon any apparatus and machinery that they have created. If you don't you can always pray for me!

But if, as I hope, you are involved in sharing the gospel personally, then I suggest that you watch out for this temptation too. If you ever start feeling that, when you are sharing Jesus, what you are doing is slick and polished and that you are doing it automatically, then it's time to have a long hard think about what you are doing. You are in danger of edging the Holy Spirit out.

A plea to honour the Spirit

What all three of the temptations that I have discussed have in common is this: they dishonour the Spirit. They either consider he doesn't exist, think that he can be manipulated, or allow him to be sidelined. What I want to do in the remaining part of this chapter is to give you three suggestions on how you can honour the Spirit in sharing your faith in Jesus.

But before I talk about how we are to honour the Spirit, can I urge you to re-read the book of Acts? Acts is a relatively short book – it takes about an hour and a half to read – and is the textbook of mission. There is so much there that is fascinating. I love the variety of the accounts of how the first followers of Jesus were used in the mission of God. In Acts, there is talk and action; there are accounts of the apostles travelling and there are accounts of them staying in one place. We see public speeches and we see private conversations, there are arrests and there are releases, there is martyrdom and there is deliverance from martyrdom, there is witness with miracles and there is witness without, there are shipwrecks and homely scenes. There is even a committee meeting or two. But behind this glorious scrapbook of the Early Church runs the great theme that threads itself through all these scenes. That theme is the mission of God, fuelled by the awesome power of his Spirit. And, as I told you earlier, you and I play our part in the twenty-first century sequel to Acts that is now being written.

Firstly, realise that you need the Spirit's power

The task of being involved in the mission of God is a daunting one at the best of times. Speaking personally, there are very few things that fill me with more fear and a greater sense of my own unworthiness and incompetence, than witnessing. Not to put too fine a point on it, I am often tempted to do a Jonah and run in completely the opposite direction. I suspect you are the same.

Yet, there is an element to the fear that is good. It reminds us that we are powerless and that we need a power supply. Now in this, witnessing for Jesus is no different from many other things in life. You may have a wonderful computer system, a stunning stereo, or even an amazing car. But without power, they are nothing but an embarrassment. You press the switch or turn the key – and nothing happens. Equally, in our lives we need power to fulfil our own ambitions or goals. And to serve Jesus we also need power.

God's Spirit gives us the power to serve and witness for God: something that we see plainly in the Bible. Even Jesus himself did nothing until he had been baptised and received power from above when the Holy Spirit came upon him. And as for Jesus, so for his followers. So when Jesus sent out his first missionary teams we read, 'One day Jesus called together his twelve apostles and gave them power and authority to cast out demons and to heal all diseases. Then he sent them out to tell everyone about the coming of the Kingdom of God and to heal the sick' (Luke 9:1-2).

The Spirit is the moving power, the energy, the inspiration and the strength behind all evangelism. The Spirit actually works in both us and our hearers. We, as those that call out, can only live, work, speak and proclaim in the power of the Spirit. Our hearers, who don't know God, can only see the truth of our lives, our words and our actions because the Spirit enables them to see who Jesus really is and know his love. In this way, the Spirit acts as an agent of translation and communication and works with both sides. From first to last, the process of mission is something that God does; even what we do is empowered by the Spirit.

The task is so great, that how talented you are naturally is irrelevant. You may have a wonderful voice, a great command of words, a powerful presence; you may even be a warm and likeable person. But if you do not have God's power, all these are of no value whatsoever in witnessing for Jesus. Equally, if you do have the power of the Spirit of God, you may have none of these natural gifts and be greatly used.

There is a delightful paradox here that I feel comes very near to the heart of what the Good News of Jesus is all about. It is that the Spirit is more likely to use weak people than strong people. Paul, battered over the years by the burdens of his ministry, knew something of this. In one letter he writes how, faced with some major affliction (the mysterious 'thorn in the flesh'), he asked God to take it away. The answer he got, he tells us, was a strange one: 'Each time he [God] said, "My gracious favour is all you need. My power works best in your weakness." So now I am glad to boast about my weaknesses, so that the power of Christ may work through me. Since I know it is all for Christ's good, I am quite content with my weaknesses and with insults, hardships, persecutions, and calamities. For when I am weak, then I am strong' (2 Corinthians 12:9-10).

God set the pattern for how the Good News is to be proclaimed at the cross. There, at the heart of the message, lies a crucified, dying man. It is the very picture of weakness and frailty. That pattern – God working through weakness – has been the one he has used ever since. It is only when we are weak that he can be powerful. Otherwise, we just get in the way.

Witnessing for Jesus without seeking and using the power, which God has provided for that very purpose, will be disastrous. You can move a car by getting your shoulder behind it and pushing. You don't get far, you soon get exhausted and frankly, you look pretty stupid. Trying to witness without God's power is pretty much the same sort of thing.

Secondly, ask for the Spirit's power

Now what I have just said may leave you discouraged. 'God's power! And how am *I* expected to get hold of that?' you say. Yet, it is here that there is a wonderful lesson to be learned, and for me it is one of the most important lessons of the Bible. When God calls and asks us to do something, he doesn't leave us high and dry. Instead, he gives us everything that we are going to need to do it.

When I think of this I am reminded of how, when God's people were slaves in Egypt and forced to build palaces and pyramids, an unusually cruel demand was placed on them. They were ordered to make bricks without one of the most vital ingredients – straw. Now God is not like one of those Egyptian taskmasters; he doesn't tell us to make bricks and give us nothing to make them with. He does not tell us that we have to be witnesses to his love in words and actions, by our prayers and our presence and then leave us on our own to rely on our own resources. He is, after all, our heavenly Father. And what father would demand that a task be done without supplying what was needed? Our resource for the task of witnessing is, as we have seen, the Spirit.

Jesus gives one of the most wonderful promises of the Bible to his disciples in precisely this context. In Luke 11:10-13, we read that Jesus told them. 'For everyone who asks, receives. Everyone who seeks, finds. And the door is opened to everyone who knocks. You fathers – if your children ask for a fish, do you give them a snake instead? Or if they ask for an egg, do you give them a scorpion? Of course not! If you sinful people know how to give good gifts to your children, how much more will your heavenly Father give the Holy Spirit to those who ask him.'

Do you see the basis for being given the Holy Spirit? It is merely to ask God our Father for him. Humbly, realising that we are short of the resources needed to live and witness for Jesus, we are to go to our Father and ask him for help. I'm sure you can see why I find that encouraging!

Can I remind you again that I am not simply talking about large-scale evangelism? You see, you could say, 'well I can see how you might need the Spirit for talking to thousands, but surely when I just talk to my neighbour across the fence, I can manage that on my own?' In fact, you cannot do that either. John Drane, a widely respected scholar and the Director of the Centre for Christianity and Contemporary Society, tells of just this sort of situation:

Several years ago, I found myself sitting on a plane next to an obviously rich and successful businessman. As we talked this man confided in me that he had problems. That very morning he had slammed the door of his home for the last time. His marriage was under stress. His growing children were giving cause for concern. And he was personally unfulfilled. The only thing to do was to leave them to get on with it, and try and find satisfaction alone somewhere else.

I was actually on my way to a conference on evangelism where I was scheduled to give one of the keynote addresses. I knew there was no way I could deliver that address with integrity if I did not share my faith in Christ with this person. But how? I had no idea. So I did what most of us do when we are in a real fix: I prayed. A silent momentary prayer that God would give me the words to say. Before I had time to think about it I found myself asking a question, 'Do you know God?' I said to him. At that very instant my whole life seemed to flash in front of my eyes.

If the question surprised me, the answer bowled me over completely, 'As a matter of fact, I don't,' my companion replied, 'But if you know something about God, I'd like to know more.' At the end of the flight, I gave him my address and we went our separate ways. Two weeks later I had a letter from the same person. In it, he told me how at his destination he had been unable to get our conversation out of his mind. He saw a church with an open door, went in, and there he prayed as best he knew how that God would somehow intervene directly in his life. In due course, his business was completed and he had to face going home again. For all his bravado, he had nowhere else to stay. In any case, he thought that would be a real test case for God.

When he finally returned, he was surprised to receive a warm welcome from his wife. Even more surprised to hear what she had to say. The morning he left home, she too had felt it was all over. As she left her children at the school gate she shared her feelings with another parent. The other person was planning to go to a prayer group that very day. It wasn't meant to be an evangelistic group, but how could an obvious need like this be ignored? So the two of them went together. The woman was immediately attracted to the warmth of the group. In fact the group prayed for the husband on the plane – at exactly the moment that I was in conversation with him. As a direct result, it seemed, both husband and wife had met God in a new and challenging way that subsequently transformed their marriage their family and their entire outlook on life. (Drane p.195ff)

I like this story, especially as it happened to a man who cannot be, by any means, described as naive or credulous. It also, by the way, gives a glimpse into the complex network of Spirit-empowered prayer, talk and action that lies behind conversions. We need the Spirit's power and we need to ask for it.

Thirdly, have faith that the Spirit will move

Now can I urge you to do two things?

First of all, I would urge you to be expectant. The Spirit can easily be deterred from acting and one way of doing that would simply be by not expecting him to work. We could call that having a lack of faith, or we could call it simply disbelieving God. It doesn't matter; either way it is not a sensible way to expect God to move in power. You can be expectant; God does keep his promises.

Secondly, and this balances my previous point, please be open on exactly how the Spirit will work. It is easy for us to imagine how things are going to work. In fact, often we imagine that he will work in exactly the way he last did. For example, nearly a hundred years after the last Welsh Revival there are still people in Wales who are expecting God to come up with a repeat performance. The danger is that in doing this that we end up restricting how God can work, because we are only open to him working in one particular way.

Can I remind you here that he is the Lord? God is the one who searches hearts, minds and cultures; he knows what is best. Pray for your friend to be converted: just don't lay down conditions. Pray for the Spirit to move: just don't tell him how to do it.

Some final words on the Spirit

Let me say just two more things.

The first is a plea, that when the Spirit does move in answer to prayer, please be very careful to give God the glory. Remember, that it is only God's power that brings people to faith; it is not us. As I have tried to make plain from the first page of this book, every part of mission comes from God. When things happen and people are converted what we are seeing is what God has done and God alone.

The second thing is that at the end of a chapter full of warnings and pleas, I would like to leave you with a word of encouragement. The task we face in sharing our faith and seeing people brought to faith in Christ is humanly speaking, impossible and we need to remember that. It is not however, divinely impossible. In the Holy Spirit, God has given all the power that you or I need to do his will in this area. If we will let God use us, I believe that extraordinary things can happen.

Exercises

1. Read Isaiah 11:1-4. This is a famous passage of prophecy looking forward to the Messiah. What is the Spirit to do in his life? Now read Isaiah 61:1-3 and compare it with Luke 4:18-21. How does Jesus see himself relating to these Old Testament passages?

2. Read Ezekiel 37. In another prophetic passage, Ezekiel looks forward to the revival of his people. As you read it be aware that the word for breath and spirit are the same. What does this tell us about the power of the Spirit? What does it tell us about what his ministry is all about?

3. Read Romans 8:1-30. How many times does the word 'Spirit' occur in this passage? If you only had this passage of Scripture, what would you know about the Spirit?

Questions

1. Of the three temptations with respect to the Spirit that I mentioned (to disbelieve in him, to manipulate him and to find substitutes for him), which do you personally find most tempting? Have you ever tried witnessing without the power of the Spirit? What happened?

2. What wrong ideas have you had about who the Spirit is and how he works? How have those wrong ideas hindered your Christian life and your witness?

3. In what areas of your life and witness would you like to see the Spirit's power? Why? What can you do about it?

NOTES:

John Drane, *Evangelism for a New Age* (0-551-02843-2, Marshall Pickering, 1994)

Chapter 18

THE SIXTH PILLAR: PRAISE

GLORIFY GOD!

At first sight, you may feel that the idea of a chapter on praise is out of place in a book on evangelism. If you do, I hope that after reading this, you may have changed your mind. But in saying that, I do not want to pretend that I have got all the answers in this area. In fact, I think that this is a part of our existence as Christians that we have not yet really thought through properly. So what I have written here are really some of my current thoughts on the matter. I should also say that these are by no means all my thoughts; there is far, far more on praise that could be written.

Before I go any further I ought to try and make some things clear:

- There are two main meanings to the word 'worship'. In its broadest sense, worship is the way that we dedicate ourselves, and all that we are, to God. The word is derived from the word 'worthship' and our worship is, in fact, recognition of the worth of God and the fact that he is Lord over every area of our lives. It is this sort of worship that the

Devil wanted to have from Jesus when he tempted him in the wilderness (Matthew 4:9). He didn't just want to be flattered or praised by Jesus; he wanted Jesus to bow down before him and give him honour and loyalty. Worship is a very serious business. Indeed, as many people have pointed out, all that we do at church, home, work, or play, ought to be part of our worship. In that sense, our witness is worship; we are obeying God.

- However, when today we talk about 'worship', what we mean is a narrower definition; it just a part of what I have just described. What we mean is the situation where God's people come together and offer him praise, in prayer and in song. In this sense, *praise* and *worship* are almost interchangeable words. Now when I use the word worship, I will be using it in this sense. Please, however, do remember that there is far more to worship than just singing songs. They are just the most obvious feature of what ought to be a whole life of worship.

- Equally, we need to remember that worship styles vary enormously even in British churches. There are places where guitars and drums play only songs written after 1990, and there are places where the organ plays nothing but hymns written before 1890. There are places where worship is scripted and planned down to the last word, three days before, and where to finish a minute late is to invite criticism. And there are places that are so spontaneous that no one knows what song is coming next and where, to even ask the time, is to invite some one to pray for your cold heart. In the context of evangelism, I am not in slightest bit interested in which sort of worship your church or fellowship practices. You probably know – or can guess – my own preferences. What I want to talk about here actually goes beyond all our differences in worship style.

- Do bear in mind that worship actually need not even be inside a building; one of the most exiting developments in recent years has been the *March for Jesus* initiative, where

Christians praise God out on the streets. It can also be in homes. I am suspicious about the way we have let our praise get reduced to a couple of fixed slots on a single day of the week. As I said earlier about evangelism, I think it suits the devil to have us restricted.

Now, having said all that, I have to frankly admit that the relationship of praise to evangelism is not an easy issue. That we should worship is plain; that we should witness is equally plain. It is how the two relate that is the difficulty.

In fact, I believe that one of the things that are wrong with our modern practice of Christianity is that we have managed to fragment everything. We now see the Christian life as being one that has various compartments: prayer, witness, worship, social involvement and so on. To misuse the famous sentence of the marriage ceremony, I believe we have managed 'to put apart what God has joined together'. I do not know where these divisions come from; it may be that the habit theological colleges and universities have of dividing things up so as to fit them into courses is to blame. Whatever the origin, I believe it has been disastrous.

Now by fragmenting our Christian life, it is all too easy to turn one part against another. So you sometimes hear in church discussions, statements such as 'there's too much worship and not enough concern for evangelism here' or 'that church is excellent in social involvement but it has been at the expense of witness'. Such a fragmentation of what we are as individuals and churches turns us into spiritual schizophrenics, whose split personalities war against each other. It is not a pleasant sight. In this book, I have tried to do what I can to re-unite things that have been separated. For instance, I tried to make the point that we should not think of mission as a separate part of our life as believers in Jesus Christ. My desire to see us live integrated Christian lives is nowhere stronger than in the area of praise and worship. And what I want to do in this chapter is to suggest to you that praise and worship have an important part in our witness and are, in fact, linked to it. This is not just my opinion, Dr. John Drane, who I quoted in the last chapter, says this: 'If worship is a central part of the Gospel, and if evangelism is about communicating the whole gospel, then clearly there can be no effective evangelism without authentic worship.' (Drane p.126)

What I want to do is to briefly, and rather tentatively, express why I think that worship is so important to the process of calling out. But before I can look at these, I want to comment on a question that is now widely raised: do worship and witness mix?

Some people argue that Christian corporate worship can put non-Christians off more than anything else. They argue that what goes on in the hymns and the songs is meaningless to those outside the church. Indeed, they say it is worse than meaningless; it is alienating. Some have gone as far as to suggest that we divide our church meetings into worship events (for the 'church family'), and 'seeker-sensitive events' (for those who are not Christians) in which there is little, if any, collective worship.

Now I understand the logic of this position, especially as people who have proposed it are keen on evangelism. My head recognises that there is a point here; the church that is praising and glorifying God can often become so involved in the process of worship that it can forget the presence of outsiders. But nevertheless, I feel very uneasy about separating what we do as church into a 'family-only' worship event and a meeting that is designed for outsiders. My objections lie along the following lines:

- Firstly, I fear that there is a risk that it could lead to a potentially deceptive situation where a church has separate public and private faces. I can imagine a situation where at the public meeting there is an attempt to show the church as we would like it to be; made up entirely of smooth, polished, professionals doing smooth, polished, worship. In contrast, at the meeting for the fellowship, who we really are emerges: we also have the sick, unemployed, and those that sing loudly out of tune. Now in an era when appearances are stage-managed, I think I would rather we took the risk of openness; I think we should adopt a policy of 'what you see is who we are'. I think there is a helpful parallel with ordinary families here. There are two ways of introducing someone to your family. One, is to have them come round for a formal meal: you will have made a special effort with the food, the teenagers will be clean, there won't be toys on the living room floor, and everyone will be on their best behaviour. The other way is to say 'Oh just come over and join us. Make yourself at home. Be part of the family.' Many people – perhaps most people – would find the second offer far more attractive.

- Secondly, by doing this we end up judging what is suitable for those who are not believers in Christ. Now I am uneasy about that; it seems to both limit the role of the Spirit and assume that all people are the same. I am helped in this by the observation that the things that intrigue non-Christians seem to be things I would not have expected and the things that put them off are equally unpredictable. When one agnostic friend of mine came to our church, he really enjoyed the bit when he had to turn around and shake everybody's hand; he used it as a time to tell people his name and introduce himself by saying a bit about what he did. He was a little perturbed though, when the only response was 'Peace', and completely phased by the middle-aged man who gave him a big bear hug. But sometimes it is the incidental things that attract: the way the noisy child is treated, the sense of community, and the air of warmth and tolerance.

- Thirdly, and most importantly, it seems to me to go against the spirit of the Bible. God's people are to be a worshipping people, we are to glorify God publicly and are declare his praises openly, and I find no hint of ever disguising that fact.

So my cautious verdict, and I will give other reasons for it, is that I think we should not have a split between meetings for seekers and meetings for the fellowship. I think that there is something about corporate worship that actually draws people to Jesus; what those things are, I will discuss below. That said though, we do need to be aware that there can be things about the style in which we do worship that can be barriers. I think we should always be reassessing what we do and asking questions as to how this or that will be received. We certainly need to make sure that people understand why we do things.

Now after that detour, let me suggest some reasons why worship is vital to our witnessing.

1. *Worship is a witness in itself*

The first thing to say is simple: it is that worship is witness. Now exactly why and how it is witness is not easy to say, but the fact is that it is.

Let me remind you that in worship we declare how great God is and we praise him. Now our praises should be for God's benefit, but nevertheless, when we praise him a side effect of that praise is that others seem to see how great he is too. It is almost as though by 'lifting up' God and 'magnifying' God we are indeed making him more visible to those around us.

But there is more. One of the problems about worship is that, because we do so much, sing, play instruments and pray, we tend to think that these activities are all that there is to worship. In my opinion, this is a very serious mistake. You see, I believe that the most important thing that happens when people gather in the Lord's name to worship isn't our songs, our words, our prayers or our rituals. It is that through the presence of his Spirit, we encounter God himself. I believe that, in genuine worship, there is a real meeting with God. And I believe that the reality of God's presence through the Spirit is an awesome evangelistic tool. We have talked a lot in this book about reasons and arguments and these are, of course, valid. But there is such a thing as the direct and overwhelming encounter with God.

Now this is not simply the language of some modern charismatics who are into emotions and are a bit fuzzy in the intellect department. The Frenchman Blaise Pascal was one of few truly great geniuses of the last millennium and, in a life spanning only 39 years, made major achievements in physics, philosophy and mathematics. He was also a deeply religious man who had undergone a life changing conversion. When he died in 1662, a paper with a testimony written on it was found stitched into his coat lining. Let me quote you part of it:

> Monday 23rd November 1654. From about half ten in the evening until half past midnight. FIRE: God of Abraham, God of Isaac, God of Jacob, not of philosophers and scholars. Certainty, Certainty, heartfelt, Joy, Peace. God of Jesus Christ, God of Jesus Christ. My God and your God. Thy God shall be my God. The world forgotten and everything except God. He can only be found in the ways taught in the gospels. Joy joy tears of joy. Jesus Christ, Jesus Christ . . .

Clearly, this great man of enormous intellect had met the living God in such an overwhelming way as to change him forever.

There is a strong biblical basis for this sort of confrontation. It is not usual (oh that it was!), but it does happen. The pattern of Scripture is that our fellowship meetings are not simply social gatherings with songs, but encounters with the living God. Just to give one example, the Apostle Paul spends some time in his first letter to the church in Corinth talking about, and encouraging, the right use of the gifts of the Spirit in corporate worship. Then he says this. 'But if all of you are prophesying, and unbelievers or people who don't understand these things come into your meeting, they will be convicted of sin, and they will be condemned by what you say. As they listen, their secret thoughts will be laid bare, and they will fall down on their knees and worship God, declaring, "God is really here among you."' (1 Corinthians 14: 24-25).

The point I want to draw your attention to, is not the specific issue of the use of prophesy, but Paul's expectation that in their meetings there was to be an overwhelming and tangible experience of God that overpowered those that were there.

The authentic spirit-filled worship of God can bring the Spirit's presence among us in a way that can be a tremendous and irreplaceable witness.

2. *Worship gives us the right perspective for witnessing*

One of the great things about worship is that it gives us a sense of proportion. By praising God, we are actually doing two things:

* On the one hand, we are saying how great God is and how wonderful and marvellous every aspect of him is. We often talk about 'lifting up' Jesus or 'magnifying' God. Both of these phrases suggest the same idea; we are to make the image and reputation of God greater. Because, in reality, God is so great, there is never any danger (as there is with human leaders) that we pass into ridiculous flattery. The more we praise human leaders, the more distant from reality we get. The more we praise God the closer we get to saying the truth.
* On the other hand, by worshipping God we are reminding ourselves that we are not remotely in the same league. He is the all-powerful God and we are merely mortal human beings made by him.

In short, what we are doing by praising God is that we are emphasising how great the difference is between him and us. Now this is profoundly helpful to our witness because, as I have been saying throughout this book, what we are about is doing God's mission, God's way, with God's power. Now can you see that the worst mistake that we can make is to blunder in and try doing God's mission *our* way with *our* power? You may have noticed how, quite frequently, to avoid this sort of stupidity I have been at pains to point out exactly how great God is and exactly how feeble we are. Now, after genuinely praising God, you and I are much less likely to make that sort of a mistake. Praising God and worshipping him is the best way I know of getting the right perspective so that witness can be done in the right way.

Incidentally, linked to this is something very helpful. If you remember, in the last chapter I said how tempting it was for us to accept the credit when the Holy Spirit did move in power. I also said how very dangerous this was; the Holy Spirit's task was to glorify Jesus, not you or me. The beauty of praise is that it makes such an attitude very hard. If you are some one who keeps praise and worship high on your agenda, then you are likely to be fairly resistant to this temptation when people are converted to Christ. Remember God can handle any amount of praise; you and are I are poisoned by even small amounts of it.

3. *Worship proclaims the victory of God*

You may also remember that, when in the last chapter I talked about healing and signs and wonders, I suggested that they were a little bit like cinema trailers for forthcoming films. Worship has a similar forward-looking function; it points ahead to the future triumph of God. If I asked you which book of the New Testament had the most about praise in it, I am fairly certain that you would not pick the book of Revelation. Worship is probably not the first thing that comes to mind when you think of that extraordinary book at the end of the Bible. Yet amid all the weird symbols and the terrible dark storm clouds of judgement, there are a number of great and glorious passages about worship that break in like sunlight. There are four main ones and the first three are to be found in Revelation 7:9-12; 11:15-19; 14:1-5. It is a shame that I do not have space to print them all, but I cannot however resist the last one.

After this, I heard the sound of a vast crowd in heaven shouting, 'Hallelujah! Salvation is from our God. Glory and power belong to him alone. His judgements are just and true. He has punished the great prostitute who corrupted the earth with her immorality, and he has avenged the murder of his servants.' Again and again their voices rang, 'Hallelujah! The smoke from that city ascends forever and forever!' Then the twenty-four elders and the four living beings fell down and worshiped God, who was sitting on the throne. They cried out, 'Amen! Hallelujah!'

And from the throne came a voice that said, 'Praise our God, all his servants, from the least to the greatest, all who fear him.'

Then I heard again what sounded like the shout of a huge crowd, or the roar of mighty ocean waves, or the crash of loud thunder: 'Hallelujah! For the Lord our God, the Almighty, reigns. Let us be glad and rejoice and honour him. For the time has come for the wedding feast of the Lamb, and his bride has prepared herself.'

Revelation 19:1-7

Now there are two points here. The first is that what we are doing in our worship meetings is something that we are going to be doing in heaven. When we praise God we are rehearsing for eternity. Praise is a foretaste of heaven. Of course we will be doing it longer, better and – from the passage above – louder. Now I think this is a witness in itself.

The second is that in praising the Father, the Son and the Spirit what we are doing is proclaiming God's triumph in the world. In praising, and especially by praising publicly, we are saying to all who can hear, that Jesus is going to win. Now I feel that this does not simply apply to the human world; I feel it has a special relevance to the demonic realm too. I am fairly certain that the Devil hates, more than anything, the celebration of his certain downfall and destruction. I think it is possibly for this reason that something like a 'March for Jesus' which takes our praise out of our buildings into the world, has a real value. By going out and publicly proclaiming the victory of God, we make it plain that Jesus Christ is ultimately the Victor. Don't ask me exactly how it works, but I am certain that as we get out and proclaim the name of Jesus there is a change in the spiritual atmosphere. Praise changes everything: streets, houses and even places of work.

4. *Worship is good for our witnessing*

Let me get personal here. Positively, praise is good for our attitude to witnessing. In praise, we look up towards God and we remember all that he is and all that he has done. Now this is very helpful for us. I have made clear, earlier in this book, that I believe our witness is to be something that is natural and that comes out of who we are and what we are. Let me make the obvious point that if you have spent time getting excited about God in praise, it is quite likely that this will bubble out later on. One of the wonderful side effects of praise is – to put it in rather a trivial way – that it re-charges the batteries of mission. Of course, that is not the point of praise; but nonetheless, it is a very useful spin-off.

Let me give you an illustration that might help. Imagine you were a public relations officer for some town and your job involved travelling around trying to attract business investment and tourism. Now, suppose that you have to go to some conference and make a presentation. Wouldn't it make a lot of sense if, just before you went, you took time to walk round some of the best bits of your town: its beauty spots, great historic sites, or recreational facilities? That way, when you got up to make your appeal for visitors or investment, your enthusiasm would be genuine. Now, in witnessing, I suggest that praise fulfils something of that role: it enthuses us.

This helps us with authentic witnessing. In fact, one of the reasons that I think people sometimes find it difficult to believe the things that we say about the Good News, is that they see so little real joy in our lives. I have little sympathy with most of the ideas of Sigmund Freud, but I remember hearing a story about him seeing a patient who tried to convince him she had a happy marriage, while all the time she was slipping her wedding ring on and off her finger. Later, when real problems surfaced, he remembered this and realised that her unconscious body language had conveyed a more accurate message than the words she had used. Much evangelism seems to be like this. We are trying to convince others of the truth of the message, but our lives are denying it. Unknown to us, we are invisibly slipping the ring on and off our own fingers. Incidentally, this is another reason why I think that non-Christians should attend our worship.

Let me say again, that we have to get excited about God. Our witness is meaningless, or even counterproductive, if it is simply cold and unenthusiastic. Indeed, the Bible does not seem to know anything of this sort of witness. And if we have to get excited about God, the best way is actually to praise him. Now, of course, in praising God we are not working ourselves up into some artificial state of excitement. Worship is not some sort of 'positive thinking' technique like the factory songs that some corporations make their workers sing together to encourage them to produce better video recorders. Our worship is simply focussing on the glorious reality of God and trying to do him justice in our words, prayers, and songs. The best witness is that which overflows naturally from a heart that has been warmed by worship.

5. *Worship motivates us to support witnessing*

If you think of a Jewish man or woman becoming a follower of Jesus in the first few decades of the church, there must have been a number of things that they would have found odd in the worship of the new religion. The most obvious difference from their old Jewish faith was the worship of Jesus as God. But another change would have been that there were no sacrifices. Of course, the reasoning for this was that the first Christians believed, as we do, that Jesus Christ himself had been the final and complete sacrifice. Now frankly – okay call me squeamish – I have never found myself nostalgic for animal sacrifices. In fact, I think I would find having to slit some animal's throat something that would take the edge off worship for me. But it is there in the Old Testament. For the Jew then, worship involved not just praise, but also sacrifice. Now, it is easy to be superior about this, yet in this messy business of sacrifices there was something important. It was the idea that it was not right to come to God, the great King, with words alone. They knew, as we do, that words are cheap. They wanted to do better, and they didn't want to come with empty hands, so they presented offerings.

This raises questions. Even accepting that Jesus is the ultimate sacrifice, are we now to offer nothing to God in our worship? Do we get off more easily in this area than people did before Christ? They, it seems, had the attitude that they ought to pay something to get an audience with God. Are we right to feel that we can get in free? The answer seems to me to be that we are still to bring offerings to God. But before Animal Rights groups blacklist me can, I say that the sacrifices are not to be animals. The Bible makes it clear that what we are to offer to God in our worship is no longer a physical sacrifice: it is to be our bodies, our lives and our actions. Paul says in Romans 12:1, 'and so dear brothers and sisters, I plead with you to give your bodies to God. Let them be a living and holy sacrifice – the kind he will accept. When you think of what he has done for you, is this too much to ask?'

I find it hard to improve on the wording of that request. God demands of us all that when we are to come to him in praise and worship we should be bringing not just words and music, but all that we have; whether it is our intelligence, our skills, our wealth, our time or our actions. We should lift them up to God and say, 'Lord you have done so much for me: I offer these to you in return. Take them and use them. It sounds painful. It is. But so was the cross.

Now it is hard to overestimate the relevance of this for mission. So often, the work of witnessing to Jesus is hindered by the fact that there are neither the people nor the resources to do the job. There are enormous possibilities for reaching people at home and overseas, but so many Christians seem to have other priorities for their time and their money.

Can I ask that the next time you come to God in worship, you seriously ask yourself what you can offer him? What will you bring him? And don't just think about money: think about all you have; think about your whole life.

Do remember the wise rule; a sacrifice is not a sacrifice if the giver doesn't even notice that they gave it.

A final thought

I believe then, that praise and witness are linked. Others agree. Listen to John Drane again; 'It is undeniable that worship and evangelism are inextricably linked together in the New Testament. Worship is the dynamic factor.' (Drane, p. 117.)

Another author, Dr William Abraham has said, 'If God is not celebrated and adored as Lord in worship, it is highly unlikely that God's rule will be celebrated and welcomed anywhere else.' (Abraham, p. 168.)

I have suggested some ways in which praise and witness are linked, but I'm sure there are others. One area that is worth exploring lies in the Old Testament. Here there is very little about evangelism as such; there are merely those wonderful hints that one day the Gentile nations will come into a relationship with God through the Jewish people. What there is however, and it is a tremendous theme, is the belief that God *will* be praised through the Gentiles. This is perhaps the greatest contribution the Old Testament brings to witness; the desire and the hope that the whole world will one day praise God (see Psalms 86:9; 102:15; Isaiah 2:1-4; 66:18-20). This is particularly the case in the Psalms; we are to praise God and praise him all over the world (see Psalms 9:11; 46:10; 105:1).

There seems to me to be no doubt that a part of our witness is to praise God. Praise is an integral part of our mission, and mission without praise will wither away. Praise is not only the best preparation *for* witness and the best response *to* it: it *is* witness.

Exercises

1. Read Exodus 20:3-4. These are the first two of the Ten Commandments. Why do you think they come first? Do these commands simply define who was to be the subject of the Israelites praises? Or are they about the focus of their lives?

2. Read Psalm 100. This is one of many psalms that centre on praise and worship.

   - What reasons are given for praising God?
   - What are the duties of those who know God?
   - What should our attitudes and emotions be?
   - Is it just Israel who is to praise God, or is there a wider command here (verse 1)?

3. Read Revelation 7:9-12; 11:15-19; 14:1-5. How do you feel about the fact that one day you will be involved in the heavenly worship? How does it affect your view of how you witness to God on this earth?

Questions

1. When your church uses the word 'worship' what is normally meant by it? Are you helped by the idea that there is both a broad 'attitude of worship' that we should always have and narrower 'acts of worship' that we perform?

2. Does your worship today cost you anything other than having to get up early on a Sunday? Would it help us to think of it as being a more sacrificial offering?

3. What do your friends and neighbours who are not believers in Christ worship by their actions and words? Do we get as excited about Jesus as our friends do about their interests? Why not?

NOTES:

John Drane, *Evangelism for a New Age* (0-551-02843-2, Marshall Pickering, 1994)

William Abraham, *The Logic of Evangelism* (0-8028-0433-0, Hodder & Stoughton, 1989)

Blaise Pascal, *Oxford Dictionary of Quotations* (OUP)/Pensées (Penguin)

Chapter 19

THE SEVENTH PILLAR: PATTERNING

DISCIPLE THEM!

Can anything follow praise? You may have thought that I should have ended the book with the last chapter. Perhaps I should, but there is one more thing that needs to be said and that is so urgent that I feel I cannot end the book without saying it.

What I have to say is this: it is not enough to lead people to Jesus Christ and then move on. We need to look after them, we need to teach them, we need to train them and we need to encourage them to share their faith as well.

Now I quite understand that it is very tempting to concentrate on evangelism. There is an excitement there, a stimulus and a challenge. Evangelism is spectacular. But conversion is merely the act of being born and for all new Christians there is a lot of growing up to do. The problem is that there can be a lot of people who turn up at the birth of new Christians and get very excited about what happens but, to continue the metaphor, not many people seem to want to stick around to change the nappies. Often, the growth of new Christians is far from being spectacular. Oh yes, it may be: as they tell their friends about Jesus, make it up with their separated partner, or decide to return stolen property back to its rightful owners. But for much of the time, spiritual growing up is just as dull, steady work as physical growing up is. Much of it is the spiritual equivalent of putting one foot in front of the other, and getting food into your mouth rather than your ear. The new Christian has to learn lots of things: to find their way around the Bible, to learn how to forgive (and to be forgiven), and how to pray. Sometimes too, it is discouraging, as the new believer slips back into old habits, makes stupid mistakes and even seems to forget that they have been born into a new life through Jesus Christ. It is precisely then, though, that we need people alongside them to help them get to their feet and move on.

At the risk of trivialising the whole matter, can I point out that neglecting people after we have brought them to Jesus Christ is not merely bad ethics, but it is also bad business practice? The best businesses will try and ensure good customer service and give a good after-sales service. The reason is simple: they want to make customers happy, so that those customers will tell others how good their cars or their video recorders are. Now that is the most down to earth of all reasons, but it is one that should not be ignored. As an evangelist I am intensely grieved when I hear of people, who having made a decision for Jesus, are then allowed to fall away and slip back into their old life style. I feel that we have failed them. Now of course, that may not be the case: it may be that the conversion was not genuine, or it may be that they deliberately chose to turn their back on all that Jesus Christ offered. Only God knows the truth of these sad cases. But the charge that is often laid against evangelical Christianity is that of emotional manipulation; of giving people some sort of spiritual high that soon evaporates, leaving them with little more than a psychological hangover. Nothing supports that rather feeble claim quite so much as people who give up the faith. 'Oh, I tried religion' you hear them say, 'but it didn't work'. What didn't work is not easy to ascertain; it certainly wasn't Jesus. But we do need to be sure that we have done all we can.

Of course, we are not in the business of selling a product, even if that product is Jesus. Remember that back in Part One I made the point that God's purposes are not just to 'save people', but to restore the whole of creation and make a new heavens and a new earth? Equally our goal is not simply to produce new Christians; it is to integrate these new Christians into the community of the church and to help them grow into becoming mature people of God.

Let me suggest that here we have three main tasks. Firstly, we need to see these Christians brought through into maturity, or at least into a level of maturity where they can be responsible for themselves. The area of spiritual maturity is a vast one, and I could write another book about it, but there are probably others who are better qualified to do so. One definition of a mature Christian is someone who is applying the truth of the Good News of Jesus Christ in every area of their life. In all that they say, do, are, and think, they belong to Jesus. An image that I have already used in another context, is to imagine our lives as houses: in one room lie our emotions, in another our ambitions, in yet another our priorities and so on. Conversion to Jesus Christ is the first step, where we open the door of our lives to Jesus Christ. This, though, is just the beginning; the real changes occur when Jesus walks through the house looking in every room and peering in every cupboard. As he does, he demands changes and sometimes we find these painful. Cherished hopes, long-held hatreds, deep hidden lusts, are all exposed and sentenced to the rubbish skip and then hopefully to the incinerator. This process of becoming more and more like Jesus is one that is only really completed by our death. No sooner have we cleaned out and repainted one room of our lives, than another needs doing. In some rooms, the reshaping and remodelling seems to have been going on for years.

Now, it is sadly quite common in churches to meet people

who suffer from the spiritual equivalent of arrested development. Spiritually, they are still very immature. This pattern occurred in the New Testament and many of the letters have sections in them devoted to the deepening, correcting, broadening and stabilising of the faith of the early Christians. And as Paul and the other writers made this maturing a priority, so ought we. Our goal, too, should be nothing less than producing mature people of God who can take a lead in churches and look after themselves.

Secondly, we need to teach believers in Jesus to be able to share the Good News themselves. As I have pointed out elsewhere in this book, that is only teaching them to be what they ought to be, normal followers of Jesus. Teaching Christians to follow Jesus has other spin-offs. One is statistical. If an evangelist can see one person brought to faith every month, then they will produce twelve Christians in one year and twenty-four in another and so one. That is fruitful growth. However, if our evangelist could train those Christians so that they themselves start producing other Christians at the same rate, then the amount of growth becomes extremely impressive as it doubles every month. You might like to try the mathematics! I make it that the entire population of Britain (some sixty million people) would be converted in two years and that of the entire world within three. Of course, such figures are hopelessly unrealistic, but you get the awesome potential of creating not just Christians, but *multiplying* Christians.

Thirdly, we need to let these new converts teach us. Now I know that this sounds a surprising thing to say but it is true. We need new converts because Christians inevitably change as they mature in their faith and get older. At the same time, the non-Christian culture around us changes. The result is an ever-widening gap between the culture and language of those of us in the churches and those people who are outside the church. Although Christians may continue to have strong commitments to evangelism, as time goes by, they can lose their rapport with the way that the non-Christian world thinks.

This reduces the effectiveness of our evangelism and, if we are not careful, we can end up being totally out of touch. New converts, in contrast, have just come from the world, so they can be effective witnesses: they still have a foot in both camps.

Now I have called the title of this chapter 'patterning', not simply because it is another word beginning with 'P'. My reason was far more important. You see it is easy enough to give new converts books, leaflets, tapes and (probably) interactive CD-ROMs with titles like 'Growing into Spiritual Maturity' and 'Now you are a Christian'. These are great resources and I do not wish to belittle them. But all the evidence suggests that people learn best and fastest by imitation. For example, you could spend weeks on a teaching programme trying to tell new believers what a Christian family ought to be like, but they could learn that (and more) in a day by being with a Christian family and watching and listening to what is said and done in some of our homes. In short, living the Christian life can be taught, but it is more easily caught. Equally, you can tell new believers how they ought to react in difficult business situations, but an example shown by someone in the workplace who has been a Christian for years can often be worth many thousands of words. We need to be patterns for Christian living. Paul, in his first letter to the Corinthians, sets himself up as a pattern for an immature church. 'I am not writing these things to shame you, but to warn you as my beloved children. For even if you had ten thousand others to teach you about Christ, you have only one spiritual father. For I became your father in Christ Jesus when I preached the Good News to you. So I ask you to follow my example and do as I do' (1 Corinthians 4:14-16).

I believe that in the days that we are living in it is especially important that we set examples for new Christians. They face difficulties that we in this country have not faced for many centuries. We are seeing people coming to faith who know nothing at all of what it is to be a Christian. You hear stories which are both exciting (and frightening), of people who come to believe in Jesus Christ, who have to be taught that lying is wrong. You hear of people who have been Christians for several months, who are unaware that Christianity makes demands over their sexual lives. Of course, it is very easy to criticise these people; but what we need to remember is that our world has changed and, in very many ways, not for the better. A hundred, fifty or even twenty-five years ago, people who were converted in this country came from a Christian cultural background; they were – to use a technical term – nominal Christians. These people knew, more or less, what was expected of them as practising Christians: they had read at least bits of the Bible, they had picked up from school, books and their culture some sort of understanding of what Christians stood for. When they were converted these people could, to some extent, be left on their own to get on with the business of being a Christian.

Now what we are seeing is the conversion of people who are effectively 'pagans' and that raises new challenges. Many, perhaps most of them, will not understand things that most of us have always taken for granted. We have to lay down new foundations and deal with things in a new way. Those of us who teach in church settings, need to be aware that much of the language that we use will be unfamiliar to new Christians. Many of our new believers will not know that there are two Testaments, most will be uncertain about even the most rudimentary facts about God, and almost all will have only the sketchiest of ideas of what they are expected to do now that they have invited Jesus into their lives. The result is that there has never been a greater demand for teaching on how to live the Christian life, and there has never been a greater demand for patterning the way to live it.

I want to make some brief practical suggestions for churches here:

- Whenever you think about doing any sort of evangelism in a church setting simultaneously think about what you're going to do for those who will come through to faith. I do not care what you call it: a 'discipleship programme,' 'Beta', 'From Now On', 'Follow Up' or whatever. But have something, and not as an afterthought. Even if you do not have a specific programme of evangelism planned, you still ought to have someone in your church who is responsible for developing a ministry for new Christians. One reason for doing this is that people who are gifted at evangelism are often, not so gifted at follow-up. In fact, there can sometimes be problems when new believers realise that their friend who brought them to Christ is now making new friends with non-Christians and seems to have lost interest in them.

- Be prepared to forgive. Most new Christians mess up at some stage or another, some times badly. This need not be fatal, after all there are many cases in the Bible of people who made spectacular mistakes but who God used later (Moses, Peter, John Mark, etc). What can be fatal however, is if this is so badly handled that the new believer thinks that they have fallen beyond recovery and give up. New believers (and maybe the rest of us) need to know two things. First, that God does expect us to live up to his standards and secondly, that when we fail and turn to him in repentance and faith he is ready to forgive and restore us. We need to mirror that in our churches and home groups. What we are asking new Christians to do is a public tightrope walk; the least we can do is to provide them with a safety net.

- Identify people within your church who you think are gifted at being able to model or pattern the Christian life for new converts. They don't, of course, have to be exactly in the same culture; in fact, as mature Christians, by definition, they will not be. There is no reason why, for example, a single retired woman with the right attitude may not be able to successfully help a single woman twenty years younger. The key things are an ability to identify with them, a willingness to get alongside, a refusal to be shocked and a desire to serve Jesus. Plus, of course, a lot of love. Without reinventing the Roman Catholic confessional, there is also a lot to be said for this relationship being one of openness and accountability. Our new Christians may need to be able to admit that they have messed up and this is, perhaps, the safest setting for this to happen in.

- Work to put together appropriate structures for new believers and particularly at making them accepted in church communities. In addition to the more formal mentoring or discipling type of relationship I have talked about above, I think it is a very good policy for mature Christians in our fellowships to develop close relationships with these new believers. It is particularly important that Christian families, as far as possible, try to 'adopt' some of these 'baby' believers, befriend them, have them round for meals and so on. Producing working marriages and families is tough enough and if you've never had a decent model to imitate – and increasingly new converts have not – it's even tougher.

- Finally, and I realise that this is a risky thing, be prepared to try and use them. Stretch them, encourage them to get involved, give them responsibilities, and treat them seriously. Now of course some people will come with so much baggage and so many problems that they will need special care and attention. But there are those to whom conversion to Christ occurs in such a way that it is as if everything has clicked into place. They hit the ground running and they are willing to apply a great deal of determination and effort to the process of becoming more like Christ. If so, then take risks with them and try to get their gifts developed.

- Oh and pray for them. You will be aware of the concept of infant mortality and the fact that young children are particularly vulnerable. The same is true of new Christians. I have heard it said that the first year is critical in setting the pattern for the rest of someone's Christian life, and I can believe it. Please do commit these new believers to God in prayer on regular basis.

Now, by saying these things it may sound as if I am making new Christians out to be liabilities and burdens to churches. I suppose in a way they are, just as new babies are burdens in families. But actually – just like children – they are a delight. People who come out of the darkness of pagan environments into the light of the Good News of Jesus Christ bring tremendous gifts with them. They have zeal, joy, enthusiasm and a questioning attitude ('why do you do this?') that is badly needed.

Please value your new converts. Encourage them, strengthen them and love them. And above all, pattern the Christian life for them.

Exercises

1. Read Matthew 28:16-20. What does Jesus command his disciples to do in the world? What things are they to teach the new believers?

2. Read 1 Timothy 4:12, 2 Timothy 1:13 and 2:2. In what areas of life is Timothy to set an example?

3. Read Philippians 4:8-9. What is Paul's desire for these Christians? In what ways has be provided a pattern for them? Did he believe in just producing converts?

Questions

1. Why does the church need evangelism and patterning? Why isn't it enough just to constantly produce new converts?

2. How important to people are examples rather than mere instructions?

3. Think of a friend of yours who you are praying for to become a Christian. If they did, what steps would you want them to take so that they could grow in Christ?

4. Is your life in the sort of state that you would want it to be a pattern for a new Christian? Why not?

A FINAL WORD

This has been a long book and in it, we have covered a very large topic. That is hardly surprising. After all, if calling out is so central to who God is and if it is central to all we should be, then it is inevitable that all sorts of matters should have arisen.

But, before closing, I want to say one last thing. I hope that you have agreed with at least some of what you have read here. If you haven't agreed with it then I would say this: would you examine why and where you disagree? Examine the Bible, think through carefully what it says and challenge yourself. There are doubtless things that I should have said that I haven't and there are probably things that I have said that could have been expressed better. I apologise for both.

If you have agreed that calling out the Good News of Jesus ought to be central to who we are and what we are; I would like to leave you with one final question. (I don't want you to answer it hastily because I do not believe that it is a question that I alone ask; I believe it is one that God asks through me. This question is addressed, not to your friends, not to your wife or husband, not to your church, but to you.) It is this:

What are you going to do about it?

APPENDIX

SOME ANSWERS TO HARD QUESTIONS

In his first letter, Peter says this: 'And if you are asked about your Christian hope, always be ready to explain it' (1 Peter 3.15). From this, I gather that asking Christians questions about their faith has a long history. Equally, seekers deserve more than a shrug of the shoulders and the statement 'just believe it'.

I must have had tens of thousands of questions thrown at me over the years. Out of that number, perhaps a dozen questions have surfaced again and again. What I want to do here is very briefly sketch out the sort of answers I might give to some of these questions.

- These are just outline answers. What I *could* say would stretch on for pages and all of these questions have had books written on them.
- In some cases, I have hinted at the answers in the main body of the book.
- The precise answer, and the tone you deliver it in, depends on the setting and the questioner. There is all the difference in the world between some question hurled out in a club such

as 'Er mate, wot about aliens then, eh?' and some clearly deep-felt question on suffering.
- In addition to the answers that I give, do note *how* I try and answer the question. For example in the first one ('Is Jesus God?') a simple 'yes' answer, although true, is misleading. You need to unpack what they mean by 'God'. Do however be wary of too much use of the phrase 'it depends what you mean'. But bouncing the question back has two other values; it forces them to think and it gives you time to think.
- It is often how you answer, rather than what you answer, that counts. The onlookers (and possibly the questioners) will be watching to see how you field the question. Are you, they are asking, at ease with hard questions? Or was your talk all words?

Let me begin with questions about Jesus.

1. *Was Jesus God?*

Before we answer such a question with a 'yes', we have to first clarify what people understand by the word *God*. When people tell me that they don't believe in God, I often ask them which God they don't believe in. I push them to describe him, her or it. The answers they give are very illuminating. Often they describe God as some distant figure, existing far away from the world and only really concerned with catching people out, and rewarding the religious, while condemning the rest of humanity to a fiery hell. Of course, such a God is an irrelevant, unjust and completely imaginary person. He bears more resemblance to a rather psychopathic Father Christmas than to the God of the Bible.

When people describe to me this kind of God my reply is 'We've got so much in common – I don't believe in that God either!' This answer surprises them and puts you on their side. You see, if people ask 'Was Jesus God?' and have in their minds such a picture of who or what they believe God to be, it would be ridiculous (and actually blasphemous) to try and identify Jesus with such a God.

What we need to ask is 'Who is this Jesus?' I believe that when people have taken time to read the accounts of Jesus' life by those who lived alongside him and who gave their lives to implementing what he stood for, they will not be able to resist the fact that he was more than just an extraordinary man. In terms of his character, his wisdom, his integrity, his love and his kindness he was unique, but it is inescapable that he also believed that not only was he the embodiment of what was best about humans, but that he is actually the unique, complete and final expression of who God is.

So I suggest that what we have to do then is not come to Jesus with our already formulated ideas about who God is, but to ask 'What kind of God do I meet in Jesus?' The God who Jesus reveals is different from any God we could create. This God is loving and caring and is like a father whose joy in life comes from having his children around him. He is one who knows the number of hairs on our head, one who heals and calms us, one who saves us, one who promises us life forever with him and one who wants to be a constant presence with us. The thing to wonder at is not how God came among us in Jesus, but who this God is, what he offers, what he demands and what he wants to be for us.

2. *Isn't the resurrection a myth?*

The resurrection is the central pivotal event in all Christianity. Without it there would be no church, no Christianity, no continued remembrance of Jesus. Everything pivots on this event.

Now we all know that death is not something you can be cured of, or recover from. No one ever has a mild case of death. When someone dies they stay dead and this is something that the writers of the Bible would have known too. After all, there was a lot of death around in those days and some of it was pretty public. So when the dead, lifeless body of Jesus was taken down from the cross on which he was hanged, outside the city wall of Jerusalem, and carried to a tomb [*note*: or 'grave', what word I'd use would depend on who I was talking to], no-one expected to see him again. The Romans weren't just efficient in road building; they knew how to kill men who were deemed a danger to state security. The tomb was sealed and that was the end of this failed messiah. Jesus was history: for the Romans, for the Jewish leaders, for the disciples. That was it. End. *Finito*.

But just three days later the tomb was empty. There was nothing there apart from the graveclothes. There was no other explanation for where the missing body might be. But Jesus' followers, the eleven closest to him, as well as those who were less close, were soon giving testimony that this same Jesus was alive. He had appeared to them in locked rooms, on walks along the road, in conversations in gardens, and at meals on the beach. They had met with Jesus and were confident that it was no ghost or vision. They had touched him, talked with him, listened to him and fully encountered him. They were all in agreement: he had risen.

The New Testament is full of the evidence that Jesus had risen. It shows this both in direct and indirect claims.

The *direct claims* are impressive. All four gospels state that Jesus rose from the dead. The nature of these accounts encourages belief that they are accounts of genuine events. There are little, almost irrelevant points, that must be eyewitness details such as the 'other disciple' outrunning Peter in John 20:4. There are also things that would have been an embarrassment to the early church: the doubts and fears of the disciples and the fact that the first appearance was to women when the testimony of women was invalid under Jewish law. There are even the apparent minor contradictions (was there one angel or two at the tomb?) that all eye-witness accounts have, but which would surely have been edited out if these had been made up. Above all, these accounts do not read like the stuff of legends; there are no awesome dramatic appearances of vast angelic choirs, no blinding lights. Other direct claims occur throughout the New Testament letters and in some ways, these are even more impressive, because these documents are earlier than the gospel accounts. For example in 1 Corinthians 15, Paul spells out in detail the reality and the importance of the resurrection. Yet, most experts agree that this was written in AD 53-55; barely two decades after the event.

The *indirect evidence* is even more compelling. Let me give one example. Everybody is in agreement that the earliest statement of Christian belief was 'Jesus is Lord'. Now this is a meaningless statement unless Jesus was, in fact, alive. There are indirect references – if not direct ones – to Jesus being raised from the dead on almost every page of the last twenty-three books of the New Testament. There is just no way that you can remove the concept of the resurrection from the New Testament. An equally strong piece of evidence is the existence of the church itself. The explosive growth of the belief that, in this obscure Jewish carpenter and his shameful death, God was directly intervening in the world is hard to explain unless there was a resurrection.

Something brought about an astonishing change in the psychology, circumstances and beliefs of the disciples so that they just had to share the Good News. We know that Christian communities had spread as far as Rome within twenty years of Jesus' death. The most obvious explanation as to what performed the change is, frankly, the claimed one; Jesus had risen.

Of course, dead people do not, in our experience, rise from the dead. But then Jesus life and teaching shows that he was a unique person, unlike anyone before or after him. That such a unique person should have a unique fate after death doesn't seem too surprising. In fact, if you believe that death is the result of sin and that Jesus was without sin, then the resurrection is not simply acceptable; it is a logical necessity (see Acts 2:24).

If you have already come to the conclusion that dead men

can't rise, then the resurrection will be something that God
cannot do. But is God so limited? Is it possible that your belief
that the dead cannot be raised is blinding you to the possibility
that here it did happen?

I suggest you look at the evidence carefully both from the
gospels and the letters of the New Testament. But if you believe
you have disproved it, or can show it didn't happen, then please
let me know as soon as possible. If that is the case, everything I
live for, speak for and work for, is in vain.

[*Note*: the evidence for the resurrection is extremely strong
and there are several lines for a possible answer. Good books
are *Evidence That Demands a Verdict*, Josh McDowell; *Easter
Enigma*, John Wenham and *The Weekend That Changed the
World*: *The Mystery of Jerusalem's Empty Tomb*, Peter
Walker]

3. *Don't all religions lead to God?*

The modern idea that all religions lead to God is, on the surface,
a very attractive one. We don't have to say anybody is wrong
and we can be wonderfully tolerant to everybody. Yet when we
examine it, this idea proves to be fatally flawed. It raises two
questions:

- Firstly, do we really mean *all* religions? What about those
  that involve human sacrifice? Or those that involve ritual
  child abuse? No, of course not, comes the answer. But the
  moment we say that, we have made a judgement, and what
  basis have we got for doing that? In practice, no one believes
  that *all* religions lead to God, only that some do. Christianity
  just narrows that further.
- Secondly, how can the beliefs of differing religions be
  logically compatible when they are so much at odds with
  each other? At a basic level, in some religions there is one
  god, in other religions many gods and in some religions, no
  god at all. These differences occur in ethics too: for instance,

some religions demand that animals are not killed, while others allow murder. They don't look to be going the same way to me.

Christians believe that, while there may be elements of truth and insight in all religions, the final and complete truth about God is only found in Jesus Christ. After all, Jesus is God made flesh, and in him we are shown the true nature and character of God. But Jesus is not just the revelation of God's truth to humanity: he is the one – the only one – who saves us. In Jesus, God has paid for the sin of all, he has acted to die for all, paid the price for all and been judged in the place of us all. The Bible is clear, Jesus is the way, the truth and life and there is no other name given to people by which we can be saved. This salvation cannot be earned through doing good things, it can't be achieved by religious devotion, practices, observance or any effort of our own; it is a gift of God's free and kind grace. It becomes ours when we have faith in him, rather than in ourselves, in others or in any other scheme.

If you understand that, you can see that it is very hard for Christians to say that all religions are going the same way. For us, God has intervened directly in the world in a once and for all way, in Jesus. Now in saying this Christians do not – or should not – feel proud or superior. We believe that it is not us who have found God; it is God who has found us.

One result of this is that Christians have always felt obliged to tell others about Jesus. We would have a quieter life if we didn't. Instead, we feel obliged to say to people everywhere that, in Jesus Christ, God shows how much he loves them and us. If we seek to follow Jesus, then our task is to communicate God's love to this world. What he has asked us to do is spread the news about Jesus and leave the rest to him.

4. *If God is a God of love, how can he send people to hell?*

Rightly, this question affirms that God is a God of love. The good news of Christianity is that God loves those he created so much that he desires them to live in his presence forever. God made no one in vain, and made everyone in his image and with the potential for an intimate eternal relationship with himself. So Paul says in 1 Timothy 2:3-4 'Pray this way for kings and all others who are in authority, so that we can live in peace and quietness, in godliness and dignity. This is good and pleases God our Saviour, for he wants everyone to be saved and to understand the truth.' God desires each one of us intimately, personally, passionately and eternally.

In Jesus, God made his desire crystal clear, as he came as one of us, to live for us, die for us, and rise again to new life for us. In Jesus, God has paid for the salvation of all, has paid the price for everyone's sin and has been punished in the place of everyone. He has taken the judgement that we have all brought on ourselves. 'Whatever we do, it is because Christ's love controls us. Since we believe that Christ died for everyone, we also believe that we have all died to the old life we used to live' (2 Corinthians 5:14). So, as far as I see it, God chooses us, all of us, in Jesus. No one is excluded from his offer of salvation; the gift is for everyone. God has, if you like, said 'Yes' to everyone. The question is, what people will do with the invitation? It demands a response. Will people say 'Yes' to God's 'yes'? Will they accept what Jesus has done, or will they dismiss it, and go on living apart from him, without his help? Jesus demands a response. Paul says this, 'He died for everyone so that those who receive his new life will no longer live to please themselves. Instead, they will live to please Christ, who died and was raised for them' (2 Corinthians 5:15).

To those who say 'No' and live that 'no', the choice has already been made. People can choose to live for themselves, or for him who died for them. But if they choose for themselves, at the end of their earthly life God will, I'm afraid, not impose on them what they did not want. If someone has chosen to be separate from God, God will honour that decision. If they have said 'No' to God he will simply let them reap the fruit of that decision.

The question of what happens to those who say 'No' to God is a very complex one. There is a strong debate going on at the present time as to the nature of hell. What is clear is that hell is a place where there is no good thing. All good things are gifts from God: peace, hope, joy, even humour and patience. In this world, you can reject God and – to some extent – keep his gifts; in the next, there will be no such option. Hell is a terrifying and hopeless eternity without God and without his gifts. In this way of looking at it, hell is essentially self-inflicted. But it is no less terrible for that.

[*Note*: You might want to re-read my comments on hell in Chapter 8].

5. *Why does God allow suffering?*

This a difficult question because there can never be any easy or glib answers when it comes to suffering. It hurts too much. The part of the Bible that really addresses the issue of suffering is the book of Job in the Old Testament. Job is a man who has a really hard time of it and suffers to the extent of losing family and friends, possessions, security and health. His three friends come to visit him and in Job 2: 11-13 we are told: 'When they heard of the tragedy he had suffered, they got together and travelled from their homes to comfort and console him. When they saw Job from a distance, they scarcely recognised him. Wailing loudly, they tore their robes and threw dust into the air over their heads to demonstrate their grief. Then they sat on the ground with him for seven days and nights. And no one said a word, for they saw that his suffering was too great for words.'

The first response to the plight of any suffering is compassion and silence. Actually, in the book of Job, the trouble actually comes when the friends open their mouths.

The second response would probably be to point out what we all know deep inside us – things aren't supposed to be this way. God didn't make the world or its inhabitants for suffering and pain. The first chapter of the Bible paints a wonderful picture of the world as it was originally created, and over everything, we read God's proclamation 'it was good'. The problems come when human beings decide to do things their way instead of God's way. And as that happens, huge complications and malfunctions enter: if you go against the grain, you get splinters. It is not that humans are being punished, but that they now have to bear the consequences of choosing against God. Everything is now out of sync. In this way, all suffering, pain, tragedy and agony are the consequences of our choosing against God. Suffering and tragedy affect everybody, to different degrees, and in an indiscriminate way. There is very rarely a direct correlation between someone's suffering and things they have done themselves. The reason for this is that our rebellion has effects that are wider than just ourselves. The fall out of this is to bring suffering on ourselves, on those following us, on animals and on the whole of creation. Children suffer from the selfishness of parents, friends suffer from the sins of friends, strangers suffer for the sin of strangers and communities suffer because of the sin of other communities. The principle is true for races, countries and continents. We all suffer the effects of the selfishness of others.

The Bible tells us of a God who, instead of being removed from the suffering of the people, hears our cries and comes to strengthen us and help us to continue to trust in him. The God of the Bible is someone who grieves over the suffering that the world brings on itself, as we suffer under the consequences of our decision to turn away from God. What is more, in Jesus, God himself came within our human condition and suffered: cruelly, unjustly, terribly and alone. So he knows what its like from the inside. We worship a suffering God.

But in this suffering, God has not simply entered into the human condition, he has acted to save us from it, to transform it and to redeem it. In his life and work, Jesus went round proclaiming the Kingdom of God: the rule of God that would bring salvation – which means 'wholeness'. Jesus brought evidence of the kind of wholeness that this Kingdom consists of by healing people, feeding the hungry, making the blind see, the lame walk and raising the dead. On his cross, notice was served on evil and suffering, and by his resurrection, the new future of the Kingdom of God was opened up and proved to be a reality. In that is the promise that, one day, God will wrap up human history and the victory of the cross and resurrection will be fully realised. The promise of the Bible is that God's future is one where suffering and evil have no place. At the end of the Bible we read this: 'I heard a loud shout from the throne, saying, "Look, the home of God is now among his people! He will live with them, and they will be his people. God himself will be with them. He will remove all of their sorrows, and there will be no more death or sorrow or crying or pain. For the old world and its evils are gone forever." And the one sitting on the throne said, "Look, I am making all things new!"' (Revelation 21:3-5).

Until that time, we are acutely aware of the pain of this present age. However, God is with us to strengthen us, to bring us hope, and to give us evidences and signs of his healing. It is always right to pray that God bring his healing, but we must allow God to do that in whatever way he sees fit.

[*Note*: There are numerous books on this. I have found three very helpful. *How Long O Lord?* by D. A. Carson and *The Problem of Pain* and *A Grief Observed* both by C. S. Lewis]

6. *Is the Bible true?*

Again, this is a question where I would urge whoever the questioner is to be clear on what they mean. If by *true* they mean that they think it can be read as if it were a twenty-first century non-fiction book such as an encyclopaedia then the answer is 'not quite'. It's not that the Bible isn't true; it's just that our ideas on what a 'true book' looks like are a bit different from those who wrote and compiled the Bible. We take 'true' to mean that the words have a precise, literal, absolute and unchangeable meaning. That is not how they are used in the Bible.

Let me give you an example. At the end of Genesis 41, if you look at the text literally it says, 'And all the world came to Egypt to Joseph to buy corn'. Now I suppose you could take that literally and imagine people trekking from all the continents to Egypt, but I don't know anybody who does, and most Bible translations tone down the words. What the writer meant, of course, is that from his perspective, it seemed that everybody from all the lands was there. We use similar loose expressions in speech. We might say of a party that 'everybody was there', or even, 'the whole world was there'. No one would accuse us of being a liar if we said something like that it. Now the language of the Bible is like the way we speak rather than the way we write; it uses a lot of images and phrases.

It is not a modern textbook and doesn't use the same conventions. It is actually rather arrogant of us to take our western, twenty-first century criteria for books and apply them to the past. No one would now criticise, for instance, a modern African author because he or she failed to conform to our western way of writing. It is equally unfair to expect someone in the past to have written the way we do now.

Above all, we need to take the writings in the Bible in the sense that the author meant. That, of course, means recognising that there are different styles of writing (poetry, history, prophecy, etc). If we make these allowances for language and culture, then yes, what the Bible says is true.

It is certainly *trustworthy*, which may be a more helpful word than 'true' here. By that, I mean it that it can be relied on and will not mislead. Take a road map. Road maps are not literally true: in mine, motorways are shown as being blue and about half a mile wide. Yet they are trustworthy for the purpose they are written: getting you from A to B.

7. *Isn't the Bible full of contradictions?*

[*Note*: This follows on from the previous question and the answer in some ways overlaps].

I find that the best place to start with this kind of question is to ask the person what particular contradictions they had in mind. Often you'll find that they haven't read anything of the Bible and have merely heard something obscure, perhaps on a television programme, which they are regurgitating. You can always give them a Bible and ask them just where the contradictions are. It might be that they take it home and read it! In fact, most contradictions in the Bible are best called 'apparent contradictions'. At the moment, we do not know whether they are real or whether they are just an illusion caused by inadequate data. Let me give you an example. Imagine that in the future only fragmentary data has survived from our era. Two documents exist. Document A, talks about a Winston Churchill who was a Conservative leader, while in Document B, Winston Churchill is referred to as a Liberal MP. On the basis that you cannot be both, a contradiction is claimed. Anyway, you can imagine the allegations. In fact, Churchill was a Liberal MP for some years before changing party allegiance. With more data, the contradiction vanishes. It was apparent, not real. Now I suggest that many of the biblical problems could be resolved if we had better data. But bearing in mind that many of the historical parts of the Bible have been demonstrated to be accurate, we are best off presuming that these discrepancies will be resolved. I think the Bible deserves to be held innocent until it is proved guilty!

But behind this lies a misunderstanding about the Bible. As Christians, we believe the Bible is the Word of God. But it is not the Word of God in the sense that a Muslim for instance would use the term for the Koran. For a Muslim, the Koran is the Word of God because they believe that God dictated it through the hand of the true prophet Mohammed. Mohammed was merely the muscles that moved the pen, and he had no say in what went into the Koran.

Now Christians have a different view of how God relates to human beings. We do not believe that God used the writers of the Bible by overruling their backgrounds and cultures so that they dictated just what he wanted. The Christian view is subtler; it is that God worked through people to say what he wanted to say. The result is that the words of the Bible are still inspired, but they reflect the personality, background and culture of the individual writers. Now when we accept this, we can see that the Bible is not simply one book. It is an account of the history of God's actions in our world, from the creation, to the forthcoming transformation of the universe when Jesus returns. It was written by various authors, from various viewpoints in various styles. It is a whole library of books.

Now if we simply approach the Bible as we might the *Radio Times*, for instance, or the *Encyclopaedia Britannica*, or even a car manual, we will find it rather puzzling. Instead, we must approach it as the unique book it is. Taken as a whole, the Bible tells of a God who is, not full of contradictions but, one who speaks rightly, who acts truthfully and who is someone we can stake our lives on.

[*Note*: There are great books published to help us understand the Bible. If someone is interested in researching and learning about the breadth and insight of the Bible, a book I would wholeheartedly recommend is *Reading The Bible For All It's Worth*, by Gordon Fee].]

8. *Hasn't science proved that God doesn't exist?*

[*Note*: this sort of question comes in various forms; 'science versus creation', 'evolution versus God', 'can we seriously believe in a six-day creation?' and so on.]

The Bible is not a science book. Neither is it one of the books that the Victorians used to love, with titles like, *Seek Within for Answers to Everything*. This means that sometimes the questions that we come to the Bible with, do not fall within its scope. Sometimes people ask about what the Bible has to say about the European Union, or dieting, dinosaurs, football matches or hairstyles! These questions, although perhaps important for us, are not the ones that the Bible actually seeks to answer. So, what is vital is that we ask the right questions of the book. This is especially true in terms of things like creation.

The key approach when looking at any book of the Bible is to understand what the writer(s) who wrote it meant, and why they wrote it. The Bible is a library of books rather than a single volume and the briefest flip through its pages reveals that there is history and poetry, songs and proverbs, laws and biography, letters and predictions, wisdom and prophecy. We have to treat each book of the Bible with integrity and with due consideration of its role within the Bible.

Genesis deals with the beginnings of our world. It does not set out to answer the scientific questions that many seek to ask today. [*Note*: I have touched on the issue of cultural arrogance in Question 6]. It is not concerned with the timescale on which the world came into being and is not bothered with the intricacies of how or when? Because of this, it is my opinion that, to have an argument about whether God created the world in six twenty-four-hour time periods, is to completely miss the truth of what these chapters say.

Equally, it is not a question of either evolution *or* the God of the Bible. As far as I understand it, Genesis certainly doesn't rule out evolution as a mechanism through which God worked. After all, God is in charge of every thing that happens. It does tell us that it was God, not some principle of nature, that caused the universe and all living things to come into being.

These chapters are some of the richest and most important in the Christian faith, and we would do well to hear what they do have to say to us, rather than getting side-tracked into what they do not say. The real purpose of Genesis is to communicate the truth that God made the world and that he made it good. These chapters speak to us of a free God, who doesn't have to create, but does so because he desires to. They tell us that, while God and the world are separate, God is not far away. He is the sustainer and upholder of all creation. The fingerprints of this generous and creative God are seen all over his creation.

What we really need to do is not, come to the Bible with our predetermined questions, but let the Bible teach us, address us and perhaps even ask us questions.

[*Notes*: There are many good books (and a few truly terrible ones) on the complex Science and Faith debate. What you read depends on your scientific background. Recent good books at high level of science and Christianity are: *Science and Theology: an Introduction*, John Polkinghorne, SPCK 1998; *Science and Religion: an Introduction*, Alister E McGrath, Blackwell 1999; and *Questions of Science*, Andrew Barton, Kingsway 1999. There are also lots of resources at the web site of *Christians in Science* http://www.cis.org.uk].

9. *Can a Christian have doubts?*

The short answer is 'Yes'. Now, I am very clear that Christians should have questions. As far as I see it, we should always be questioning and seeking to understand the Christian faith more. We should be striving for more wisdom and insight.

Doubts, however, are something else. All Christians, to differing degrees, will have doubts on different matters concerning their faith. Often, these doubts can be as to whether God is really present with us through our darkest hours, and whether we really are loved and saved by him. What is important in times of doubt is that we focus our beliefs, not on our own capacity to believe, but on the truth of what the Bible communicates to us. For example, I might doubt my worth in God's eyes, I might believe that God could not really be concerned with me. But in this scenario, my feelings are not a reliable guideline as to what the truth of the gospel is.

I believe that this is why Jesus, in one of his most famous stories, encouraged men and women to build their lives, not on their feelings, but on his words. He said that if we build our lives on his words we would be like those who built our houses on a solid foundation of rock. But if we didn't, it would be as if we were constructing a house on sand (Matthew 7:24-27). Only the house built on rock would last.

In this story, Jesus assumes that there will be storms in our lives, but encourages us to build our lives on his word. If you are having doubts, or you know someone who is, I believe that Jesus would encourage you to hear his words and to trust them. Often, in times of doubt, people give up on church and they give up on talking to others. I would always encourage those who feel they are in a time of doubting to stick in there with church, and try to talk it through with Christians that they know and trust.

10. *Isn't the church full of hypocrites?*

The sharp and deadly one line response to this is 'Yes, but don't worry; we can always find space for one more.' A safer answer might be along the following lines. *Hypocrite* was a word originally used for an actor who played two parts in a play. It has come to mean someone who says one thing and does another. So you see, in one sense, we are all hypocrites – we all do things that are the opposite of what we say we want to. Hypocrisy is a disease that each member of the human race suffers from. And as much as we might want to, there is nothing that we can do to help ourselves. As the apostle Paul confessed frankly, ' I don't understand myself at all, for I really want to do what is right, but I don't do it. Instead, I do the very thing I hate. I know perfectly well that what I am doing is wrong, and my bad conscience shows that I agree that the law is good. But I can't help myself, because it is sin inside me that makes me do these evil things' (Romans 7:15-17).

That's why we all need saving. And we need saving by someone who is different, someone who hasn't got the same problem of hypocrisy that we have. Jesus is the only person who was never a hypocrite. He did what he said and said what he did. He told his followers to turn the other cheek when they were struck; which is what he himself did. He told them to love their enemies and forgive those who ill-treated them, which is exactly what he did. Jesus, the most true, faithful and honest man who ever lived, died for we hypocrites. He died for us to forgive us and to make us into people of integrity. Consequently, words like *holiness*, *in the likeness of Christ*, *purity* and *faithfulness* are all used to describe Christians in the New Testament.

It is, of course, a huge shame that there is hypocrisy in the church. But can I remind you that it is not the church that offers salvation, it is Jesus Christ and it is to him alone that we bear witness.

11. *Does it matter what you believe as long as you are sincere?*

This view is widely held by people that I talk to today. They have no trouble with my being a Christian, but just don't see that what I believe should affect them. It is one of the biggest signs of the individualism of the age.

Yet, it is a strange question because it obviously *does* matter what you believe. Let's say I go to my local train station because I believe that I can get a train from Chorleywood direct to Newcastle. Now I might really believe that I can get a train to Newcastle, but actually, I'll be waiting all day, all week and all month. No trains go from Chorleywood to Newcastle. However much I might believe that they do, makes no difference. I can be sincere, but sincerely wrong.

Linked to this question – and possibly lying behind it – is the idea that what I am doing by appealing to people to become Christians is asking them to take some blind leap of faith. This needs examining. Of course, belief is not a peculiarity of Christians. We all actually exercise belief or faith in many areas of life, even in things we do not understand. When I fly, I have faith in aerodynamics; when I switch on the television, I trust in electronics. In my case, both of these are examples of something that is pretty much blind faith. I suspect I am not alone here. In fact, it is hard to prove anything at all. I mean, can you prove you exist?

What is important, however, is that we exercise an appropriate level of faith. I would not, for instance, trust a drunk driver to get me home and I would not trust my six-year-old son Benjamin to do our week's shopping. To do that would not be faith, it would be stupidity. In fact, most of us trust something, or someone, because we have evidence that faith is a suitable response. I fly, because the evidence suggests that it is a worthwhile risk; I switch the TV on because I have never come across anybody who has been electrocuted doing that. My faith in both cases is reasonable. So we can apply these general ideas on belief to belief in God:

- Firstly, a belief, however strong, doesn't make something true.
- Secondly, we need to have appropriate faith. There is no point in trusting something or someone beyond their capacity to deliver.
- Thirdly, a reasonable faith needs is one that has something to base itself on.

Now, from all that I have tried to set out in this book, I have endeavoured to show that Christianity isn't a 'take it or leave it' business. It is not a reckless leap of faith off a fifty-storey building. 'Just believe' is not a Christian statement.

God has asked us to take a whole-hearted and irreversible step of faith in Jesus as our Lord and Saviour. But he has left us evidence to encourage us to do that. The character and person of Jesus indicate that he is trustworthy: the claims of Jesus are verified by historical events and two thousand years of Christians have found him to be someone they can trust with their lives. In short, it is entirely reasonable to become a Christian.

And finally ...

In Part Three, I suggested three very useful answers to use
when you are stuck with difficult questions. Let me repeat them
here. I would suggest that you try to keep them in reserve for
when all else has failed you. The possible answers are:

- 'I'm sorry, I don't know the answer to that. What I will do
  though is read up on it and also ask someone who might
  know the answer. And I'll get back to you.' Of course when
  you say that, do what you promised. Wrong answers or
  ignorance may not put people off Christianity, but broken
  promises do.
- 'I'm sorry, I don't know the answer to that. But does it mean
  a lot to you?' The advantage of this answer is that it
  continues the conversation and gets them to open up. You
  may actually find out that the real concern is not what they
  said but actually something else.
- 'That's a good question and I'm sure it has an answer, but let
  me ask you one in return. If I *could* answer your question,
  would you become a follower of Jesus?' All too often they
  will look sheepish at this point because you have caught
  them out; the issue is not that of the mind, it is of the will.
  Mind you, it can be a bit heavy: use this one gently. And
  don't forget the loving them bit.

BIBLIOGRAPHY

Alpha Course Manual (1-8988-3800-3, Holy Trinity Brompton)
William Abraham, *The Logic of Evangelism (0-8028-0433-0,*
Hodder & Stoughton, 1989)
Andrew Barton, *Questions of Science* (0-8547-6779-7,
Kingsway, 1999)
D A Carson, *How Long O Lord?/Reflections on Suffering*
(0-8511-1584-5, IVP)
John Drane, *Evangelism for a New Age* (0-551-02843-2,
Marshall Pickering, 1994)
Gordon D Fee and Douglas Stewart, *How to read the Bible for
all its Worth* (0-8620-1974-5, Scripture Union)
Jill Johnstone, *You Can Change the World* (1-8507-8108-7,
OM Publishing)
Patrick Johnstone, *Operation World* (1-8507-8120-6, OM
Publishing)
C. S. Lewis, *A Grief Observed* (0-5710-6624-0, Faber)
C. S. Lewis, *The Problem of Pain* (0-0062-8093-5, Fount)
Josh McDowell, *Evidence That Demands a Verdict*
(0-7852-4219-8,Thomas Nelson, 1999)
Alister E McGrath, *Science and Religion: an Introduction*
(Blackwell, 1999)
Janet Morley (Desmond Tutu), *Bread of Tomorrow/Praying
With The Poor* (0-2810-4559-3, SPCK)

Blaise   Pascal,   *Oxford   Dictionary   of   Quotations*
(OUP)/*Pensées* (Penguin)
John Polkinghorne, *Science and Theology* (0-2810-5176-3,
SPCK, 1998)
Peter Walker, *The Weekend That Changed The World*
(0-5510-3135-2,Marshall Pickering)
John Wenham, *Easter Enigma* (0-8536-4765-8, Paternoster
Press).

If you would like to know more about the Ministry of J. John, or order books and resources, please contact:

The Philo Trust
60 Quickley Lane
Chorleywood
Herts
WD3 5AF

01923 286286
01923 286186 (F)

or email us – admin@philotrust.com

The Philo Trust is the charity which supports the Ministry of J. John. The word Philo is Greek for brotherly love.

The Philo Trust was launched as a registered charity in 1980. Since then it has enabled J. John to lead nearly 200 missions throughout the UK and overseas, developing many innovative approaches to communicating the message of Christianity.

J. John is also a prolific writer, currently having 14 titles in print in 13 languages.